THE WORLD & THE FIRST & THIRD WORLD & THE

ESSAYS ON THE NEW
INTERNATIONAL ECONOMIC ORDER

Edited by
Karl Brunner

Contributions by
Peter T. Bauer
Karl Brunner
Harry G. Johnson
Rachel McCulloch
Daniel Patrick Moynihan
Basil S. Yamey

UNIVERSITY OF ROCHESTER
POLICY CENTER PUBLICATIONS

Center for Research in Government Policy and Business
Graduate School of Management
University of Rochester
Rochester, New York 14627

THE WORLD
FIRST THIRD
WORLD THE
&

ESSAYS ON THE NEW
INTERNATIONAL ECONOMIC ORDER

Library of Congress Catalog Card Number: 78-62660

First Edition 1978

ISBN: 0-932468-00-4 Cloth

0-932468-01-2 Paperback

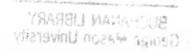

Contents

Preface

There has recently been a major shift in the relationship between the industrial countries of the West and the Countries of the Third World. Western countries which were once viewed as generous benefactors to countries characterized as underdeveloped or less developed now find themselves assailed for various sins by many leaders of the Third World. Wealth transfers from the First World to the Third World are no longer being viewed as gifts but rather as a right or even as reparations for past injustices. Moreover, the proposals for a New International Economic Order are promoted by many Western officials, particularly those who will be the brokers in any further transfers of wealth from their countries to the Third World.

The essays in this volume explore the growing confrontation between the First World and the Third World. In addition to critically examining the factual basis for the claims made in support of a New International Economic Order the papers examine the motives of the Third World leaders and explain the apparent acceptance of the Third World arguments by the West. The essays in this volume are certain to challenge many commonly held viewpoints.

While this volume was in production, Harry Johnson, who contributed three papers to this volume, passed away. Although Harry was a man of broad interests he always exhibited a particular concern for the advancement of the less developed countries. The world, First and Third, has lost a man capable of bringing reason and economic analysis to bear on a wide range of problems.

In addition to acknowledging my debt to the individuals who have contributed essays for this volume I wish to especially thank Ron Hansen and Marty Zupan for their diligent editorial assistance.

Karl Brunner

The First World, the Third World, and the Survival of Free Societies

A New Marxian-Leninist Manifesto

The history of man is largely a story of oppression, poverty, and war, with the somber fabric occasionally relieved by the freedom of open societies. The institutions of a free society offer man a chance to grope for human dignity and human achievement. They open opportunities to improve standards of living and the quality of life in ways rarely experienced by man. The historical record of Western societies offers in this respect a remarkable illustration. "Capitalism" fostered energetic application of human resources and imaginative innovations. The range of freedom expanded, arbitrary government power shrank, opportunities for broad groups rose, and the human lot improved substantially.

The Ideological Assault

But the freedom of open societies remains forever fragile. Their very existence threatens the institutions and conceptions of the many tyrannies, whose survival requires that the

I gratefully acknowledge useful comments made on a first draft by Allan H. Meltzer. The manuscript was prepared during a visit at the Hoover Institution, Stanford, Calif., during the 1977/78 period.

freedom of an open society be denigrated, perverted, and "re-interpreted" as the "slavery of a lost society." Although the details of such assaults may vary over a wide range, the most pervasive and effective forms share a common strand. They exploit man's perennial desire for universal orientations and certainties in a world confined to fallible views and chances.

The essentially human attempt to alleviate "the burden of reality"—recognized and used to advantage by the assailants—comes to endanger man's striving for freedom. In this respect, the "ideological warfare" suffered by free societies emanates from fundamental religious conceptions embedded for thousands of years in man's mind. It functions to weaken the intellectual attraction and emotive force of the freedom experienced under open societies. It constitutes, moreover, an effective shield supporting and protecting the tyrannies in the very name of freedom and humanity.

A systematic political campaign reinforces the "ideological warfare." This campaign diminishes the power and influence of the free societies and subtly affects their domestic institutions. The trend seems poorly understood, little appreciated, or, in contrast, even welcomed by Western bureaucracies and the intelligentsia. The rhetorical camouflage of "Orwellian inversions" may obscure perception. Recognition is probably also veiled by the nature of the political mechanisms increasingly used in the onslaught on free societies. The United Nations was constituted at the end of the Second World War with great expectations as an instrument of peace and political stability in the world. It was supported in the United States over many years and with a considerable emotional investment. Under these conditions, it is difficult to perceive that the United Nations has gradually changed conceptions and operations as its membership has changed. Its institutional apparatus has evolved into an instrument systematically exploited by a majority for their political-economic purposes.

In recent years, the political thrust of the United Nations organization has been increasingly focused around the idea of a "New International Economic Order" (NIEO). Its various strands are not really new, having been proposed and discussed in UN agencies for almost two decades. But they have emerged with a new design anchored in a broad sociopolitical conception. With their new ideological coherence, these ideas have found an attentive response in the General Assembly. They increasingly influence, moreover, the operation or the agenda of many international agencies. The NIEO proposals would modify the purpose and role of the United Nations. The contrast between the poverty of the Third World and the affluence of the First World is politically offensive and morally unacceptable to advocates of the NIEO. Their determined attempt to interpret these differences in wealth as a serious "danger to peace" serves to legitimize the attention of the United Nations and to justify the new focus of its expanding institutions.

The program advanced under the NIEO encompasses a wide and open-ended range of proposals and instruments.[1] The array and diversity of proposals under the program of the NIEO reflect a broad strategy to exploit all possible avenues and institutional opportunities for the central purpose: a massive transfer of wealth from the Western countries to the Third World.

The strategy emerges in the activities and operations of the Food and Agricultural Organization (FAO) in Rome, in the International Labor Organization (ILO) in Geneva, in the secretariat of the United Nations Conference on Trade and Development (UNCTAD) and the series of conferences sponsored by this agency. But the crucial and unifying strand of the strategy was probably most explicitly revealed in conferences and negotiations concerning exploitation of the rich resources of the ocean beds. The representatives of the Third

---

1 It includes a set of "integrated" international cartels to "regulate the price" of major Third World exports. These cartels are to be operated with the aid of a common fund financed by the Western countries. The free societies of the West are also expected to impose domestic constraints on the development of substitutes for major products supplied by the Third World. Other devices would stabilize Third World revenues from exports. The NIEO also proposes a systematic pattern of preferential tariffs, subsidies, and regulations of international trade for the benefit of the Third World. The First World is, moreover, expected to support or encourage "joint ventures" in the Third World, with the more or less tacit understanding that the First World's contribution establishes no relevant property rights. Any Western ventures by private groups with expectations of profit are exhibitions of a "neocolonialism" endangering the just aspirations of the Third World. Special agencies should be instituted to "facilitate the flow of technologies" from Western countries to the Third World. Similarly, the media and communication systems require apparently substantial changes. This too requires Western resources, properly channeled via United Nations agencies in order to satisfy the "legitimate national interests" of the United Nations' majority voting bloc.

World opposed access by private corporations, asserting that ocean-bed resources "belong to mankind". This declaration supposedly justifies the political proposal of a single monopoly organizing the extraction of ocean-bed resources and "owned by the people of the world through their respective governments." Such rhetoric never fails to impress portions of the media and the intelligentsia. But the significant aspect of the proposal is that the monopoly would in fact be controlled by the voting blocs of the Third World. The required resources and technologies are to be supplied, on the other hand, by the First World. The development of ocean-bed resources should thus proceed under institutions that allow the Third World to impose implicit taxes on U.S. and other Western citizens, extracting a wealth transfer irrespective of the wishes and rights of those citizens.

The Erosion of Freedom

Negotiations designed to structure the exploitation of ocean-bed resources in accordance with an international agreement were suspended in 1977. The United States foreclosed for the moment this access to Western wealth. But the central idea still guides the NIEO and influences the array of other proposals or the operations of international agencies. The unifying theme is the development of a political mechanism offering partial control over Western resources. That mechanism requires a gradual modification of international institutions in two directions. In the first stage, the secretariats, offices, committees, agenda, and broad decision-making are to be controlled by representatives of the Third World. The second stage would then achieve a gradual expansion of UN functions, with a corresponding encroachment on the domestic affairs of Western countries.

The threatened erosion of institutions in free societies seems difficult to perceive, however. Recognition of the process linking the operation of international agencies with the domestic scene in Western countries is obscured by the diffuse nature of the political mechanism. There are no dramatic evolutions, and the process moves with many unobtrusive and almost innocuous little steps. But the cumulative effect of the trend is not beyond understanding. Senator Daniel P. Moynihan has recognized the basic issue, noting that "what is going on is the systematic effort to create an international society in which government is the one and only legitimate institution." The NIEO's vision is dominated, according to Moynihan, by "an encompassing state, a state which has no provisions for the liberties of individuals."[2]

The erosion of free societies required by the realities of an NIEO has been explicitly acknowledged and presented as a human achievement by some Western advocates. Gunnar Myrdal contends that "rationality" demands the imposition of coercive institutions to forcibly lower the real consumption of Western societies and thus to extract the massive transfer of wealth deemed morally appropriate. Parliamentary democracy and the Western institutions assuring the chances of freedom and human opportunities would barely survive in Myrdal's world. Charles W. Haynes, former secretary of the Carnegie Endowment for International Peace, appears as an ardent advocate of the NIEO in the United States. He understands that it would require "a full abandonment or at least a sharp curtailment of the consumer-oriented society." This phrase must be recognized as a moralizing obfuscation of the proposed systematic dismantling of the institutions assuring men the pursuit of their own ends by their own lights. This consequence of the proposal is more easily discernible once the required institutional rearrangement is pondered in some detail. Haynes essentially admits that the freedom still enjoyed in Western societies must be sacrificed, but he is confident that "free societies will accept the restraints" to be imposed by an NIEO.[3] The former secretary of the Carnegie Endowment for International Peace is apparently little deterred by such a loss of freedom. Patient and nonideological negotiations carried on at high government levels should lead to the "peace" of a new international order. The demand for a "nonideological" approach really means that the West must renounce its commitment to the institutions of a free society. Such renouncement implies, moreover, Western acceptance of the ideological theme governing the views and policies of the Third World.

---

2 Daniel P. Moynihan, "A Diplomat's Rhetoric," *Harper's*, January 1976, p. 41.

3 Charles W. Haynes, "Can We Build on Fear?" *New Catholic World*, September-October 1975, p. 226.

This theme finds little explicit recognition in the Western nations. The prevailing disposition is to interpret the New International Economic Order as a diffuse program bearing on international trade and investments, with an array of somewhat "boring" detailed technicalities. The details, however, are not so irrelevant, for they reflect a basic purpose and emerge from an encompassing ideological position. It is important to penetrate "beyond the trees" of technicalities affecting exchange of technologies, communications, preferential tariffs, etc., "to the woods" providing structure and meaning to the amorphous mass of details. A remarkable article by Senator Moynihan, published in 1975 and included in this volume, directed the attention of a broader public in the United States to the essentially ideological theme embedded in the "institutional revolution" permeating the United Nations. His recognition of the theme was flawed, however, by a serious misconception of its nature. It was presented as a descendant of Fabian socialism and interpreted as a broad heritage of the educational exposure of the Third World elite to English cultural experiences. Although Fabian socialism may have, at best, prepared the way for the contemporary ideological theme, the central notion of that theme is essentially Marxian in character and contains a discernible Leninist flavor. This Marxian-Leninist orientation permeates the political or social conceptions and rhetoric of the Third World, occurring independently of the Communist parties. It explains and motivates crucial parts of domestic arrangements and dominates the details and patterns of international policies. The NIEO thus emerges as a New Marxian-Leninist Manifesto expressing the political thrust of the Third World and gradually institutionalized by the United Nations.

The Marxian Theme

The Marxian-Leninist theme presents man as an entity conditioned by the embedding social organization.[4] The crucial characteristics of society are its *Produktions-Verhältnisse*, the occurrence or nonoccurrence of private property "in the

---

4 The reader is referred to Karl Brunner and William Meckling, "The Perception of Man and the Conception of Government," *Journal of Money, Credit and Banking*, February 1977.

means of production". Private property assures the emergence of class conflict, determines exploitation, and obscures consciousness about deeper realities. Conflict, exploitation, oppression, and injustice thus occur independently of the personal volitions of members of the "capitalist class". Owners of private property are compelled by their role in the social process to exhibit specific attitudes, valuations, and behavior patterns. It follows from this fundamental perception of man and society that only a radical change of the system, the abolition of private property, can remove oppression, conflict, exploitation, and assure the transition from "necessity to liberty". Such a "revolutionary expropriation of the exploiters" modifies the "social condition of production" and transposes man into a new world without conflict and oppression. The Leninist extension of the Marxian vision, with its stress on imperialism and the political "avant-garde", has found a particular echo in the Third World, as have the Stalinist additions pertaining to the role of organizations and "control techniques". The commitment to a Marxian-Leninist doctrine assures that any human progress or improvement of the human condition under capitalism is really an "accident" and in contrast to the essential trend or inherent conditions of capitalism "determined by the fundamental laws of society." In a corresponding view, all failures and "Gulagian events" in societies that recognize Marxian principles are remedial accidents not essentially inherent in the social process conditioned by socialist institutions.[5]

Implications and Advantages

The ideological theme dominating thought and policies in the Third World yields several important implications for the New Manifesto. The first emphasizes the inherent impossibility of reforming or improving the "system"; attempts along such lines would obstruct the necessary and final revolution. These endeavors are thus particularly evil and

---

5 It may be objected that the Marxian literature acknowledges the historical progress associated with capitalism. Indeed, one does find appropriate passages in the work of Karl Marx and in Marxian publications describing the human progress from "feudalism" to "capitalism." But one also notes that the attitude described in the text dominates contemporary Marxian views about current socialist and capitalist societies.

repugnant according to advanced insights into the "laws of society" offered by historical materialism. This explains the virulent hatred reserved by Marxian faithfuls for social-democratic intellectuals, politicians, and parties. The second implication is a close corollary of the first. Recognition of the "basic social laws" implies that the total destruction and overthrow of the system is the foremost priority of political action. All existing institutions should be systematically used for and applied to this radical purpose. Another implication naturally confines "imperialism" to political and economic relations with capitalist countries. The central imperialist country in this view is necessarily the United States. The political program requires, therefore, that the United States be weakened and its sociopolitical institutions be gradually modified. Moreover, all operations of private foreign corporations in countries of the Third World are necessarily "neo-colonial expressions" of Western imperialism. The following message is unavoidable under the circumstances: "In one world, as in one state, as I am rich because you are poor and I am poor because you are rich, transfer of wealth from rich to poor is a matter of right; it is not an appropriate matter for charity. The objective must be the eradication of poverty and the establishment of a minimum standard of living for all people. This will involve its converse, a ceiling on wealth for individuals and nations, as well as deliberate action to transfer resources from the rich to the poor within and across national boundaries."[6]

According to Marxian doctrine, differences in wealth are symptoms of exploitative class relations. Massive redistributions thus weaken the system of private property, reinforce class conflicts, and eventually destroy the class structure. The same theme emerges also in the views attributed to Mr. Boumediène from Algeria: "The raw material producing countries insist on being masters in their own houses. Developing countries must take control over their natural resources. This implies nationalizing the exploitation of these resources and controlling the machinery governing their prices."[7] The metaphor of "master in the

---

6 Peter Bauer offers this quote from Nyerere's speech in "Ordering the World About: The New International Economic Order," *Policy Review*, Summer 1977.

7 Quoted from "The New Economic Order," *New Internationalist*, 1975.

house," with the emphasis on "nationalization" of resources, conveys the basic idea that countries of the Third World must abolish private property and establish the socialist institutions required to "remedy poverty and oppression." Boumediène, Nyerere, and other representatives of the Third World cultivate a ritualistic "anti-imperialism" that combines a nationalist fever and socialist intentions formulated in a Marxian context.

The prevalence of this ideological theme among the members of the Third World is hardly a matter of chance. Its propagation offers substantial advantages to the "ruling elites" of the Third World. The doctrine justifies the replacement of markets based on private property with a complex set of political institutions to control the use of resources. This transformation contributes to the survival of oligarchies and protects the tyrannies established in many countries of the Third World. A society based on private property and markets does not guarantee that dictatorship will never emerge. The "open institutions" of markets and private property seriously constrain, however, the power and manipulative range of a dictatorship and offer greater opportunities for its removal. The socialist institutions that emerge with the abolition of private property concentrate power in a small oligarchic apparatus suffering little exposure to challenge from outside groups. Moreover, the Marxian theme justifies the power monopoly with satisfying humanitarian language. It exploits the intelligentsia's disposition to confuse words and reality in order to obtain the docile group of clerics that centers of power always require.

The events in Tanzania in past years provide, in this respect, a stark illustration. Coercive collectivization of agriculture has uprooted millions of inhabitants and forced a large social group into a Russian mold. This mold, with its characteristic pattern of disincentives, has produced in Russia a permanent agricultural crisis. Agricultural production also fell, of course, in Tanzania, and we can safely expect its agriculture to flounder and stagnate for many years in the future. But it should also be clear that such collectivization offers vastly increased opportunities for political control over the rural sections of the country. It has become substantially more difficult in the Tanzanian countryside to express or organize opposition to Dr. Julius Nyerere and his political apparatus. As Jean-François Revel notes: "democracy provides a legal mechanism whereby in the normal political process, without civil war or coup d'etat, one administration can be replaced by another, if the majority... so decides. Such a system is captivating to few if any of those who hold power. Once they are informed that their socialist conscience forbids them in the interest of the revolution to permit any provision for their own replacement in power, that conscience will also prevent them from allowing any criticism whatever of themselves."[8] Such criticism, under the circumstances and according to the interpretation of reality guided by the ideological theme, simply has no function. This implication of the basic theme partly explains the Third World's endeavor to exploit UNESCO as an instrument of information and communication policy. The essential purpose is to control the flow of information, in a sense safeguarding and strengthening the prevailing power structure.

The pervasive ideological theme yields another advantage. It offers opportunities to disguise any mismanagement or failure in domestic policies by attributing all problems to capitalist countries. Responsibility for economic stagnation and drift is shifted by the ruling oligarchies to the "insensitive and selfish" behavior of the United States and Western Europe. The theme also backs up, with a penumbra of intellectual pretensions, the insistent drum-fire of demands that the "right" for massive transfers of wealth be honored and actually implemented by the West. Recent conferences, sponsored by various agencies, have thus increasingly revealed cautiously conciliatory and "concessionary" gestures by Western countries.

Flaws in the Marxian Scheme

The political and economic usefulness of the ideological conception governing the NIEO does not establish its validity. It seems appropriate at this stage to examine critically some of its major strands. We note first some facts generally accepted by independent observers not yet ensnared by a new *credo quia absurdum est*. All historical realizations of

---

8 Jean-François Revel, *The Totalitarian Temptation* (New York: Doubleday, 1977), p. 107.

Marxian societies suffer under a typical pattern of economic problems. One may well speak about a "structural crisis of socialism". Agricultural production probably reveals the most obvious case. The problems are lessened to the extent that ideological purity is sacrificed and private property survives as it does, tenuously, in the agricultural sectors of some Eastern European countries. The peculiar incentive system confronting managers and bureaucracies induces a wasteful use of resources and low-quality production of those goods with little immediate significance for the political apparatus. Queues, shortages, and huge, rigid bureaucracies are permanent characteristics of socialist societies. Moreover, oppression and poverty have not been relieved by the "destruction of the system" and the appearance of "socialist institutions". On the contrary, the systematic pattern of intense oppression occurs as an endemic social disease of Marxian societies. The brutalities of Gulag Archipelagos do not appear in capitalist countries, but they do exist in the Marxian societies. Most Western Marxian scholars would find it difficult or impossible to teach or publish in such a society.

Recognition of the "Russian model's" failure induces two very different responses among Marxian intellectuals in the West. One group has apparently decided that the failure results from ideological impurities. The ideological lapse from eschatological commitment produced a "pragmatic bureaucratization"; ideological pragmatism neglected the emergence of the New Man in a New Society through the purgatory of sustained "cultural revolution". This group looks hopefully to Yugoslavia or to China's Cultural Revolution and may turn to Albania or may admire international terrorism. Their hope will always shift with the eventual accumulation of information about historical realities. We are reminded of the Christian sectarians forever proclaiming (sequentially) another day of reckoning just ahead of us. Other groups, with less religious fervor, grope for alternative forms of "socialist institutions". They contend that "Stalinization" is not a necessary feature of a socialist society evolving according to Marxian precepts. Their discussions usually center around vague ideas of "universal sovietization"—a pervasive system of participatory self-management applied to all forms of social organization. The remarkable fact about this "groping for socialist answers" is the implicit admission that Marxian analysis yields little information about the actual operation of socialist societies. This failure of Marxian analysis reflects a fundamental flaw in the conception of the "social conditions of production," defined in terms of man's ownership relation to the means of production. The underlying sociological model of man, traditionally used by Marxians, equates self-interest with the profit motive fostered by the ownership of property in a capitalist society.[9] Self-interested behavior is thus not a pervasive characteristic of man, according to Marxian views, but the result of a specific social condition in a particular historical context. We can recognize at this juncture the fundamental cognitive flaw of the analysis, a flaw subtly influenced by the metaphysical, or religious, traditions incorporated into Marxian thought.[10] An alternative conception of man, advanced by the Scottish philosophers of the 18th century, has been systematically developed over the past 200 years and forms the central core of economic analysis.[11] By this analysis, self-interested behavior, understood in a broad sense, is fundamental to man's nature and is thus *invariant* with respect to historical changes and social conditions, although these conditions affect the *specific* responses and prevailing patterns emerging from the self-interested attention of individuals enmeshed in a specific social context. It follows that abolishing private property yields no *fundamental* change in man's attitude. Any set of "socialist institutions" creates new, and characteristic, patterns of incentives and disincentives. Responses to them, however, remain unanalyzed in the Marxian scheme because of its denial that self-interest is a fundamental human characteristic. We note, in particular, that the abolition of private property does not remove private control over and private use of resources. Available resources are administered somehow, and they are administered by

---

9 Further elaborations may be found in Brunner and Meckling, "Perception of Man."

10 These aspects were extensively explored by Ernst Topitsch, *Vom Ursprung und Ende der Metaphysik; eine Studie zur Weltanschauungskritik* (Vienna: Springer, 1958).

11 An excellent survey of the issue can be found in William Meckling's "Values and the Choice of the Model of Man in the Social Sciences," *Schweizerische Zeitschrift für Volkswirtschaft und Statistik*, 1976.

individuals. The arrangements used determine the opportunities for private use of resources. Socialist institutions thus encourage a *private* use of *public* resources at the expense of the general public.

The basic view of man incorporated in modern analysis, when compared with that of the Marxian sociology, is substantially more compatible with historical experience. It explains, in particular, the failures of the historical realizations of Marxian societies, whose socialist institutions suffer, as it were, a permanent "capitalist crisis." It explains most particularly their human failure and the systematic inhumanity produced. It explains also why the search for a "socialist society with a human face" remains essentially a religious illusion, ending ultimately in the misery and brutality of a Stalinist society. The Western European hope for a Marxian society based on "self-management of all resources" will remain a dream without reality. The analysis emerging from the insights of the Scottish philosophers informs us that the institutionalization of Marxian dreams effectively destroys the historical aberration of freedom and restores the universal human condition of oppression, war, and poverty.[12]

Several more specific strands of the ideological theme behind the NIEO deserve some attention. Nyerere expressed the Marxian belief that the wealth of Western nations is due to the poverty of the Third World. Exploitation of the Third World produced, in this view, the living standards of the West. The pervasiveness of this belief follows from its "obvious" simplicity. It corresponds to the simplistic impression that nobody could live on the other side of the earth without falling off. The relevant facts are very different. Its relations with the West contributed in general to the economic development of the Third World. We also hear laments that the West consumes an inordinate share of the world's wealth, although we never hear that the West also produces an "inordinate share" of this wealth. Peter Bauer has examined these and related issues in a series of papers, and the reader is referred to his articles included in this vol-

---

12 A more detailed examination of the issue beyond this short summary will be presented in a forthcoming paper, "Substantive Issues in Ideology," prepared for the Fifth Interlaken Seminar on Analysis and Ideology, 1978.

ume. Justification of the NIEO in terms of an established "right" based on "past exploitation" should eventually be recognized as a theme without support in reality. It remains, however, a powerful ideological weapon to lure the support of a gullible Western intelligentsia for persistent raids on the wealth of Western nations.

We note in this context the medieval misconception of trade as a zero-sum game. Nyerere and his cohorts fail to recognize that wealth is produced by human endeavors in response to incentives and opportunities. Since voluntary trade and transactions actually bring mutual benefits to all participants involved, the resourceful groping for and coping with opportunities by participants in the social game yields substantial rewards. This resourcefulness is an essential characteristic of a social organization based on markets. It assures continual increase in wealth and also distributes the gain, under competitive conditions, over widening social groups. It is precisely Nyerere's institutional dream of an NIEO that would transform the social organization into an essentially zero-sum game. The political institutions of such a society intensify conflict and maximize the rewards to be extracted from political power.

Some arguments offered in justification of the NIEO emphasize specific supplementary aspects more or less linked with the basic theme. Called up as evidence of the need for a transfer of wealth are a persistent decline in the terms of trade confronting the Third World and a decline in its share of international trade. Neither is really supported by relevant observations. The findings of a group of experts selected by UNCTAD from "developed and developing countries" and using the data prepared by UNCTAD yield no support for the notion, well advertised in UN circles, that the Third World suffers under the "old economic order" an inherent decline of the terms of trade. The report concludes: "There was general agreement that the statistics presented to the group did not provide any clear evidence of a long-term deterioration in the terms of trade of developing countries."[13] It is also noteworthy that neither

---

13 The information is based on a report filed by Edwin Dale in *The New York Times*, March 25, 1975. The reader may also note the detailed discussion of this event by Edwin J. Feulner in *Congress and the New International Economic Order*

the terms of trade nor the movements in shares of trade can be systematically linked to the economic welfare of the countries involved. Falling relative prices do not imply under all circumstances a fall in the real incomes of the producers involved. The link is substantially controlled by additional elements affecting technological developments, productivity, and relative input prices in the production process. Similar considerations apply to the movement of trade shares. Many factors determine trade shares with very different influences on real income. The movement of trade shares by itself offers no information without further detailed examination. We may indeed infer, with good reason, that real incomes are lowered by a fall in trade shares produced by domestic export taxes, export controls, domestic obstacles in one form or another imposed on imports, or foreign obstacles to domestic exports. But this consequence results jointly, with the declining trade shares, from the underlying specific events. Lower real incomes are not caused by lower trade shares but by the events indicated. But many other events lower trade shares of countries and simultaneously *raise* their real incomes.

Transfer of wealth is also supposed to alleviate poverty and support economic development. The NIEO program, however, provides for transfers from Western nations to the *governments* of Third World countries. Our analysis of the political institutions prevailing in these countries implies that the resources extracted from the advanced nations are predominantly used to benefit the ruling oligarchies. They will be distributed among selected social groups supporting the regime, and they tend to strengthen the existing power apparatus. The ruling oligarchies experience little incentive under the established sociopolitical institutions to distribute the benefits over broader groups, independently of political status. Poverty will be alleviated for a few at the cost of diminished future opportunities for the majorities. A similar pattern characterizes economic development. Political incentives dominate the choice of projects and their mode of execution or operation. The result is usually a wasteful use of

(Washington, D.C.: Heritage Foundation, 1976), p. 62. After the report containing results quite unpalatable to UNCTAD was leaked to *The New York Times,* it was suppressed and "eventually released with contradictory conclusions."

resources with comparatively little permanent or broad effect on real incomes and economic opportunities.[14] The vehement opposition of representatives of the Third World or advocates of the NIEO to a program of broad opportunities for private investment under reliable "rules of the game" should be noted in this context. A flow of private investment would benefit wider population groups and raise real income with a lessened dependence on the political intentions of a confined power structure. The development of projects and the expansion of job opportunities beyond manipulation of the political apparatus raises opportunities for potential political competition and offers a basis for independent criticism of domestic policies. In contrast, wealth transfers for governmentally controlled "economic development" minimize the potential competition for political office and maximize the means of political control.

The Western Response

Even well-informed citizens of Western nations fail to recognize a connection between the thrust for a New International Economic Order, the "institutional revolution" within the United Nations, and the future evolution of their own societies. A "sophisticated" or disillusioned attitude finds that the United Nations and its array of agencies is a "do-nothing speech club" with cocktail parties, chauffeured limousines, and plush offices. Common opinion also has it that neither the General Assembly nor its many agencies possess compelling decision-powers affecting our lives and welfare. This complacent view of the matter is dangerously misconceived. The attribution of a "do-nothing" character to the United Nations follows from a belief that the international organization's function is the protection of peace and the resolution of conflict, as expounded in the official rhetoric that launched it and still sustains its propaganda apparatus in the United States. When this naïve belief is confronted with the unending series of regional wars, conflicts, and threats of wars, the natural conclusion is that the United Nations really does nothing. This attitude also fosters a

14 Peter Bauer's contributions in this volume elaborate the theme.

perennial hope that it will eventually "do something," that is, will act in accordance with official rhetoric. And so we hear that the international organization is man's last hope, requiring our prayerful support. This attitude misses the relevant reality rather completely. Rachel McCulloch investigates, in her contribution to this volume, the gradual modifications in the UN structure, governing ideas, and mode of operation. The problem does not follow from the United Nations' doing nothing, but from what it actually does. And we need to recognize that the problem is embedded in the very structure of the institution.

The Role of Passive Diplomacy

Western representatives, politicians, and media do not perceive sufficiently, thus far, the increasingly focused trend in the operation of international agencies. They appear cautiously reluctant to recognize facts, understand their deeper meaning, or acknowledge a systematic underlying pattern. In his article included in the present volume, Senator Moynihan discusses the bland obliviousness of Western representatives steeped in "traditional diplomatic courtesies". Speaking of the human-rights issue in a more recent article, he notes the capitulation of the West in the ongoing ideological war: "The issue of human rights has long been at the center of international politics. In fact, from the time the Soviets commenced to be so hugely armed that their 'peace' campaign lost credibility, and Khrushchev opted for Russian involvement in 'liberation' struggles, this issue has been acquiring greater and greater salience. Which is to say that in human-rights terms the Western democracies have been attacked without letup....Western democracies, having allowed themselves to be placed on the defensive, finally ceased almost wholly to resist. In the language of diplomatic instructions, this lack of resistance was known as 'danger limitation'. In truth, it was something very like capitulation...." Senator Moynihan also notes the basic flaw in the Carter administration's "human-rights approach". The secretary of state essentially refuses, in the senator's view, to place the problem in the relevant political context, and insists on dealing with it as a separate and isolated "humanitarian issue".[15] Under the circumstances, the issue may easily fade among the files of a bureaucracy with little interest in or appreciation of the fundamental confrontation of our time. Concern with ideology seems a de facto monopoly of the tyrannies in the Second and Third Worlds, a monopoly conceded by Western governments. The rising cult of the Third World among the Western intelligentsia and government agencies reinforces the distorted vision reflected in Western policies and actions. A growing awareness of the fundamental sociopolitical issues staged by the Second and Third Worlds would reflect "a new American will to resist the advance of totalitarianism." But Senator Moynihan worries, quite properly, that the "permanent government" can be expected to push in the opposite direction, toward a policy of "reassurances and accommodation" to our enemies.[16]

The passive disposition of our State Department bureaucracy has been noted by various observers. In August 1976 a UN agency sponsored an international conference on crime in Geneva. The Western nations were subjected throughout the conference to a flood of hostile harangues. The Second and the Third Worlds joined in a common ideological onslaught on the free societies, in rhetoric drenched with Orwellian inversions. The experience offered an excellent illustration of the systematic exploitation of any institution, irrespective of its official or announced purpose, to wage a full-scale sociopolitical war on the Western nations. This barrage was endured with silent passivity. Hostile resolutions even found their way through committees chaired by Western representatives. Independent observers reported that delegates from Western countries "did not wish to engage in polemics."[17] They behaved according to a pattern of "traditional diplomacy" and maintained a pos-

---

15 Daniel P. Moynihan, "The Politics of Human Rights," *Commentary*, August 1977, pp. 20, 23. In the last section of the present discussion some reservations are offered concerning Senator Moynihan's interpretation of "human rights" as the fundamental sociopolitical issue of our time.

16 Ibid., p.

17 The facts of the Geneva conference on crime were reported in detail by (zi.), the correspondent of the *Neue Zürcher Zeitung*. The reports corroborate in substantial detail the general description advanced by Senator Moynihan in the essay included in this volume.

ture of "reassurances and accommodation". The same pattern suffused the State Department bureaucracy with respect to the International Labor Organization in Geneva. What is remarkable is that continued participation was advocated even after the ILO sessions held late in the summer of 1977. The sessions revealed with brutal clarity that the majority of the ILO has effectively abandoned its original purpose. A voting bloc from the Second and Third Worlds rejected the documents, prepared in line with the original function of the organization, reporting on the administration of treaties and conventions in member countries. This action and the pervasive sociopolitical confrontation revealed vividly the new political role imposed on the ILO. It has essentially become another "institutional weapon" to be used against the free societies by combined forces of the Second and Third Worlds.[18]

The consequences of our disposition to reassure and accommodate reach beyond verbalizations and declarations. The rhetorical barrage reflects political pressure bearing on a wide and open-ended list of demands presented to the Western nations. A disposition to "accommodate" necessarily produces a series of concessions. Any particular event or occurrence in the series may have modest or even negligible significance, but their cumulative effects over many years still emerge with a serious weight. Moreover, even minor concessions supplemented with an array of new committees, commissions, or agencies open new avenues for the exploitation of the "institutional weapon." The new institutions tend to evolve very differently from the manner expected or officially announced by Western bureaucracies. The experiences already assembled under international agreements or with negotiations developed in the spirit of the NIEO are quite informative.

Institutional Extensions

Several years ago the European Economic Community negotiated with a group of Third World countries the so-called Lomé agreement, which initiated an arrangement designed

---

18 It should be noted that President Carter eventually decided against the advice of his foreign-policy bureaus and terminated U.S. membership in the ILO in late 1977. The decision does not excuse the remarkable blindness cultivated in this matter by the State Department.

to stabilize the revenues from major exports supplied by participating members of the Third World. The new bureaucracy of the Stabex system rapidly adjusted its operations to the incentives built into the institutional arrangement. Independent observers note difficulties encountered in obtaining relevant information; Stabex operation proceeds behind a protective veil.[19] Such nontransparency expresses a natural interest of the bureaucracy to increase its opportunities to control resources and manipulate their use with minimal pressure from outside monitoring. We note also the systematic disposition on the part of the bureaucracy and political commission to interpret the agreement and its execution in increasingly extensive terms. Stabex operations have been extended to compensate *any* losses or reductions in export revenues, including those clearly attributable to the *domestic* policies of the export countries. One country initiated, for instance, a trade monopoly over lumber, and another set minimum prices on sisal. In both, exports and revenues fell, with prompt compensation by the Stabex system. The two cases are very instructive indeed. Both policy measures involved a transfer of wealth to selected groups in the respective countries. The major transfer by the trade monopoly probably accrues to the government sector, its bureaucracy, and associated "elites". Moreover, this transfer proceeds at the cost of citizens in the Common Market countries. The complexity and nontransparency of the arrangement assures that few voters in Western Europe will know about the taxes systematically imposed on them by the Third World.[20] The reader may object that the amounts involved are possibly "small". But the two events, however small, illustrate the long-run consequences of the bureaucracy's disposition. The extensive interpretation shapes new opportunities for Third World countries to impose policies on their societies that will effect transfers of wealth to the governing class and its associates and sup-

---

19 Otto Matzke, a correspondent of the *Neue Zürcher Zeitung*, publishes regular reports on the operation of international agencies. These reports offer some unique and insightful information.

20 A ministerial commission sets a plafond on the Stabex system's five-year budget. The extensive interpretations thus push actual expenditures to the plafond. The bureaucracy's incentives also make it very likely that the operating committee will approach the ministerial commission for additional funds before the first five-year term is ended.

porters, with the expectation that any losses in revenues produced by such measures are shifted to the Western European taxpayer. It raises, thus, the incentives to develop "innovative policies" endangering exports for the benefit of selected domestic groups. It should be clear that such transfers of wealth from the West neither alleviate mass poverty nor contribute to economic development. They essentially reinforce and benefit the existing political structure and raise the consumption of the government sector. They encourage further misallocation of resources and lower whatever economic progress could otherwise be achieved. It is noteworthy that the Federal Republic of Germany opposed the "extensive interpretation" but eventually yielded under general political pressure from its associates in the Common Market.

The bureaucracy's extensive interpretation of the agreement covers more dimensions. The number of countries with rights to receive transfers has been increased from 46 to 52. The list of products with guaranteed export revenues has naturally been enlarged, and in some cases revenue is guaranteed even for exports to countries beyond the members of the Common Market. The separate events are modest or even trivial per se, but they indicate the step-by-step process evolving under the incentives built into the agency.

This experience bears significantly on the so-called North-South dialogue. It is hardly reasonable to expect that any arrangement emerging from this "dialogue" will not suffer systematic extensions over the years, with increasing opportunities for the Third World to manipulate implicit taxes on citizens of the First World. Another case in point is offered by the protracted negotiations over the constitution of a common fund to finance an "integrated commodities program". In these meetings, the Third World has consistently advocated arrangements with extensive or essentially open-ended mandates and with substantial powers vested in the bureaucracy or crucial voting committees. The Third World thus pushed in recent negotiations (summer 1977) for a wide-ranging interpretation of "buffer stocks" that would permit open-ended interventions by the new control agencies in the market for raw materials. This feature would support the new bureaucracy's disposition to raise "regulated" prices beyond any level determined by "narrow" stabilization purposes. The proposals include, moreover, that plans for diversification, technological development, productivity increases, market research, commercial development, etc., etc., be subsumed under the activities financed by the "common fund". As in the Stabex system, the taxpayers of Western countries will have no vote in these arrangements. Neither will the Western governments have any opportunity to control or even to monitor the use of funds extracted from their citizens to further Third World schemes.

Responsible monitoring of the resources obtained from the West will be prevented or obstructed by the "anti-imperialist" claims to self-determination and "sovereignty over resources". Self-determination and sovereignty include, of course, a "right", represented by suitable institutions, to raid the Western taxpayer. It also includes the expectation that Western governments will prod and cajole private corporations under their jurisdiction to invest in countries of the Third World, under conditions dictated by those countries requiring that indigenous managers be employed. And, most particularly, the investor should expect no returns and fully accept the risk that the ventures, once successfully operating, will be expropriated with little or no compensation. Proposals of "joint ventures" mean, in a similar vein, that the Western investor may neither control the management nor expect a return on his investment. It is remarkable to note the occasional willingness of Western governments to accept the Third World's suggestive rhetoric in this matter and convey "appropriate" signals to private industry.

Similar willingness is evident in the events surrounding negotiations aimed at a "consensus document" on the occasion of the Seventh Special Session of the General Assembly in 1975. The session opened with a speech by Secretary of State Kissinger, read at the time by Ambassador Moynihan. A round of discussions had been initiated with the Third World's submission of a broad list of demands. The United States responded with a set of proposals developed in Kissinger's paper. Several weeks of "hard bargaining" eventually yielded a consensus resolution. "However, neither Ambassador Moynihan nor Assistant Secretary Enders, nor the Congressional advisory group mentioned that the specific language of the resolution was much more forceful in advocating certain proposals over others. The proposals which were advocated least strongly were those generally advanced by the United States."[21] Nevertheless, Assistant Secretary Enders reported, in the best diplomatic tradition, that the document resulted from "a genuine process of negotiation in order to get an agreed result from which we could all go forward." The consensus was established, however, with "many United States concessions (e.g., transfers of real resources, international monetary reform, and even a study of indexing for rather tenuous consideration of United States proposals)."[22] Several things should be noted about the U.S. proposals. They would enlarge the network of international agencies involving the First World in the Third World's economic policies. The comparatively muted response to the proposals probably reflects the smaller opportunities for eventual political control of the organizations envisioned by the United States. But even such institutions, once in operation, would offer incentives for modification and extension according to a now-customary pattern. Second, Enders' emphasis on "going forward" from the "agreed result" extends hope and "reassurance" to the Third World for future accommodation. Finally, by proposing such international agencies, the United States helps the NIEO and its underlying theme. It has basically accepted the Third World's position and opened the initial round in a state of permanent negotiations bearing on "concessionary transfers". Although the United States officially disavowed some of the characteristic language expressing the Third World's ideological theme, it did accept the documents, thereby conveying legitimacy to the basic theme.[23]

A previous paragraph noted the breakdown of negotiations over the exploitation of ocean-bed resources, a breakdown essentially due to the extreme position of the Third World. It seems highly unlikely that this suspension will persist, and one may surmise that the State Department is preparing for new rounds of negotiations. It appears useful, under the circumstances, to examine the U.S. position in

21 Edwin J. Feulner, *Congress and the New International Economic Order*, pp. 13, 14.
22 Ibid., p. 15.
23 Ibid., p. 68.

this matter. The State Department opposed, under Secretary Kissinger, the full monopoly of a joint international government "enterprise", instead advocating that private corporations should have limited access for a limited period. This proposal concedes too much and again accepts the basic thrust of the NIEO. It offers a major machinery beyond the control or influence of Western nations affecting the use of Western resources. It is, moreover, blind to the incentives unleashed. The limited realm of private corporations would be continuously threatened. The very existence of this realm, created by an international political body, would open opportunities to raise issues about the geographical range and the duration of the "corporate privileges" to exploit "the people's wealth". Any acceptance of the U.S. proposal would thus unleash a series of intermittent negotiations that would erode private rights via "a process of genuine bargaining". Such erosion of property rights would produce another transfer of wealth at the cost of investors, workers, and consumers in the United States. Any signs indicating willingness or interest on the part of the State Department bureaucracy to resume international negotiations in this matter should therefore be viewed with some apprehension.

A Tentative Explanation of Western Accommodation

The pattern of accommodation and "concessionary" moves gradually acquires a sharper focus. This development, and our apparent helplessness or indifference to changes in the role of international organizations, still requires some explanation. This section tentatively advances three reasons, which may partly interact or overlap: a fundamental lack of relevant ideological conception on the part of our foreign service bureaucracy; the incentives and rewards operating on this bureaucracy; and lastly, the partial acceptance by some groups among the intelligentsia, the media, Congress, and also the administration of central elements of the ideological theme embraced by the Third World.

The Conceptual Vacuum

The Western countries show little awareness that a political war has been unleashed on the free societies. The systematic exploitation of the "institutional weapon" for broad sociopolitical purposes hardly penetrates public consciousness. The Western world recognizes no underlying theme that weaves into a unified pattern the mass of technical detail confronting its representatives and negotiators. But there is such a theme, and it guides the persistent search for new issues, the choice of technical or organizational details, and the change in the use and operation of international institutions. It should be explicitly emphasized that this ideological theme bears on fundamental issues, on matters of *substance* and *fact* affecting the survival of free societies.

For the most part, foreign-service bureaucracies in Western countries refuse to recognize the signals. "Traditional diplomacy" conditions the bureaus to an isolated, piecemeal approach centering on technical detail per se, with substantial neglect of the sociopolitical thrust reflected by the detail. In a persistent confrontation with an opponent trained to view all issues and the most negligible detail as a component of a coherent "ideological theme", the conceptual failure of the West encourages piecemeal "concessionary bargaining". It also fosters the "concessionary reinterpretations" and adjustments of agreements or institutions.

The United States Treasury, in contrast to the State Department, has occasionally approached some comprehension of the basic issue. It appeared to understand during the Kissinger era that the United States should actively advance its sociopolitical case for the institutions of a free society and also shape its policymaking in accordance with this case. The evidence suggests that Secretary of State Kissinger rather failed, in matters concerning the NIEO, to see "the wood for the trees". The "ideological theme" underlying the NIEO was brushed aside as "a sterile debate". The Secretary of State also concluded, apparently after a discussion with his aides, that the issues raised by the NIEO were "just a big bore." This evaluation by political and diplomatic leaders hardly encourages a bureaucracy to penetrate beyond the range of "traditional diplomacy" into a realm of systematic sociopolitical confrontations. But Kissinger does not stand alone in this respect. Willy Brandt, the former chancellor of the Federal Republic of Germany, expressed in the late summer of 1977 the hope that the issues surrounding the NIEO might be safely "de-ideologized". Appropriately enough, the preparations for a new international committee provided the background for this expression of hope, which was supplemented with a declaration emphasizing the need for "concessionary transfers." Brandt's comments reveal the entrenched Western blindness to the fact that the NIEO *is* the instrument of an ideological assault on the West. It is also remarkable that the Third World's ideological thrust, well designed to engender guilt feelings among Western intelligentsia, has never really been answered by the West. No major political leader in a Western country has raised his voice to present a case for the free societies or to emphatically reject the barrage of accusations. Minor politicians daring a rejoinder suffer verbal abuse in the media for "their insensitivity".

A remarkable illustration of the West's failure to understand the issue and to articulate with courage and determination its case on behalf of free societies appears in President Carter's commencement address delivered at the University of Notre Dame in 1977. The President assures us that "we will cooperate more closely with the newly influential countries in Latin America, Africa and Asia. We need their friendship and cooperation as the structure of world power changes." With a new confidence in our own future we are now "free of the inordinate fear of communism which once led us to embrace any dictator who joined us in that fear." President Carter also lends some support to the "new international economic order" with the words of a previous president of the United States: "More than a hundred years ago Abraham Lincoln said that our nation could not exist half-slave and half-free. We know that a peaceful world cannot exist one-third rich and two-thirds hungry."[24] We observe just in passing the distortion of facts expressed by "one-third rich and two-thirds hungry." President Carter follows intellectual fashion and speaks as if the world's incomes were concentrated at two extreme end-points of a distribution. The facts are very different, however; real incomes, including those of countries beyond the First World, are distributed over a wide scale and exhibit a substantial middle ground. Considerably more serious is President

---

24 Moynihan's "Politics of Human Rights" brought this speech to my attention. The reader is particularly referred to pp. 24 and 25 of his article.

Carter's failure to comprehend the current ideological assault upon the United States. There appears a serious misconception about the confrontation with the Second World over its deliberate ideological imperialism. It requires no "inordinate fear of communism" to understand the pervasive sociopolitical and intellectual war waged on Western positions. The "confidence" that dismisses "inordinate fears" easily fails to appreciate the nature of the conflict. The statement quoted also legitimizes the New Marxian Manifesto, with no apparent awareness that it is an instrument in the worldwide battle to transform the free societies according to the prevailing totalitarian pattern.

The attitudes and views of the Second and Third Worlds reveal a common strand affecting our destiny. The "old problem" of communism and the "new problem" raised by the NIEO confront the West with the same basic issues. This seems little understood in President Carter's dismissing "dictators who feared communism" and offering "friendship and cooperation" to dictators in the Third World. The facts indicate, however, that the old and the new problem both express the sociopolitical war on free societies. Recognition of their unity would direct President Carter's attention to an important connection between the sentences quoted. Our contemporary tyrannies subject their citizens to a state of slavery described by Revel as approaching a "prenatal stage controlling things and people in the same manner,"[25] but the *contemporary* world of "half-slave and half-free" apparently lies beyond our president's perception. Also beyond his comprehension is the fact that the sociopolitical institutions of those tyrannies—from Uganda or Tanzania to Russia and China—obstruct economic development and entrench the poverty of the masses.

This judgment seems contradicted by President Carter's attention to "human rights." The administration's interpretation of the human-rights issue offers, however, another illustration of the conceptual failure or vacuum pervading

---

25 The full statement was, "Since, moreover, nationalization or, more exactly, state ownership of the economy is the only socialism known to centralized authoritarian regimes, this kind of unofficial or lay Stalinism is, under a pseudo-revolutionary pretext, a throwback to the so to speak prenatal stage of political power, where no distinction was made between control of people and ownership of things." Revel, *Totalitarian Temptation*, p. 100.

our political institutions. The nonpolitical or purely human-itarian interpretation of the issue artificially separates the problem from its relevant sociopolitical context. The Second World should have shown the nonsense in such attempts at separation. The very idea of isolating a "humanitarian issue" is a remarkable exercise in prayerful naïveté about the realities of social and political forces. President Carter's approach and reaction to the Russian stance on human rights reveals a serious misconception in this matter. The French government's fear of provoking the Russian leader-ship expresses, on the other hand, a keen appreciation of the essentially political nature of the issue.

The "nonpolitical" reinterpretation of human rights is probably conditioned by a subtle and influential misconcep-tion of the social problem, a misconception apparently shared to some extent by Senator Moynihan. To regard human rights as the issue of our time with the greatest bearing on the structure of a free society is to misconstrue the nature of the problem. Recent trends in political lan-guage have sharply separated human rights from property rights. Moreover, most discussions of human rights reveal a subtle shift in the meaning of the term "rights" used in these contexts. In the earlier understanding, the rights of individual members of a social organization, including their rights to property—which are, after all, the rights of humans with respect to specified objects—either circumscribe the range of admissible individual action relative to specific objects and persons or confine the range of governmental action in definite ways. But in its modified meaning, "rights" have come to represent an allocative claim to specific resources: "the right" to housing, to food, to a job, to medical care, etc. Such "rights" also imply, however, detailed claims on society's members. Such claims are im-posed by coercive political institutions with the role of determining and supervising the details of resource alloca-tions between individuals or between production units and industries. It follows that the extension in the meaning of the word "rights" actually endangers the institutions sup-porting the freedom experienced in Western societies. The fashionable notion suggests policies and arrangements im-plicitly advocated by the NIEO and its underlying ideolog-ical theme. But under the institutions protecting the power monopoly of an oligarchy, the "new rights" are converted into obligations to the ruling apparatus. The emphasis on "human rights" as a political component of our foreign policy is therefore neither sufficient nor really appropriate. It also offers excellent opportunities for suitable reinterpretations according to a Marxian theme.[26] Still, Senator Moynihan deserves credit for grappling with a central issue of U.S. policy. He directs our attention to the fact that there is a sociopolitical confrontation in our time and advises that our policy be formulated in full awareness of the ideological battle. Indeed, the sociopolitical case for a free society should be a cornerstone of U.S. foreign policy. This requires a characterization of free societies, not in terms of the now-ambivalent "human rights" concept, but in terms of the relevant institutions assuring the freedom and opportunities we have known. These institutional arrangements include severe constitutional constraints on the range of governmental powers and activities, private property, and a dominant reliance on the market mechanism to guide the allocation of resources.

The Bureaucracy's Incentives

It seems doubtful that the conceptual failure of the West explains the political behavior previously described. One naturally wonders why the conceptual vacuum persists. The answer, I suspect, lies in the pattern of incentives embedded in the bureaucratic structure of the foreign services.

People do change beliefs and attitudes whenever the stakes are sufficiently large. Changes are quite costly, however, requiring unpleasant efforts and separation from accustomed habits. They also involve substantial investment in learning new procedures and acquiring new information. Such costs are taken on by most people only in case the return expected is sufficiently large. The bureaucratic structure of nonmarket organizations tend to raise

---

26 A report published by Marvin Stone on the editorial page of *U.S. News and World Report*, January 16, 1978, is noteworthy in this context. We read: "Communist boss Gierek told me during an hour-long interview in his Warsaw office: 'It seems to me that you Americans make one cardinal mistake in believing that human rights was invented by your side.' In his view human rights means the right to food, a job and shelter." In such terms a prison society satisfies the criteria of human rights most adequately.

the costs and lower the returns associated with its individual members' investments in changing their views or the surrounding beliefs. The pattern of incentives assures the survival of the inherited "admissible range of procedures and views" to which the higher echelons of the permanent government have become attuned.

Another important aspect concerns the manner of determining achievement and success in the performance of duties assigned by the bureaucracy. There is a strong presumption that a negotiator or representative at a conference should be able to exhibit some "result," some instrument emerging from the process with appropriate signatures attached. The training of a career person in the foreign service is geared to a permanent stance of ready-and-willing negotiation. This implies a conditioning that blurs, in general, the crucial underlying contours. The mind is immediately channeled into an approach that screens out relevant features of reality beyond manageably isolated packages of technical detail, which offer definite advantages in separating out and converging toward resolvable issues.[27] The "achievement incentive" that induces negotiators or conference delegations to "come back" with a signed document of sorts is reinforced by the media. This was made starkly visible in the spring of 1977 on the occasion of Secretary of State Vance's visits to Moscow and the Middle East. It was quite unlikely that these visits would produce any serious results. They should have been understood as a step in the continuous long-run exploration of avenues and positions. Nevertheless, when Secretary Vance repeatedly "came home" without waving the obligatory piece of paper, the media decided that he had dismally failed in his endeavor. The achievement incentive probably also contributes to the congratulatory optimism of U.S. delegations, described in Senator Moynihan's article included in this volume. Signed-and-sealed documents with implicitly threatening content

---

27 Some proposals bearing on political prisoners and raised by the United States at the time are instructive in this context. The sour and almost hostile response by Western and particularly by English representatives reflects the apprehension of foreign-service career personnel toward procedures and issues violating their traditional conditioning and job perception. Moynihan, "Politics of Human Rights."

and language are interpreted as a major success for the United States.

The achievement incentive emerges most particularly in long and drawn-out negotiations. The bureaus and delegations involved, including the appointed top echelons of the respective administration, experience mounting pressure to demonstrate some results to Congress, the media, and the public. The pervasive incentives affecting the foreign-service bureaus also produce a subtle confusion between ends and means. The diplomatic political means of "successful negotiation" replaces the relevant end expressed by a nation's welfare and political position. Events or issues endangering the "progress of ongoing negotiations" are resented by the bureaus involved even if suspension of negotiations would improve the nation's welfare or allow a deeper reflection on the relation between proper means and relevant ends. The strategy of the Third World under the NIEO manifesto is actually well suited to benefit from this achievement incentive. The confrontation with persistent and wide-ranging lists of demands forces United States delegations, given their conditioning and incentive structure, to reject in "a process of genuine bargaining" the more extreme demands and to concede the lesser demands. The process blurs their vision and the reports in the press. One obtains an impression of having gained something, when actually concessions are made without any relevant, or with very dubious, returns. This sequence offers, of course, substantial opportunities to both Second and Third World countries to influence the ultimate outcome via manipulation of the demands addressed to Western countries.

Another dimension of the incentive structure of a domestic foreign-service bureaucracy requires some attention. This bureaucracy is in regular contact with the bureaucracies of other countries or of international agencies, and there are occasional movements of personnel between national and international bureaus. Foreign-service personnel are involved with the preparation of position papers outlining avenues of exploration and the nature of eventual negotiations or conference participation. They are exposed more substantially and more regularly to foreign and international bureaucracies than to their domestic public or legislative bodies. They are thus exposed to various pressures from their colleagues in foreign and international offices, and these pressures subtly and gradually affect evaluations made and positions suggested by the domestic bureaus. The result is a mutually reinforcing mechanism of narrowly defined achievement incentives with a corresponding exclusion of any broader perspective or sociopolitical analysis of the issues confronting us.[28] Lastly, the stance of permanent negotiation built into the program of the NIEO and the operation of international agencies naturally appeals to the conditioned self-interest of the bureaus. It increases opportunities for their specific professional skills. Similarly, an expanding network of international agencies enlarges the range of work for given bureaus or leads to the creation of new bureaus with new career possibilities.[29]

The Marxian Theme in the West

The effects of the West's conceptual failure and of the traditional incentives of a bureaucracy are reinforced by a third element. This strand involves the very opposite of a lack of vision. It refers to a sociopolitical vision that is substantially related to the Marxian theme underlying the New International Economic Order. Unfortunately, American political terminology, with "liberal-conservative" and "left-right", has more emotive than cognitive usefulness. The positions

---

28 The pressure mechanism is illustrated by the Federal Republic of Germany's eventual acceptance of the extensive interpretation of the mandate of the Stabex system. Further examples are provided by the interaction between the more "progressively accommodating" Scandinavian bureaucracies and other Western representatives in preparation for new rounds in the North-South dialogue centered on the common fund and raw-material buffers. Lastly, Switzerland, generally considered by "opinion makers" as the least progressive country, produces a remarkable observation. A few years ago the voters rejected, under a "facultative referendum" and by a large majority, a program of foreign aid for the Third World. The unease and discomfort of the Swiss government was quite noticeable. It was subjected to criticism, comments, suggestions, demands, etc., at usual and regular contacts with the bureaus of other countries. Within three months of the referendum's outcome, the Federal Council of Switzerland declared that the Swiss government would have to find some means to execute a transfer of wealth in spite of the voters' expressed wishes. Eventually, in October 1977, the Council publicly announced some suitable proposals, which, adjusted for the size of the U.S. economy, would involve about $3.2 billion.

29 These last remarks explain the State Department's attitude with respect to the ILO. Once negotiations and representation are assigned a value independent of the sociopolitical context and their consequences for a country's long-run position, one easily concludes that the United States should remain at the ILO and "maintain contacts."

so labeled encompass very different views, and the terms blur the issues. The crucial point is that central building blocks of the Marxian theme expressed in the Third World's manifesto and the Second World's ideological imperialism appear as important centerpieces of the sociopolitical vision governing influential sections of the Western intelligentsia. In particular, the "sociological model of man" has been warmly embraced in some Western intellectual circles.[30] Since, according to this model, man is determined by his social conditions, emphasis is put on the need for liberation from his bondage to the one-dimensional, confining, and suffocating values of a commercial world. The sociological model necessarily directs attention to "government" as the instrument of liberation. It thus produces a political view favoring, on balance, the suppression of private property rights or markets and supporting the growth and extension of the government sector with its bureaucratic apparatus. It also fosters a pronounced egalitarian attitude, with implicit advocacy of the coercive institutions required for implementing egalitarianism. One hardly need emphasize that private business, and particularly private corporations, are approached, under the intellectual circumstances described, with hostility or at least deep reservations. This contrasts sharply with the embrace offered to political institutions and bureaucratic agencies.

My argument will necessarily touch sensitive nerves. But I urge the reader to ponder, beyond an immediate reaction, the essential facts. There should be sufficient observations available to evaluate my thesis. The issue is not whether "liberal" thinkers, intellectuals, or politicians are "Marxists" or advocates of a New Marxian Manifesto. They need not be. The issue is whether the sociopolitical vision inherent in some "liberal positions" is dependent on crucial ideas forming the centerpiece of the ideological war on Western societies.

What are the consequences of this situation? It produces feelings of guilt, visible among Western intelligentsia and examined in some detail by Peter Bauer in one of his contributions to this volume. A view attuned in basic respects to the ideological theme propagated by the Second and

---

30 This issue was discussed in Brunner and Meckling, "Perception of Man."

Third Worlds can hardly resist the exploitation strand of that theme. Thus it cannot resist a sense of responsibility for the gap in wealth or "worldwide hunger and starvation". Western feelings of guilt provide a useful instrument in the ideological battle surrounding the NIEO. They offer opportunities to the Third World to extend the range of "institutional weapons" and to enlarge their demands with the reasonable expectation that guilt feelings blur the West's perception. Western advocates of Western guilt contribute to the political pressures on Western bureaus and representatives. They implicitly accept the principle of "concessionary transfers" and naturally implore us to cultivate the proper attitude of "forthcomingness" rightfully expected by the Third World. The implicit Marxian theme in various strands of Western thought necessarily weakens Western determination. It obstructs, in particular, a proper recognition of the increasing dangers to the survival of free societies. The implicit vision tends to support or actually applaud and reinforce the assault on the United States. While there may be disagreements on the details and technicalities of the NIEO, its central theme and basic political thrust are accepted. Some groups in the West may even be coming to appreciate the political opportunities emerging under the circumstances. U.S. involvement in the diplomatic and bureaucratic tangle of the NIEO promises to yield institutional implementations within the United States that would hasten the trend toward a socialist society desired by these groups. It should be a matter of some concern, therefore, that foreign policy officials who are ideologically sympathetic to the theme behind the NIEO have apparently come to carry more weight in the Carter administration. This development replaces the conceptual vacuum, noted above, with a serious conceptual failure that reinforces the effect of bureaucratic incentives. The likelihood of alternative stances to our foreign policies, encouraging the survival of free societies, hardly seems improved under the circumstances.[31]

---

31 The reader may find of some interest an article by Chalmers Johnson, "Carter in Asia: McGovernism without McGovern," *Commentary*, January 1978.

Is There an Alternative?

The United Nations is frequently presented as man's last hope to prevent the doom of a holocaust. Peace is necessary for the survival of man, and the international organizations are the only means to maintain the chances of peace. We are thus compelled, the argument proceeds, to contribute to the proper functioning of international organizations with a suitable accommodative disposition. A more specific argument with respect to the NIEO bolsters this view. We hear that a refusal by the Western nations to "engage in a process of genuine negotiation" within the framework and premises of the NIEO would unleash disastrous international consequences. An undertone of veiled and dire threats frequently creeps into the discussion.

Both the general and specific arguments badly misconstrue the real situation. The relation between peace and international organizations is substantially more problematic than the standard line assumes. The structure and operation of the international organizations offer opportunities and incentives to search for "issues" or to play up potential conflicts. The forum provided by an international organization can be used to develop rhetoric and actions encouraging popular support for the ruling oligarchy. In this setting, accommodation by a substantial group of countries neither pacifies opponents nor wins friends. "Reassurances and accommodation" produce just the opposite, strengthening the opportunities associated with a demanding and aggressive policy by others. Political friends or allies also realize that political friendship yields little benefits under the circumstances. The reality of international organizations and their effect on "peace" is therefore substantially more complex than the United Nations propaganda line admits. Opportunities for conflict and for avoiding major conflagration in the world depend ultimately on the political perception and will of the United States. Although a less accommodative and reassuring stance may not decrease conflicts, it would change their nature and pattern. It would lower the return on aggressive demands thrown at the West and would induce a more circumspect choice of conflicts to be negotiated. We need to understand that conflicts are not imposed by extraneous social forces, but express to a substantial extent political choices. These choices are, moreover, conditioned by opportunities determined by the mode of operation of the agencies involved and by the behavior of major countries. A significant modification of these opportunities affects the choices of potential conflicts under consideration and the actual conflicts pursued.

These considerations extend to the specific argument that points to awesome dangers in any refusal to develop a "concessionary disposition". But the threatening undertone of the argument requires additional attention. The dire threats of repercussions are not very clear and really make no sense. Suppose the United States explicitly rejects the underlying ideological theme of the NIEO evidenced in the language of resolutions, documents, proposals, or even agreements. We may be told that the Third World will form a voting bloc with the Second World. But that has already happened to a large extent. This bloc dominated the meetings of the ILO in the summer of 1977 and the Geneva conference on crime a year earlier. But what else could happen? Do we have visions of African armies marching on Washington, or are we concerned that the African nations may be driven into the Russian orbit, or are we afraid of inviting retaliation by a worldwide raw-materials cartel that would force us to our knees? We may safely disregard the first fear, and the others are extreme versions of a distorted, political perception.

It has been observed by several commentators—among others, by Peter Bauer in this volume—that the Third World does not exhibit monolithic unity or uniformity of interests and situations. It is a highly complex array of societies and countries, with remarkable differences in economic experiences and a substantial variety in levels of real income. The raid on the wealth of Western countries is really the only major cohesive force among the countries of the Third World. We should recognize, therefore, the significant fact that the accommodating policies of the major industrialized nations supported and nurtured this cohesiveness by encouraging exploitation of the opportunities discussed above. Less accommodation and reassurance, implicit in a policy based on rational considerations and maximizing the survival opportunities of free societies, lowers the rewards from the single strand of cohesiveness among the large mass of Third World nations.

U.S. policy should thus reject the NIEO and its underlying theme and develop a clear alternative that supports the long-run viability of free societies. Such an alternative requires four general items. First, the United States needs a stable, predictable, and reliable line of domestic policies that avoid the worldwide destabilization produced by United States policies in the past years. Second, the United States should lead the Western nations in opening their economies by lowering all barriers to international trade. Third, all obstructions to the movement of private investment need to be removed. An increasing number of countries in the Third World might, under the circumstances, reexamine their own economic policies and increasingly shift toward economic development based on innovative explorations and efforts pursued by private investors. Mounting confidence in the reliability and stability of the rules of the game offered by Third World countries would substantially raise the flow of private investments and would thus expand job opportunities and living standards in participating countries. We are led to the fourth and last point: U.S. policymakers and representatives must recognize the fundamental sociopolitical issue confronting us and learn to articulate forcefully and without defensive apologies the case for free societies. This should be complemented by relentless attention to Third World domestic policies. This attention includes proposals for institutional reform or alternative economic policies, to be submitted to various Third World countries for their consideration. The Tanzanian and other governments are certainly at liberty to disorganize their economies and lower the quality of life for their citizens, but our articulation should make explicit the consequences of their domestic policies. Our constructive advice may well go unheeded, but an incisive presentation forms an integral part of our coherent articulation.

This alternative program probably impresses the traditional activist as meager and "insensitive." He need not worry. The political chances for its acceptance as U.S. policy are small. But the apparent insensitivity and modesty of the proposal would assure a rising "quality of life" for large masses in many countries. In contrast, the "concerned activism" pursued in accordance with the New Marxian Manifesto entrenches mass poverty, raises the potential of war and conflict as a means of acquiring resources, and intensifies a worldwide system of oppression under the guise of humanitarian concerns.

Rachel McCulloch

Economic Policy in the United Nations:

A New International Economic Order?

Introduction

A New International Economic Order?

Citizens of the advanced countries have been perplexed and dismayed by the recent mood in the United Nations. With increasing vehemence, representatives of the Third World have expressed their dissatisfaction with the pace of economic development in the poorer regions of the globe. These leaders have castigated the United States and other wealthy countries for their indifference to the needs and aspirations of the poor nations. Indeed, the rich countries

Reprinted, with some changes, by permission of the author and North-Holland Publishing Co., from *International Organization, National Policies and Economic Development*, ed. Karl Brunner and Allan H. Meltzer, Carnegie-Rochester Conference Series on Public Policy, vol. 6. Copyright 1977 by North-Holland Publishing Co.

This is a revised version of the paper presented at the Carnegie-Rochester Public Policy Conference (Rochester, N.Y., April 1976). The extensive comments and criticisms of the conference participants are gratefully acknowledged. I am also indebted to Jorge Dominguez, Stephen Krasner, J. Iluston McCulloch, and Joseph S. Nye for their comments on the earlier version, and to Barbara Norwood and Karl Sauvant for helpful conversations.

stand accused of actively perpetuating poverty through their neocolonial economic policies.

A voting majority of poor countries in the UN General Assembly has sought to convert the claims of the developing nations into economic rights and the desired responses of the developed nations into duties or obligations rather than matters of discretion. As yet, the developing countries have gained control of the international machinery for publicizing and legitimizing their demands, but not of the means for compelling the developed countries to provide the tangible resources needed to carry out these programs. However, the rhetoric emanating recently from UN forums darkly threatens the use of new economic weapons, and these threats have gained credibility in the years since the stunning economic assault on the industrialized nations by the Organization of Petroleum Exporting Countries (OPEC). A more subtle but perhaps ultimately more effective form of pressure relies on appeals to the guilt feelings of the rich by implying that their present economic status could only have been attained through past and present exploitation of the world's poor.

The often acrimonious debate between rich and poor nations has centered on Third World demands for establishment of a New International Economic Order (NIEO). This vaguely defined objective entails adoption of a number of economic and social proposals intended to redistribute world wealth in favor of the countries termed poor or developing. Ironically, neither designation of the would-be beneficiaries of these redistribution schemes is particularly appropriate. The bloc of self-styled "poor" nations includes countries with per capita incomes higher than those of a fair number of industrialized nations. Likewise, the label of "developing," accurate for some, constitutes mere wishful thinking for others better described by the older term "backward regions."

NIEO became an official part of UN vocabulary in May 1974, when the Sixth Special Session of the General Assembly adopted a Declaration on the Establishment of a New International Economic Order over the objections of developed-country representatives. This was followed in December 1974 by General Assembly approval of the Charter of Economic Rights and Duties of States, which spelled out in greater detail a number of principles intended to promote the establishment of the NIEO.[1] For the developed countries, the Charter was unacceptable in both tone and substance. Particularly objectionable were provisions affirming each state's "full permanent sovereignty" over its natural resources and economic activities, specifically including the right to nationalize foreign property under terms set by domestic rather than international law. Furthermore, while the Charter reserved to primary-commodity exporting states the "right" to associate in producers' organizations, consuming nations were enjoined from common retaliatory action under the "duty" to respect that right by refraining from applying economic and political measures to limit it.

At least three distinct aspects of the NIEO deserve attention. First, there are the specific proposals which have been advanced and—perhaps more crucial—the view of economic reality upon which they rest. Second, there is an explicit rationale for massive redistribution. And, finally, there are the changes in the role and structure of the United Nations implied by the NIEO. The specific proposals themselves contain little that is new. Most can be traced to venerable ancestors in UN documents dating from the early days of the organization. Some, such as the proposals regarding trade in primary commodities, predate even the founding of the United Nations. A few of the proposals are actually rather sensible and efficiency-creating, such as those which call for lower barriers to trade flows. Others, such as the commodity buffer-stock arrangement hotly debated at the May 1976 United Nations Conference on Trade and Development (UNCTAD IV), are potentially harmful to the world economy and perhaps even to their intended beneficiaries.

It is less the specific proposals than the way in which the overall program has been put forward that makes the NIEO unacceptable to many in the industrialized countries. The proposed measures have been justified in terms of *restitution* for past wrongs perpetrated under colonial, quasi-colonial,

---

1 General Assembly Resolution 3201 (S-VI), adopted without vote on May 1, 1974; and Resolution 3281 (XXIX), adopted on December 12, 1974, by a roll-call vote of 120 in favor to 6 against, with 10 abstentions.

and neocolonial regimes. By rooting their reform proposals in this rationale, the advocates of the NIEO have called forth a flurry of denunciations from articulate neoconservatives like P. T. Bauer (1976), Daniel Patrick Moynihan (1975), and Irving Kristol (1975). These critics argue that, far from impoverishing their colonial subjects, the industrialized countries have actually been the source of much of the wealth currently to be found in Third World nations. History offers considerable support for this position; colonial ties served as the potent vehicle for international transfers of knowledge and capital. Yet the argument goes too far; the colonizers quite rationally sought out those areas which offered greatest natural advantage in terms of resource endowment or location. The landlocked countries, the regions of inhospitable climate, and the resource-poor lands are not poor merely because they missed the Midas touch of the colonial powers. However, the question of responsibility is a distracting one. Shrill demands for restitution have diverted the attention of critics from what may be a far more important issue in terms of long-range significance—the future of the United Nations as an economic policymaking body.[2]

The particular proposals included under the NIEO umbrella have shifted significantly over the past three years. However, a basic aspect of the NIEO as a whole is that it would effect an important increase in the power of the United Nations as an economic policymaking body. Interestingly, even those who have rejected many of the specific NIEO proposals have been more receptive to the general objective of investing the United Nations with greater power to make and carry out worldwide economic policy. For example, this is precisely the theme of the May 1975 report of the group of experts, headed by Richard Gardner, on structural reform in the United Nations (United Nations 1975). In focusing on an array of specific proposals, friends and critics alike have failed to appreciate that the NIEO is fundamentally an attempt by the developing nations to move the locus of international economic policymaking into the United Nations, which until now has been able to

2 Moynihan did raise this question in his much-quoted *Commentary* (1975) article (reprinted in this volume). However, he later lost interest in the subject, having immersed himself in the broader (but related) question of the future of democracy.

play only a hortative role in determining changes in the international system. This raises a basic question. If the United Nations begins to exert a serious influence on world economic policy, what kind of policy is likely to be forthcoming?

This issue is examined from a number of perspectives in the sections which follow. Below, an example is used to provide a tentative characterization of the United Nations as an economic policymaking body. The next section reviews the recent economic and political developments leading up to the current confrontation in the United Nations; the following section describes the evolution and structure of the United Nations as an economic policymaking body; and the final section summarizes the substantive economic issues currently before the United Nations and attempts an assessment of the major proposals now under consideration.

The Economics of Restitution

In characterizing the probable consequences of an important further expansion in the capacity of the United Nations to undertake international economic policymaking, it is illuminating to begin with a case somewhat removed from the NIEO. In November 1975, just after the Seventh Special Session, the General Assembly passed Resolution 3391 (XXX), entitled "Restitution of works of art to countries victims of expropriation."[3] The resolution was passed by a majority of 96 to none, with 16 abstentions. It calls on members "to make restitution of works of art, monuments, museum pieces, manuscripts, and documents, which are part of a nation's cultural heritage, to their countries of origin." Recognizing a special obligation incumbent upon countries which have acquired valuable works of art as a result of colonial rule or military occupation, the resolution affirms that "prompt restitution of such objects, without charge, was calculated to strengthen international cooperation inasmuch as it constituted reparation for damage done." A similar resolution adopted in 1973 was largely ignored.[4] For this reason, the 25 sponsoring nations decided that the General Assembly should reiterate its appeal.

3 See *UN Monthly Chronicle*, December 1975.
4 General Assembly Resolution 3187 (XXVIII).

In introducing the resolution on behalf of the sponsoring nations, Zaire said that restitution of works of art should be understood in terms of the role they could play in awakening each people to its own identity and creative genius. Egypt, a cosponsor, urged prompt restitution of works of art removed during colonial administrations. Greece urged the termination of the practice of removing works of art from any country under any pretext.[5] Poland and the Byelorussian SSR recalled the destruction of their cultural heritage by Nazi invaders. Algeria stated that it had been plundered on the eve of independence.

On the whole, the tone of the resolution and the implied view of economic transactions give a surprisingly accurate picture of UN policy on broader economic issues. In terms of its economic content, the resolution has four noteworthy features.

1. *Property relationships.* The resolution contains an implicit assumption that a broad class of present property relationships necessarily reflects past exploitation. No attempt is made to distinguish acquisitions made through force or theft from routine legitimate purchases, or even removal to protect treasures from destruction in time of war or natural disaster. There is an automatic presumption that restitution or reparation is due. Since the property rights in question are viewed as illegitimate, they can be arbitrarily reassigned. Furthermore, private property rights are now seen to exclude the right to transfer ownership to foreigners.

2. *Intent.* The primary aim of the resolution is to promote a redistribution of wealth between developed countries and developing countries.

3. *Price.* In the resolution, price serves a distributive rather than an allocative function. The "just price" for this transaction is set at zero, a determination based on the relative wealth of the transactors.

4. *Economic efficiency.* By casting into doubt the status of future transactions, the resolution whittles away the possible mutual gains from future exchange. A developing

---

5 This would include, one must assume, saving the Parthenon friezes from being burned for lime.

country may well wish to trade a few treasures for a few tractors. The would-be partner to such a transaction is deterred at least marginally by this devaluation of the security of property relations. As with many UN proposals, the attempt to get a bigger piece of the pie leads to a shrinking pie.

The emphasis on redistribution, rejection of price as a mechanism of resource allocation, failure to appreciate the economic function of secure property rights, and other similar features have been interpreted by some critics (e.g., Moynihan 1975) as evidence of a coherent socialist philosophy at work within the United Nations. However, this characterization appears to be valid only in the very limited sense that nearly all religious and philosophical systems must be regarded as socialistic. The functions performed by property rights, prices, and markets are not well understood even by those who uphold the principle of the free market. The failure of UN delegates to challenge myths about the capitalist system appears to mirror the general lack of sophistication on this subject in other intellectual discourse.[6]

Apart from its characteristic economic underpinnings, the resolution also serves as an example of current UN effectiveness as a policymaking body. The measure was passed by an overwhelming majority of countries, 96–0. As in many other cases, the majority comprised the developing-nation members along with some sympathetic Second World countries; the abstainers were all industrialized nations. However, despite the overwhelming majority approval (on two separate occasions), the resolution has had no effect. The General Assembly, sometimes given the benign label "Town Meeting of the World," has no power to enforce its policy recommendations except to the extent that resolutions deal with the operation of the United Nations itself. The current situation in which poor nations have a vast majority of the votes and rich nations pay the bulk of the total cost of the operation affords little or no possibility for the United Nations to force an objectionable policy upon the developed countries. The NIEO would en-

---

6 For a sophisticated and tough-minded presentation of the case for capitalism, see Brunner (1976).

hance the ability of the majority to implement policies without changing the basic character of the policies chosen.

Political Evolution of the Debate

Realignment of Perceptions

Few of the specific proposals advanced as part of the NIEO can be called new. What *is* new about the NIEO is that these proposals are now receiving the serious consideration of the industrialized countries, without whose active cooperation little reordering of the international economy is likely to come about. Heightened attention to the expressed needs and desires of the developing nations followed closely on the heels of the 1973 Arab oil embargo and the subsequent success of OPEC in achieving spectacular increases in the price of oil. These events have had far-reaching repercussions.

First, the OPEC venture altered drastically the perceptions of Third World countries concerning their own economic prospects. In marked contrast to the hardship and national sacrifice stressed in traditional development success stories, the OPEC members had benefited from a process entailing rapid results and minimal effort—indeed an irresistible combination. The possibility of achieving instantly the desired results of economic development through a redistribution of existing wealth, rather than through the far slower process of creating new wealth, presented a fresh and alluring vision of the future. The OPEC route to prosperity also had a second virtue which no doubt strengthened its appeal in the eyes of Third World leaders. Unlike traditional development strategies, prosperity brought about largely through higher export prices requires little internal economic transformation and, thus, far less risk of political instability and challenges to current leadership.

OPEC's successes also conveyed an eloquent message to the industrialized countries. The OPEC members had managed to engineer a vast improvement in their joint fortunes without the assistance or consent of their "benefactors." This outcome had a predictable impact upon the perceived balance of economic power between the industrialized bloc and the Third World. While perhaps only a minority in the developed countries continue to view OPEC as the first in a continuing sequence of successful producer cartels controlling world flows of raw materials, many more have acknowledged the latent collective power of the supplier nations to impose serious, if temporary, dislocations on the international system.

Without OPEC's dramatic show of force, it seems unlikely that the NIEO could have moved so swiftly to the forefront of world affairs. However, much of the tone and substance of the current confrontation between the industrialized countries of the "North" and the developing nations of the "South" had already been set by the time of the Arab oil embargo. The confrontation of the rich nations by the poor nations, long implicit in international economic relations, became highly visible at the Summit Conference of Non-Aligned Nations held in Algiers in September 1973. Only the fourth international meeting of the nonaligned since the 1955 call by Tito, Nehru, and others for a "third position" in the cold war, the conference was far larger than its predecessors. Participants included leaders of 76 nonaligned states, as well as observers representing at least a dozen other countries and national liberation movements. Convened by Algerian President Boumediène with the express purpose of formulating a common economic position for its members, the conference marked a shift of the nonaligned movement from political to economic issues as its primary organizing principle.

The theme of the conference was expressed by banners proclaiming, "Poor of the world, unite!" A draft declaration prepared by the Algerians urged the world's majority to rid themselves of the colonial yoke, to achieve real independence by eliminating foreign monopolies and assuming control of natural resources.[7] Conference participants stressed the gains to the Third World from solidarity in confrontations with the industrialized nations. An economic declaration issued on the last day emphasized two specific economic goals: improved terms of trade for commodity exporters and full national control over natural resources. The declaration urged member nations to form producer associations for major products "to halt the degradation of their terms of trade, to eliminate harmful activities by

---

7 *New York Times*, September 3, 1973.

multinational companies, and to reinforce their negotiating power."[8]

While economics dominated the agenda at Algiers, the Arab states introduced a number of political issues as well. Highest on the list was unified action against Israel, but Asian and Latin American representatives, mainly interested in common economic action, declined to support Arab proposals for economic sanctions.[9] And, although the conference took place just a short time prior to the Arab oil embargo, the use of oil or other commodities as political weapons was not discussed. However, the success of OPEC in achieving steady increases in the producers' share of oil profits was cited as an example of the economic benefits to be derived from common action through commodity producers' associations.

Neither the issue of terms of trade nor that of full control over natural resources by the developing nations was new. The alleged deterioration of the terms of trade experienced by raw-material producers was stressed by followers of Dr. Raúl Prebisch, first secretary general of UNCTAD. Sovereignty over natural resources and the accompanying right to nationalize foreign holdings and determine compensation under national rather than international law had been the subject of General Assembly debates since 1962. Even the strategy of common economic action had long been favored by the so-called Group of 77, the semiofficial caucus of developing nations in UNCTAD. The real significance of the Algiers conference lies in the emergence of a clear North-South polarity, a conscious political decision to pit the underdeveloped world against the industrialized world, whether capitalist or communist.[10]

Development of the Issues

The Algiers Conference of Non-Aligned Nations marked the beginning of a two-year episode of intensified North-South confrontation over economic issues, both within the United Nations and in other international forums. However, the

---

8 *New York Times*, September 11, 1973.

9 *New York Times*, September 10, 1973.

10 However, the substance of the nonaligned economic position clearly predates Algiers. See Jankowitsch and Sauvant (1976).

underlying areas of conflict had been established much earlier in such documents as the General Assembly's 1961 resolution designating a United Nations Development Decade.[11] That document provides an interesting comparison with more recent resolutions bearing on the same basic issue of international economic cooperation for development. The 1961 resolution reviewed in positive terms the progress already made through the efforts of both developed and developing countries but noted a growing gap between per capita incomes in the rich and poor nations. The resolution called for intensified efforts on the part of both; an overall objective of a minimum annual rate of growth of aggregate national income of 5 percent was set. The specific recommendations included policies to assure primary-commodity exporters the opportunity to sell more of their products at "stable and remunerative prices," as a means of providing greater opportunity for self-financing of economic development. Likewise, the resolution called for policies to "ensure to the developing countries an equitable share of earnings from the extraction and marketing of their natural resources by foreign capital, in accordance with generally accepted reasonable earnings on invested capital." An accompanying resolution called for substantial increases in the flow of international assistance, to "reach as soon as possible approximately 1 percent of the combined national incomes of the economically advanced countries."

An interesting feature of the resolutions passed in conjunction with the United Nations Development Decade is the absence of certain important rhetorical elements present in most recent UN documents. The poverty of the Third World is nowhere attributed to past or present colonial or neocolonial exploitation by the industrialized countries. There is no call to "redress existing injustices." Rather, the resolutions affirm past progress while urging both rich and poor nations to intensify their efforts. Likewise, calls for international measures to supplant markets are also absent. The market appears in the resolutions as a positive force for development, impeded in its benign function by tariffs and other trade barriers. Many of the specific recommenda-

---

11 General Assembly Resolution 1715 (XVI), December 19, 1961. Also see Resolutions 1706–20 adopted the same day.

tions made in the resolutions constitute movements toward freer trade. Especially notable in this connection is the resolution on "International trade as the primary instrument of economic development."[12]

The Development Decade saw major institutional evolution within the United Nations as the organization responded to pressures from the new majority of developing nations.[13] The mammoth UNCTAD I held in Geneva in 1964 shifted world attention at least transiently to the needs and objectives of the Third World. But substantive accomplishments were few, while rising aspirations on the part of Third World leaders increased the gulf between aims and achievements. In 1970, the General Assembly passed a resolution proclaiming a second United Nations Development Decade.[14] The preamble to that document, while duly noting past efforts, expresses frustration with achievements to date. Furthermore, the growing per capita income gap between rich and poor is underlined in tones of reproach: "While a part of the world lives in great comfort or even affluence, much of the larger part suffers from abject poverty...." The preamble goes on to state that the success of international development programs rests in large part on elimination of colonialism.

In terms of development objectives, the resolution on the second Development Decade goes into greater detail than its predecessors. Growth targets are set not only for national income as a whole but for annual expansion of agriculture, manufacturing output, domestic saving, imports, and exports. In terms of policy recommendations, the section on international trade represents a move away from the strong free-trade orientation of nine years before. The document proposes "a set of general principles on pricing policy" for primary commodities. Also notable in the resolution is a call for serious consideration of the establishment of a link between allocation of new Special Drawing Rights (SDR) and the provision of international development finance. This proposal reflects an increasing emphasis on

---

12 General Assembly Resolution 1707 (XVI), December 19, 1961.

13 See the next section for a detailed account.

14 General Assembly Resolution 2626 (XXV), October 24, 1970.

the part of developing countries on resource flows which are automatic, unconditional, and untied.

By the time of UNCTAD III in 1972, an air of increasing militancy was evident in the Group of 77, by then including nearly one hundred less-developed countries (ldc's). Strong dissatisfaction was expressed with U.S. delays in implementing the Generalized System of Preferences. The ldc view of the industrialized world—and of the United States in particular—as its willing partner in efforts to promote economic development had been seriously eroded. That erosion resulted from both unrealistic expectations in the Third World and the primary preoccupation of developed-country policymakers with their own national concerns. The combined effect was to strengthen the emerging position that development could only be achieved if the developing countries themselves gained a more significant role in international institutions, a process which had already begun in the United Nations during the previous decade. The stage was now set for a major ldc challenge to the economic and political power of the industrialized world. Rather than continuing to argue over the size of their slice of the world economic pie, the developing nations now looked for control of the knife (Gregg 1972).

Confrontation and Escalation

Press coverage of the Fourth Summit Conference of Non-Aligned Countries at Algiers emphasized an apparent lack of unity of purpose among the members represented. Much attention was given to doubts expressed by some conferees themselves concerning the feasibility of carrying out common action for economic or political ends.[15] However, the capacity of the nonaligned to take unified action to achieve joint objectives was swiftly reassessed by the industrialized world just weeks later when the Arab oil embargo began. The subsequent quadrupling of the world price of oil convinced the richer nations that it might be timely to give developing-country grievances a fresh hearing. While the primary concern of the industrialized countries was to negotiate a reduction in the price of oil from its unprecedented new level, the producing nations demanded that the

---

15 *New York Times*, September 4–12, 1973.

agenda of any conference to discuss oil prices include other commodities as well. Meanwhile, other raw-material producers emulated the tactic of joint action so successfully exploited by OPEC. In the favorable climate of strong demand fueled by rapid economic growth in the developed nations, new producers' organizations bargained aggressively to get higher prices for their raw-material exports. While none of these efforts was as spectacularly successful as the OPEC coup, some developed-country observers noted the successes and argued that it was only a matter of time before effective cartels would exercise control over the markets for most primary products.[16]

In early 1974, the General Assembly unanimously decided to hold a Sixth Special Session to discuss raw materials and development, even though a special session on development and economic cooperation was already scheduled for 1975.[17] The Sixth Special Session, held in April and May 1974, thus became the first to be devoted principally to economic issues. The Declaration on the Establishment of a New International Economic Order,[18] adopted without a vote at that session over the objections of the United States, Germany, France, Japan, and the United Kingdom, brought into the United Nations many of the attitudes and aims which had been expressed a few months earlier at Algiers. For the developed countries, the most significant sections of the Declaration were those affirming "full permanent sovereignty of every State over its natural resources and all economic activities," including the right to nationalize foreign-owned property under domestic law, the right to "restitution and full compensation for the exploitation and depletion" of resources, and the right to regulate and supervise activities of multinational corporations in the national interest. The Charter of Economic Rights and Duties of States,[19] adopted over the objections of the United States and other developed countries by the General Assembly in its regular session a few months later,

16 Bergsten (1974a, 1974b) was the leading proponent of this view.
17 *IMF Survey*, September 29, 1975.
18 General Assembly Resolution 3201 (S-VI).
19 General Assembly Resolution 3281 (XXIX).

added fuel to the fire by reserving to developing nations the right to form commodity exporters' associations in order to pursue common economic and political ends while appending the duty of consuming nations to refrain from measures which would limit the effectiveness of producers' groups. The Conference of Developing Countries on Raw Materials, held in Dakar in February 1975, reaffirmed the principles of Algiers and added a call for establishment of an indexation mechanism to "maintain and strengthen the purchasing power" of commodity exporting nations.[20] Also emphasized in the Dakar Action Program on raw materials were measures to increase processing of raw materials in developing countries, to improve the competitive position of natural products versus synthetics, and to promote diversification of the economies of developing nations. Furthermore, the conference "invited" industrialized nations to agree to a moratorium on debt contracted by the developing nations until their development objectives had been achieved, as well as to rescheduling or outright cancellation of debts contracted on "unfavorable terms."

The Second General Conference of the United Nations Industrial Development Organization (UNIDO) held in Lima the following month produced the Lima Declaration[21] reaffirming most of the Dakar proposals and setting a specific and ambitious target for industrialization of the developing nations. Noting that the developing nations constitute about 60 percent of world population while production of manufactured goods in those countries makes up only about 7 percent of the world total, the Lima Declaration called for an increase in that share to 25 percent by the year 2000. This announced goal caused chagrin in Western Europe and the United States as industrialists there envisioned manufacturing capacity idled by competition from Third World exports (Janssen 1976). These reactions largely failed to take into account the expansion of developing-country purchasing power which would inevitably accompany such a dramatic growth of industrial output—the degree to which developed-country production of manu-

---

20 The Action Program and resolutions on economic matters of the Dakar conference are reproduced from UNCTAD (1975a).

21 Reprinted in *UN Monthly Chronicle*, May 1975.

factures would be displaced rather than augmented could be quite small.

Did the frequent repetition and elaboration of unrealistic and even outrageous demands reflect the inexperience and lack of sophistication of the new leaders of the Third World coalition? Or were they part of an effective strategy for wresting economic concessions from indifferent or hostile governments in the industrialized nations? Some years hence, the autobiographies and posthumously published diaries of elder statesmen el-Qaddafi, Bouteflika, and Echeverrìa may yield some insights into the significance of this interesting historical period. However, in terms of results, the techniques appear to have been at least somewhat effective.

In early 1975, members of the European Economic Community (EEC) endorsed the Lomé Convention with 46 African, Caribbean, and Pacific developing nations. Among the far-reaching provisions of this package was an export-earnings stabilization scheme for primary-commodity producers (Bywater 1975). Then, in the spring and summer of 1975, a series of speeches by Secretary of State Kissinger signaled a thaw in American policy toward the Third World. In particular, the speeches indicated U.S. willingness to consider commodity agreements on a "commodity-by-commodity" basis (Frank 1975). Although the concessions fell far short of ldc demands, representatives of developing nations privately indicated their willingness to back down on some issues in exchange for positive moves on the part of the United States. As the Seventh Special Session of the General Assembly approached, the State Department spent a frenzied summer formulating specific proposals which could gain the approval of both the developing nations and free market oriented Treasury officials. Secretary Kissinger's speech, delivered at the Seventh Special Session by U.S. Ambassador Moynihan, was less important for the comprehensive package of economic proposals it contained than as the first clear signal that the United States was willing to make some concrete concessions to Third World demands.

Economics in the United Nations

Transformation of UN Membership and Focus

The developing countries are now seeking an important increase in the power of the United Nations to determine economic policy for the international community—a change which would enhance their collective leverage in the world economic system. This objective implies a major transformation of the United Nations from its present status. However, the role of economics in the United Nations today is already significantly different from that envisioned by the founders.

The United Nations of 1945 was primarily an organization to secure world peace; political rather than economic issues were to be its central concern. Nevertheless, the provisions of the Charter reflected the conviction that preservation of world peace necessarily entails responsibility for world economic and social problems. Events leading to World War II had vividly underlined the contribution to political instability made by economic discontent. Thus, from the very beginning, the United Nations was supplied with a mandate for action to promote economic and social progress. However, the reality of today differs from the conception of the founders in important respects. Economic and social activities have expanded to dominate the total operating budget of the United Nations—at least four-fifths of the $1.5 billion now spent annually by the UN system goes to support economic and social programs (United Nations 1975, intro.). Furthermore, the economic and social activities undertaken are almost entirely redistributive in character, their primary and nearly exclusive focus being the countries of the Third World. Finally, the divergence of political and economic influence within the UN membership has greatly undermined its effectiveness in economic and social undertakings.

Like the current drive for the NIEO, the rapid changes which have already transformed the United Nations' role in economic activities are a reflection of dramatic changes in the membership of the organization. In 1945, ldc's exerted little independent political influence within the United Nations; today they constitute an overwhelming majority of the membership (Kotschnig 1968). Of the newer members, most have small populations and underdeveloped economies. Insulated from the main currents of world politics by their geographic remoteness and economic backwardness, these countries have viewed participation in the United Nations primarily as a means of generating the external resource flows required to finance their internal economic transformation.

All members of the United Nations are members of the General Assembly. Each sovereign state casts one vote.[22] The number of ldc members in the United Nations need not by itself have generated an automatic majority vote on every issue. However, remarkable solidarity has been maintained through the persistent efforts of the leaders of two largely overlapping groupings, the "nonaligned nations," in number about 110, and the Group of 77 ldc's, also numbering over 100.[23] A group position on each issue is hammered out in private meetings; members then adhere strictly to the official position in all public and semipublic meetings. Efforts by the United States to appeal to particular constituents within the group, such as the "most seriously affected" (poorest) nations, have so far yielded little but frustration. Tentative private expressions of interest are rapidly followed by a public stonewall as group pressure is applied to the straying parties.

The actual powers of the General Assembly are few. The Assembly can make recommendations on any matter except those on the agenda of the Security Council, but apart from ones which concern the internal affairs of the organization, the resolutions of the General Assembly carry no legal force; they are binding neither on the member states nor on the citizens of those states (Goodrich 1974, chap. 2). The General Assembly thus functions mainly as a forum in which member states can express their views and formulate general principles for the activities of the organization.

The obvious disparity between voting power in the General Assembly and financial obligations to the United Nations

---

22 On the majoritarian voting system, see Claude (1971, chap. 7).

23 The Group of 77, originally 75, first came to prominence as an economic bloc of developing nations at UNCTAD I in 1964. The nonaligned originated in 1955 as a political "third position" and only evolved into an economic Third World bloc in 1973. In a 1976 Harvard Law School speech, Professor Clyde Ferguson called the merger of these two blocs the most significant event of the Sixth Special Session.

has tended to undermine the role of the General Assembly in matters of economic policy. The developed nations, and particularly the United States, have responded to the automatic developing-country majority by deflecting substantive decision making to such preferred forums as the World Bank and the International Monetary Fund (IMF), in which members "vote money"; i.e., votes are proportional to financial commitments. The United States has also endeavored to diminish the influence of the United Nations by creating special-purpose organizations to meet the requirements of new programs. Dr. Kissinger's speech prepared for the Seventh Special Session in September 1975 called for the creation of a host of new intergovernmental bodies to implement U.S. proposals, rather than suggesting that these efforts be channeled through existing UN machinery.

"Forum shopping" sometimes serves a useful function; successful negotiations can depend not only on the basic issues but on the composition of delegations as well. But, as with attempts to create cleavages among the 77 through appeal to special-interest groups, the success of the forum-shopping strategy has been limited by the solidarity maintained by the developing group. The positions enunciated by developing-country representatives at the (non-UN) Conference on International Economic Cooperation (CIEC) in Paris are identical to the developing-country positions held in New York. Furthermore, the militant and newly rich OPEC countries are now demanding and obtaining a larger role in these organizations.[24] Thus, the developed countries may no longer be able to shut out the unwelcome views of their economic adversaries, even in the clubs previously kept exclusive by high membership fees.

Economic Machinery of the United Nations

In designing an appropriate structure for international economic cooperation, the framers of the United Nations Charter were circumscribed in their task by the prior existence of a number of specialized intergovernmental agencies (Goodrich 1974, chap. 10). These included the International Labor Organization, the United Nations

---

24 New York Times, August 31, 1975.

Relief and Rehabilitation Administration, the United Nations Food and Agriculture Organization, the International Monetary Fund, and the International Bank for Reconstruction and Development. The domain and autonomy of each special-purpose body was protected by the commitments of various governments and interest groups. Recognizing that much of the future pattern of intergovernmental cooperation had already been set by this existing network of specialized agencies, the authors of the Charter adopted a "functional" approach to economic issues, with powers and responsibilities widely dispersed within a decentralized system.[25]

The Charter called for the creation of six principal organs: the General Assembly, the Security Council, the Economic and Social Council, the Trusteeship Council, the International Court of Justice, and the Secretariat. The Economic and Social Council (ECOSOC) was intended to serve as the economic counterpart of the Security Council and as the focus for the coordination of economic programs and projects undertaken throughout the UN system. In performing this function, ECOSOC confronted at least three major obstacles. First, the task of coordinating the activities of an increasing number of autonomous and semiautonomous bodies—by 1974, these included 14 specialized agencies plus numerous special programs, interagency bodies, and subsidiaries of ECOSOC itself—was of a scale and complexity far beyond what could be successfully undertaken with ECOSOC's modest powers and resources. Furthermore, in contrast to the Security Council, which had been invested under the Charter with primary responsibility for the maintenance of international peace and security, ECOSOC's authority in the economic sphere was subordinated to that of the General Assembly.

Problems raised by this lack of primacy in the economic area were further compounded by the new members' dissatisfaction with ECOSOC's composition. Originally constituted as a group of 18 member states, ECOSOC was considered unrepresentative of the changed membership and dominated in its operations by traditional Western theories

---

25 For an evaluation of functionalism as an approach to peace keeping, see Claude (1971, chap. 17).

of economic development. The efforts of the newer members to gain more effective representation of their economic interests resulted in two expansions of ECOSOC. However, tripling the number of states represented did not increase its effectiveness in achieving the objectives of the members. Rather, the membership expansion has had the effect of "making the Council increasingly a replica of the Assembly itself and as a consequence bringing into question the need of its existence" (Goodrich 1974, p. 66).

The Charter provision for bringing existing and newly created autonomous specialized agencies into relationship with the United Nations allows each agency to retain its own membership structure, financial arrangements, and operational character. While this relationship has the advantage of great flexibility, it also seems in practice to lead to an excessive proliferation of international bureaucracy; with many groups working to achieve the same general purpose, competitive empire building can absorb a considerable fraction of total effort and resources. Of the 14 specialized agencies, the most important in terms of total resources are the International Monetary Fund (IMF) and the International Bank for Reconstruction and Development (World Bank). With votes allocated in proportion to financial commitments, the IMF and World Bank have avoided the policy paralysis characteristic of the United Nations, where the majority which approves new programs lacks the capacity to provide the resources required to make them effective. However, both agencies have been under continued pressure from Third World members to increase the amount of credit available to poorer countries and, more generally, to increase the role of these countries in the policymaking process.[26]

UNCTAD, UNIDO, and UNDP

Within the United Nations itself, dissatisfaction on the part of the newer members with the pace of economic and social progress in general and with the existing machinery in particular has led to a rapid proliferation of the number of

---

26 The IMF has recently taken important steps in this direction: a general increase in the availability of credit, liberalization of the compensatory finance facility, and establishment of a trust fund to provide poor countries with increased credit at low rates of interest (to be financed by sale of gold).

separate bodies attempting to act in each substantive area. The earliest important result of this process was the creation of the United Nations Conference on Trade and Development (UNCTAD), in effect a poor nations' pressure group at the United Nations.[27] During the late 1950s and early 1960s, "the dreams of rapid economic development to follow in the wake of independence were rudely shattered" (Gardner 1968, p. 100). Falling prices for some primary commodities and disappointing levels of foreign aid flows contributed to the pressure from the ldc group for fundamental changes in world trading patterns. Under the charismatic leadership of Dr. Raúl Prebisch of Argentina, pressure mounted for a new body specifically representative of and responsive to the needs of the developing nations. A 1961 General Assembly resolution proclaimed an official United Nations Development Decade.[28] Shortly thereafter, ECOSOC began to formulate plans for a United Nations Conference on Trade and Development to be held in Geneva in 1964. Action by the General Assembly later in the same year gave UNCTAD the status of a permanent organ of the United Nations.

UNCTAD's major role has been as a forum for discussion and analysis of issues related to economic development, largely but not exclusively those aspects of development linked to patterns of world trade. As in the cases of the General Assembly and ECOSOC, UNCTAD decisions and recommendations, except those dealing with the internal affairs of the body, are not binding on the member states. Rather, the aim of UNCTAD has been to change world opinion regarding the key issues of trade and development. One case in which this process has been relatively successful in influencing national policy is that of tariff preferences for ldc's. Under the leadership of Prebisch, UNCTAD urged that manufactured exports of developing countries be given preferential treatment in developed countries' markets. A decade later, such preferential schemes have been enacted by most industrial countries.[29] Even the United States,

---

27 On this role of UNCTAD within the United Nations, see Nye (1974).

28 General Assembly Resolution 2626 (XXV).

29 On UNCTAD efforts to promote the Generalized System of Preferences, see Wall (1971). Provisions of the various national schemes are reviewed in *IMF Survey*, June 23, 1975.

initially opposed to this violation of the "most-favored-nation" principle of nondiscrimination, has now extended tariff preferences on a wide class of imports from developing countries. However, UNCTAD has experienced considerably less success in reshaping developed-country attitudes toward commodity agreements and levels of foreign aid commitments, two other issues which have been focal points of lobbying activity.

The United Nations Industrial Development Organization (UNIDO), a second body specifically designed to serve the needs of the developing countries, was created by the General Assembly in 1965.[30] Modeled after the example of UNCTAD (Elmandjra 1973, p. 56), UNIDO was established to promote industrial development and to accelerate the process of industrialization in the developing countries. UNIDO maintained a relatively inconspicuous public profile until its Second General Conference, held in Lima, Peru, during March 1975. That conference made headlines by calling for an increase in the developing countries' share of world industrial production from its fairly constant level of about 7 percent during the previous decade to 25 percent by the year 2000. Even more newsworthy were statements affirming "the inalienable right of every State to exercise sovereignty over its terrestrial and marine resources... [which] specifically includes the right to nationalize in accordance with *national* laws."[31] As the conferees no doubt intended, the specter of widespread nationalization of foreign investments without recourse to international law caused shock waves throughout the developed world. (By this time, expropriation with unsatisfactory terms of compensation was already a well-established practice in many parts of the developing world. The purpose of international resolutions like the Lima Declaration is to lend legitimacy to the status quo.) The Lima Conference also formulated a plan to convert UNIDO into a specialized agency, "as a means of increasing its authority, autonomy and resources."[32]

---

30 The functions and structure of UNIDO are spelled out in General Assembly Resolution 2152 (XXI), November 17, 1966. On the background of UNIDO, see also *UN Monthly Chronicle*, February 1975.

31 *UN Monthly Chronicle*, April 1975.

32 *UN Monthly Chronicle*, February 1976.

The United Nations Development Program (UNDP) was formed in 1965 by the merger of two previously existing bodies, the Expanded Program of Technical Assistance and the Special Fund.[33] Its primary activity is the provision of technical assistance to developing nations. Unlike UNCTAD and UNIDO, UNDP has no membership but only "participating" governments and specialized agencies. Its Governing Council is constituted so as to give approximately equal voice to financial contributors and aid recipients (Claude 1971, p. 132). UNDP activities are financed entirely by voluntary contributions. Predicting a "liquidity crisis" in 1976, the incoming UNDP administrator recently urged all participating governments to pay their pledges early and to make additional voluntary contributions. In a somewhat different reaction to impending financial stringency, the Governing Council asked the administrator to "reduce the top-heaviness of the UNDP management structure at headquarters, limit staff promotions to the most deserving cases, upgrade posts only on a highly selective basis and stabilize the numbers of positions" in the organization.[34] These contrasting responses to a situation of limited resources provide a nice illustration of the desirable check on empire-building tendencies imposed by a policymaking body which must pay for its policies.

Proposed Structural Reforms

The December 1974 General Assembly resolution[35] called for a special session devoted to development and international economic cooperation. It also authorized the secretary general to appoint a small group of experts, nominated by governments and selected on a broad geographical basis, to prepare recommendations for structural changes in the UN system to improve its effectiveness in dealing with problems of international economic cooperation. The experts' report, completed in May 1975, proposes a number of important structural reforms (United Nations 1975). The proposed reforms are designed to improve coordination and reduce fragmentation of effort within the system, to increase the transfer of resources to the developing coun-

---

33 See Elmandjra (1973, p. 59) on the background and structure of UNDP.

34 *UN Monthly Chronicle*, February 1976.

35 General Assembly Resolution 3343 (XXIX), December 17, 1974.

tries, to improve methods of reaching international agreement, and to give developing countries a larger voice in international economic decision making.

The most important proposed change is the creation of a new post of director general for development and international economic cooperation. This new official would be second in rank only to the secretary general and would provide leadership to the entire UN system in economic matters. A key part of the proposal is that whenever the secretary general is a national of a developed country, the director general would be from a developing country. Also proposed were two deputies for the new director general. The first, who would come from a developing country, would head a streamlined ECOSOC. A second deputy from a developed country would be in charge of the proposed United Nations Development Authority, consolidating all special-purpose UN funds for preinvestment activity.

The report explicitly recognizes that no structural changes can take the place of the "political will" of the member states in carrying out their obligations under the United Nations Charter. Less explicitly, the experts recognize that the willingness of the developed countries to channel resources to developing countries through the UN system depends on the confidence that these countries feel in the decision-making apparatus of the organization. For this reason, considerable emphasis was placed on developing new consultative procedures for promoting agreement on controversial issues. As envisioned by the experts, each issue would be tackled by a small negotiating group, representing all positions, which would attempt to reach a mutually acceptable solution. The resulting decision would then go before the General Assembly in the form of a resolution and presumably receive unanimous endorsement by the full membership. Such a process, if successful, would enhance the authority of the General Assembly by encouraging a greater degree of voluntary implementation of decisions by the member states. Whether or not serious conflicts are actually susceptible of resolution through consultative procedures, the proposed method could hardly be less effective in achieving consensus and action than the present sequence of confrontation, resolution, and nonimplementation.

Other noteworthy proposals of the experts would increase the voting rights of the developing countries in the IMF and the World Bank, phase out UNCTAD and its machinery following the establishment of a comprehensive new international trade organization, and improve the quality of UN personnel through creation of a staff college providing common training to officials from the various agencies.

Issues and Prospects

Issues at the Seventh Special Session

Unlike the United Nations documents generated during the two-year period preceding the Seventh Special Session, Resolution 3362 (S-VII) was adopted by the General Assembly only after prolonged and serious negotiations involving representatives of all interested parties. While the resolution bears a close resemblance to the working paper prepared in advance by the Group of 77, the effects of objections from the industrialized nations and the impact of the Kissinger speech are clearly visible in the tone and substance of the final document.[36] Although the United States and some other developed countries entered formal reservations to certain sections, the content of the resolution is to a large extent representative of the current status of North-South negotiations within the United Nations. The sections below review the major issues and proposals now under consideration. The issues are grouped under the seven main headings used in the resolution.

International Trade

As in the 1960s, international trade heads the list of ldc concerns in negotiations with the industrialized nations. In this area, the proposals reflect certain basic preconceptions concerning trade between developed and developing nations. Foremost is the venerable conviction that primary-commodity exporters face an inevitable long-run deterioration in their terms of trade. Implicitly, this is translated into the belief that commodity producers will, in time, receive dwindling real benefits from their raw-material exports. The empirical evidence is mixed. Results depend critically on

---

36 These documents are all reproduced in *International Legal Materials*, November 1975.

weights given to different commodities, on the period considered, and on whether commodity or factoral terms of trade are examined.[37] A secondary concern of commodity producers is the volatility of their export prices, a result of low demand and supply elasticities for these goods.

The second important preconception concerning trade is that the present world structure of barriers to trade and the process for producing changes in those barriers are skewed against the interests of ldc exporters. Here two issues are raised. First, "cascaded" tariff structures yield high effective protection rates on processing activities in the developed countries, discouraging the processing of raw materials in the producing nations. Second, the General Agreement on Tariffs and Trade (GATT) multilateral negotiating procedures, based on reciprocal tariff reductions, offer little chance for reductions of tariffs on the products of greatest interest to ldc manufacturers, generally those which can benefit from abundant unskilled labor. In addition, it is exactly these industries which are also protected by the nontariff barriers and "escape clause" actions of developed countries. The developing nations correctly regard this developed-country practice as retarding the growth of their exports of the very goods in which their present factor endowments give them a comparative advantage.

Commodity exports currently generate about three-quarters of total ldc export earnings; for many countries, exports of a single commodity make up the bulk of total earnings. The specific proposals with regard to exports of commodities have two objectives: to raise and stabilize export earnings and to increase the degree of processing in the countries of production. The most controversial of the proposals currently under consideration is indexation of raw-material prices. Although indexation is generally regarded by experts as impossible to enforce, it still enjoys strong support within the Group of 77. However, the United States remains adamantly opposed to this measure.[38] Furthermore,

---

37 An expert group convened by the secretary general in 1975 and headed by Professor Hendrik S. Houthakker found no clear evidence of a long-term deterioration in the net barter terms of trade of developing countries. Some of the experts later withdrew their support of the group's conclusions.

38 This was one of the specific reservations from U.S. approval of the Seventh Special Session resolution.

the poorest developing nations, which are importers rather than exporters of food and other commodities, would be adversely affected by indexation. Other proposals presently under consideration or already implemented are buffer-stock arrangements, compensatory financing, and long-term producer-consumer commitments. These are all elements of the UNCTAD Integrated Program for Commodities.[39]

Buffering arrangements entail buying and selling on the part of a central agency in order to maintain price within a specified range. The resources required to carry on such an operation depend crucially on how the range is determined. The lowest expected costs are for a buffering arrangement which merely smooths out price fluctuations around a long-term trend.[40] If the buffering arrangement is intended to raise as well as to stabilize price, the expected cost rises accordingly. To reduce cost of operation, buffering may be combined with export or production quotas for participating producers; however, such controls are typically difficult or impossible to enforce. Furthermore, the cost of maintaining price within a given range is likely to rise over time, as high prices stimulate substitution by consumers while attracting new producers. Consequently, unsuccessful buffering arrangements may be destabilizing; breakdown is likely to be followed by a period of depressed prices and extreme fluctuations until supply and demand adjust to changed market conditions.

The only buffer-stock arrangement presently in operation is that for tin, which has succeeded to the extent of moderating minor price fluctuations but which has lacked the resources required to resist major price changes.[41] Under the UNCTAD Integrated Program, buffer stocks would be maintained for as many as 18 primary commodities; the costs would be shared by consumers and producers.

Markets for most primary commodities are "buffered" to some extent by private transactions by firms or individuals

---

39 For details of the program, see UNCTAD (1975b). For an assessment, see McCulloch (1978).

40 It should be noted that, even for a purely stabilizing buffer, there is a nonzero probability that cost will exceed any fixed sum.

41 The Tin Agreement has also been the only user of financing available through the Buffer Stock Facility of the IMF. Eligibility requires that both producer and consumer nations be participants in the buffer arrangement.

who expect to profit by buying when prices are low and selling when prices are high.[42] Buffering also results from decisions regarding the timing of inventory accumulations on the part of manufacturers requiring raw-material inputs. The existence of private buffering activities limited by interest rates and storage costs implies that the expected return to national or international buffer-stock arrangements will be below the private return on capital. However, the extent of private buffering may be depressed below the socially optimal level as a result of anticipated government intervention when prices are unusually high. Such intervention prevents private transactors from realizing the full economic value of speculatively held stocks.

U.S. officials have remained cool toward proposals for buffer-stock arrangements.[43] The Kissinger speech emphasized the alternative approach of earnings stabilization through compensatory financing, which would reduce the disruptive consequences of price fluctuations without direct intervention in commodity markets. This is implemented by loans or grants which compensate for shortfalls of export earnings below their trend level. Export-earnings stabilization may be provided on a commodity-by-commodity basis or for total earnings by country. Dissatisfaction with compensatory financing arrangements is likely to center on interest rates and schedule of repayment; depending on terms, the funds received through such a facility may constitute close substitutes for commercial borrowing, soft loans, or outright grants.

Two major systems of compensatory financing are already in operation. The first is the IMF facility, expanded in January 1976 along the lines suggested in the Kissinger speech. The IMF arrangement provides for stabilization of members' overall export earnings. In contrast, the Stabex plan adopted by the EEC as part of the Lomé Convention in 1975 stabilizes earnings on a commodity-by-commodity basis; 46 developing nations are covered by the program,

---

42 There is an ongoing debate as to whether private profit-seeking transactions may be destabilizing. A recent article by Cooper and Lawrence (1975) stresses the contribution of speculative purchases to the commodity price boom of 1973–74.

43 Although Kissinger's 1975 speeches indicated a softening of this position, Treasury Department officials continue to make public pronouncements undermining the State Department stance on commodity agreements.

and for the poorest of these, payments received constitute aid grants (Bywater 1975).

Long-term agreements between producers and consumers are typically an important feature of the private markets for primary commodities. The weakness of this measure for reducing uncertainty lies in the problem of enforcing the contracts. UNCTAD proposals would expand the extent of such agreements by tying together agreements for a broad group of commodities on an all-or-none basis.

Expansion of raw-material processing in the producing countries is another high priority issue for the Third World. In this case, the desire for higher revenues from raw-material exports is reinforced by the longer-run goals of industrialization and export diversification. The developing countries have correctly identified the contribution of the tariff structures of industrialized nations to the small fraction of total processing which now takes place in the producing nations. However, even if developed countries are willing to make the required changes in their tariff barriers, the desired shift in the location of processing may be quite slow. The current mood in most developing nations is likely to discourage substantial new foreign private investments; financing for such ventures would have to come largely from the World Bank Group or other multilateral lending agencies.

With regard to trade in manufactured goods, the major issue for the developing nations is expansion of the Generalized System of Preferences. Now that most of the industrialized countries have implemented preference schemes, ldc representatives are pressing for broader product coverage, higher ceilings on amounts qualifying for special treatment, and elimination of the ten-year cutoff written into the original schemes. Also, since the extent to which tariff preferences give developing-country producers an advantage over their competitors in developed countries depends on the level of the most-favored-nation tariff, there is concern that the Multilateral Trade Negotiation now in progress will erode the preferential margin. The developing countries have therefore asked for compensation through measures such as increased product coverage. In addition, two further proposals have been made regarding nontariff barriers. First, the developing countries have requested preferential treatment with respect to nontariff barriers of the developed countries, a proposal endorsed in the Kissinger speech. The developing countries also want exemption from the countervailing duty actions of the industrialized nations; this would allow the ldc's to use export subsidies as a means of promoting development goals.

The effectiveness of preferential access to markets as a means of promoting industrialization is limited by two important considerations. First, the present schemes generally exclude the very goods, such as textiles and shoes, of which developing-country producers are most likely to succeed in expanding production and exports. Since developed countries already face severe domestic problems arising from the declining competitiveness of these industries, they are unwilling to force an even more rapid adjustment to changes in comparative advantage. Unless the industrialized countries can make great strides in easing the required internal adjustments, it is unlikely that the desired liberalizations of tariff and nontariff barriers will be soon forthcoming. However, even if preference schemes are expanded, the resulting increase in manufactured output and exports may be modest. Current attitudes in many developing countries are likely to dampen the enthusiasm of potential investors. As in the case of processing of primary commodities, the necessary capital for expansion of manufacturing will have to come largely through multilateral channels.

Transfer of Real Resources
A major demand of Third World leaders is, not surprisingly, for larger resource transfers on more attractive terms. The relevant section of the resolution passed by the Seventh Special Session opens by stating that "concessional financial resources to developing countries need to be increased substantially, their terms and conditions ameliorated and their flows made predictable, continuous and increasingly assured." Among the specific proposals are that the developed countries increase their development assistance to meet the official Second Development Decade target of 0.7 percent of GNP; that the SDR-aid link proposal be revived, along with other automatic transfer mechanisms; that funds available through multilateral lending facilities be increased; that aid be provided on softer terms and untied; and that

measures be devised to decrease the burden of debt already incurred, especially for the "most seriously affected" countries.[44]

The developing countries seek to divorce aid flows from the national policy objectives of developed countries. The emphasis is on multilateral, untied flows which are automatic rather than discretionary. Given the current structure of the international monetary system, it is unlikely that the SDR-aid link will soon be implemented. Some observers have suggested an alternative source of automatic flows, namely, royalty payments associated with exploitation of seabed resources (Gardner 1976). This has not, however, been proposed by the Group of 77, presumably because the 77 have not been able to resolve the very important differences of interest within the membership on the issue of ocean resources.

With regard to the prospects for increased official development assistance, the trend in developed countries over the past few years has been in the opposite direction. Between 1960 and 1975, U.S. official development assistance fell from .53 percent of GNP to .20 percent. Somewhat smaller reductions over the same period occurred in France, Germany, and the United Kingdom. While some developed countries did increase their aid as a fraction of GNP, for the First World countries as a group the figure fell from .52 to .29 percent (Howe and the Staff of the Overseas Development Council 1975, pp. 256–58). Furthermore, it is unlikely that this trend will be reversed in the near future. Foreign aid was sold to the voters as a way of gaining friends among the developing nations; these friendships have patently failed to materialize, and the recent outbursts of extremist rhetoric do not augur well for larger legislative appropriations for aid. An exception is humanitarian (rather than development) aid to countries suffering the effects of major natural or man-made disasters.

Science and Technology

As in the case of real resources, the developing-country

---

44 The Dakar conference (see previous section) called for an indefinite debt moratorium or outright cancellation of existing debt. However, an ldc meeting in Manila in preparation for the May 1976 UNCTAD IV took a more moderate stand, calling for consideration of debt rescheduling; only in the case of the "most seriously affected" was outright cancellation proposed.

objective in this area is increased transfers on more attractive terms. It is widely accepted in the Third World that the present system of technology transfers through government, international agency, and multinational corporation channels has two serious shortcomings. First, the technology transferred is deemed inappropriate to the needs and objectives of the host countries. In addition, the transferred technology is typically utilized in such a way as to engender host-country dependence on skilled labor and other inputs which must be imported from the industrialized countries. This tends to minimize local involvement in scientifically advanced enterprises and to limit the real benefits accruing to the host country.

The proposals made under this heading center on major efforts to develop local scientific and technological capabilities and, as a shorter-run measure, increased attention to the adaptation of imported technologies to host-country requirements. An international code of conduct governing the transfer of technology would be developed as a means of promoting the special needs of the developing countries. The proposals in the resolution would entail a considerable expansion of the role of the United Nations in facilitating international transfer of technology. In contrast, Kissinger's speech calls for the creation of several new special-purpose intergovernmental bodies, presumably outside the United Nations, to implement proposals in this area.

Industrialization

The General Assembly resolution endorses the Lima Declaration and Plan of Action of UNIDO[45] and urges the member states to take individual and collective action to implement them. (The United States entered a specific objection to this section of the resolution.) A number of concrete proposals to promote industrialization is appended. Included is the recommendation that developed countries facilitate ldc industrial growth by improving their own internal policies for shifting productive resources toward sectors less competitive with those likely to expand in the ldc's as industrialization proceeds. As previously noted, the implementation of this recommendation presupposes a

---

45 Texts are reproduced in *UN Monthly Chronicle*, May 1975.

new solution to one of the major policy problems now faced by developed countries. The prospect for speedy action is not bright.

Food and Agriculture

A major long-run goal of the Third World is a rapid increase in food production in the developing countries. In past decades, the trend for at least some of these countries has been in the opposite direction. A number of countries which were once self-sufficient in food production have taken advantage of U.S. food aid to shift resources from agriculture toward industrial production. Rapid population growth has reinforced the movement toward greater dependence on food imports. To increase Third World self-sufficiency in food and fertilizers, the resolution proposes increased aid for development of agricultural capacity. As a transitional measure, expanded food aid with soft financing, channeled through multilateral agencies, is proposed. A world grain reserve, also endorsed in the Kissinger speech, would be established.

Cooperation among Developing Countries

The proposals in this section of the resolution call for increased UN support and assistance to developing countries in strengthening and expanding regional and interregional cooperation. Particular areas for cooperation singled out are utilization of technology, funds, resources, and skills to promote investment, and regional trade liberalization measures.

Restructuring of the United Nations System

The structure of the United Nations has already been transformed in many respects in response to pressure from the Third World. The resolution endorses further basic structural reforms which would make the organization "more responsive to the requirements of the provisions of the Declaration and Programme of Action on the Establishment of New International Economic Order as well as those of the Charter of Economic Rights and Duties of States," two documents which the United States specifically excluded from its approval of the resolution as a whole. No detailed recommendations for restructuring are included in the resolution, but it is suggested that the Report of the Group of Experts (United Nations 1975) be considered along with other materials in formulating proposals.

Other Issues before the United Nations

The Group of 77 has maintained its solidarity in negotiations with the industrialized countries by refraining from negotiations on any issue for which a bloc position has not been formulated and endorsed by the membership. Two potentially important projects now underway within the United Nations therefore receive no explicit discussion in the resolution adopted at the Seventh Special Session. These are the development of an international code of conduct governing the activities of multinational corporations and the ongoing negotiations on the law of the sea.

Multinational Corporations

While ldc attitudes toward foreign direct investment range from outright hostility to utmost cordiality and highly preferential treatment, there is a strong sense among developing nations that the managers of multinational corporations are pursuing objectives which may well be in conflict with their own national policies. In many cases, a variety of abuses is alleged, from interference with the internal affairs of host countries to transfer-pricing practices which lower host-country tax revenues. The United Nations Center on Transnational Corporations has undertaken to develop a code which will govern relations between host countries and multinationals and is also training accountants from developing nations to help them deal more knowledgeably with foreign investors (United Nations 1976). These measures could introduce additional obstacles to the flow of private foreign capital into the Third World. However, successful efforts to curtail abuses and to specify internationally approved guidelines concerning controversial practices, such as nationalization of foreign property and phase-out requirements, could eliminate some sources of potential misunderstanding between host countries and investors and thus actually increase private capital flows to the Third World.

In this connection, it may be possible to link the question of adequacy of tax payments with that of fair compensation for nationalized foreign property through the use of a self-assessed tax system similar to that proposed for domestic property taxation. Under this scheme, the foreign investor would set a value on total assets located in the host country; this value would then be used both as a basis for taxation (in place of an income or profits tax) and would also be considered the "fair value" to be paid in the event of national takeover of the enterprise. An internationally enforced system along these lines could go far in decreasing mutual suspicion on the part of host countries and investors.

Law of the Sea

Much of the current debate over law of the sea concerns fishing rights. However, the total value of those rights is dwarfed by comparison with rights to extract oil and other minerals from the seabed. Agreement on a position regarding law of the sea has been hampered by the very large and divergent interests of such groups as the landlocked countries; the coastal economies; the "most seriously affected," which could become beneficiaries of international royalty payments; and the oil- and mineral-producing nations whose export earnings could be seriously eroded by development of alternative sources.

A recent proposal by the Trilateral Commission would institute a revenue-sharing plan to provide a relatively automatic and nonpolitical source of financing for development. Under this arrangement, a fraction of the revenues generated by exploitation of seabed minerals beyond a distance of 12 miles from shore would be paid into an international institution such as the World Bank. This would augment funds available from other sources. The plan is, in effect, an aid link to exploitation of offshore mineral resources. This proposal would probably gain the support of the landlocked ldc's but might well be opposed by coastal developing nations and also by some industrialized countries, including the United States. The sums involved are substantial. One source estimates that a 10 percent royalty rate could generate as much as $1 billion a year by 1980 and $3 billion a year by the year 2000. (In comparison, total official development assistance is now about $15 billion annually [Gardner 1976]).

Prospects for the Future

The current drive for a New International Economic Order is intended to transform the United Nations into a more effective policymaking body for the world economy. This increased effectiveness would be used to implement policies likely to inflict substantial damage on the world economy, leaving a smaller global pie to be allocated among competing groups. In the absence of enforcement powers, the techniques being employed to gain the assent of the industrialized countries, which must pay a large part of the cost of these new programs, are the usual carrot and stick. A stick is used in the form of threats—weapons such as "commodity power," which can disrupt if not permanently harm the economies of industrialized countries. And the carrot—would not a more prosperous world be better for all? Don't the industrialized countries value equality of opportunity, not only for their own populations but also for the vast majority who happen to have been born in the poorer parts of the globe?

The end of this campaign is not in sight. Some Third World intellectuals view the current phase as the beginning of a program likely to extend over 20, 30, or more years— comparable to the length of time required to allow the former colonies to achieve independence. What should the United States be doing? Some have argued that the United States should leave the United Nations. Others feel that it is important to keep the dialogue going. I do not think that decision has more than symbolic importance, since the current turmoil in the United Nations simply reflects real changes which have already occurred in the world community at large. However, with respect to economic policies there are three points worth making.

First, if the United States goes along with policies which ultimately decrease the amount available for the world to share, U.S. problems can only grow worse. This is true for specific programs but also (and perhaps more significantly) for proposals which would increase the potency of the United Nations as an economic policymaking body without altering the kinds of policies likely to be adopted. The United States should eschew short-run policies of partial accommodation as exemplified by the Kissinger speech at the Seventh Special Session. Instead, the United States ought to throw its full support behind policies likely to increase rather than decrease overall efficiency of the world economy. Of the proposals now before the international community, I would particularly endorse elimination of cascaded tariff systems which discriminate against local processing of raw materials in their countries of origin, of high tariffs and nontariff barriers protecting labor-intensive manufacturing activities, and of developed-country "anti-inflationary" export controls. It must be recognized, however, that elimination of these world efficiency-reducing measures necessarily entails finding new solutions for some difficult domestic problems.

Second, it is plain that the U.S. Congress is unlikely to reverse itself and suddenly begin to increase the level of resources devoted to assisting Third World countries, especially those which remain hostile in their attitudes toward the United States. Just as the Congress chose to exclude the members of OPEC from the Generalized System of Preferences under the Trade Act of 1974, it will wish to reward countries which are friendly and refrain from helping those which are hostile. But, in the past, the Congress has been singularly heavy-handed in pursuing this kind of discrimination. U.S. policymakers have given the developing countries little room in which to pursue their own economic and political objectives. The neoconservatives (and others) have argued that the industrialized countries should allow the developing nations to make their own choices, but without guaranteeing to provide them with additional resources when, as a result of those choices, their economic performance is disappointing. This is an attractive line to take, but unfortunately it cannot be carried to its logical conclusion. Most residents of developing nations have no opportunity to voice their approval or disapproval of government policies through free elections or a free press. Likewise, most have little alternative in terms of international emigration. Thus, it is illogical to hold individual citizens responsible for the policies of their "leaders." The United States may therefore rationally choose to provide emergency aid even when the emergency results from following a policy it has openly condemned; the case of India comes to mind. It should be emphasized that the interests of the leaders, who usually represent a bureaucratic elite in most developing countries, may be very different from those of the population as a whole. For example, it is notable that no document emanating from the Third World calls for lower barriers to international immigration—a force important in increasing economic welfare and protecting political freedoms in past centuries.

Finally, is it in fact likely that the United Nations will be transformed in the near future from a town meeting into an important economic policymaking body? It seems probable that most substantive decisions concerning the future of the international economic system will continue for some time to be made *outside* the United Nations, in intergovernmental bodies such as the IMF and World Bank where countries "vote money." Policies can only be as effective as the means to finance them, and a policymaking body which does not take this into account is unlikely to be effective. But it ought also to be recognized that the world is changing very rapidly. The United States should be looking *now* to the future of the international economic community and using its considerable international power and prestige to advance policies which expand rather than shrink world wealth.

REFERENCES

BAUER, P. T. 1976. "Western Guilt and Third World Poverty." *Commentary* 61, no. 1 (January), pp. 31–38. Reprinted in this vol.

BERGSTEN, C. F. 1974a. "Commodity Power Is Here To Stay." *Brookings Bulletin* 11, no. 2 (Spring), pp. 6–8.

———— 1974b. "The New Era in World Commodity Markets." *Challenge* 17, no. 4 (September/October), pp. 34–42.

BRUNNER, K. 1976. "The New International Economic Order: A Chapter in a Protracted Confrontation." *Orbis*, (Spring). Reprinted in this volume.

BYWATER, M. 1975. "The Lomé Convention." *European Community*, no. 184 (March), pp. 5–9.

CLAUDE, I. L., Jr. 1971. *Swords into Plowshares*. New York: Random House.

COOPER, R. N., and LAWRENCE, R. Z. 1975. "The 1972–75 Commodity Boom." In *Brookings Papers on Economic Activity*, 3: 671–732. Washington, D.C.: Brookings Institution.

ELMANDJRA, M. 1973. *The United Nations: An Analysis*. London: Faber and Faber.

FRANK, R. S. 1975. "Economic Report: U.S. Takes Steps To Meet Demands of Third World Nations." *National Journal Reports* 7, no. 43 (October 25), pp. 1480–89.

GARDNER, R. N. 1968. "The United Nations Conference on Trade and Development." In *The Global Partnership*, edited by R. N. Gardner and M. F. Millikan. New York: Praeger.

———— 1976. "Offshore Oil and the Law of the Seas." *New York Times*, March 14.

GOODRICH, L. M. 1974. *The United Nations in a Changing World*. New York: Columbia University Press.

GREGG, R. W. 1972. "UN Economic, Social, and Technical Activities." In *The United Nations: Past, Present, and Future*, edited by J. Barros. New York: Macmillan.

HOWE, J. W., and the Staff of the Overseas Development Council. 1975. *The U.S. and World Development, Agenda for Action 1975*. New York: Praeger.

IMF Survey, various issues.

International Legal Materials, various issues. Washington, D.C.: American Society of International Law.

JANKOWITSCH, O., and SAUVANT, K. P. 1976. "The Evolution of the Non-Aligned Movement into a Pressure Group for the Establishment of the New International Economic Order." Paper presented at the XVII Annual Convention of the International Studies Association, Toronto, February.

JANSSEN, R. F. 1976. "Bridging the Chasm to the Third World." *Wall Street Journal*, February 13.

KOTSCHNIG, W. M. 1968. "The United Nations as an Instrument of

Economic and Social Development." In *The Global Partnership*, edited by R. N. Gardner and M. F. Millikan. New York: Praeger.

KRISTOL, I. 1975. "The 'New Cold War.'" *Wall Street Journal*, July 17.

McCULLOCH, R. 1978. "Commodity Power and the International Community." In *The New Economics of the Less Developed Countries*, edited by N. M. Kamrany. Boulder, Colorado: Westview.

MOYNIHAN, D. P. 1975. "The United States in Opposition." *Commentary* 59, no. 3 (March), pp. 31–44. Reprinted in this volume.

NYE, J. S. 1974. "UNCTAD: Poor Nations' Pressure Group." In *The Anatomy of Influence*, by R. W. Cox, H. K. Jacobson, et al. New Haven: Yale University Press.

UNCTAD. 1975a. "Conference of Developing Countries on Raw Materials: Action Programme and Resolutions on Raw Materials and Other Primary Commodities." TD/B/C.1/L.45, February 17, 1975. Reprinted in part in *International Legal Materials*, March/April, pp. 520–42.

———. 1975b. "An Integrated Programme for Commodities: Specific Proposals for Decision and Action." Report by the Secretary-General of UNCTAD. TD/B/C.1/193, October 28, 1975.

UNITED NATIONS. 1975. *A New United Nations Structure for Global Economic Co-operation*. Report of the Group of Experts on the Structure of the United Nations System. E/AC.62/9. New York.

———. 1976. *Research on Transnational Corporations, Preliminary Report of the Secretariat*. E/C.10/12. New York.

UN Monthly Chronicle, various issues.

WALL, D. 1971. "Problems with Preferences." *International Affairs* 47, no. 1 (January), pp. 87–89.

Harry G. Johnson

The New International Economic Order

The "new international economic order" is one of those propaganda slogans that have come to figure large in politics in our day. An attractive encapsulation of a series of objectives of a deliberately ambiguous or vaguely defined sort, it is a phrase designed to give those who are unfamiliar with it the feeling that they are "one down" on those who use it familiarly and to give those who use it the advantage of seeming to be advocating something at once concrete and highly moral. The term in fact has three general connotations: that there is something fundamentally wrong with the existing system of international economic relations, which needs to be corrected by a change in the system or "order"; that that something wrong can be blamed on the past and present policies of the Western advanced countries, which have been blatantly immoral and need to atone for their pasts; and that the proposed change in the international order requires a massive shift of international political power from the major countries to the voting Assembly of the United Nations. The latter two questions I shall discuss later, concentrating for the moment on the changes involved in "the new order" itself.

Woodward Court Lecture, University of Chicago, Chicago, Illinois, October 5, 1976. Reprinted by permission of the author.

Evaluating a Slogan

The "new international economic order," considered as a set of proposals for changing the present international economic order, can be evaluated most succinctly by remarking that it is not new; it is not international; it is not economic; and it is not "an order." Let me develop these points in turn.

Time-Worn Ideas

First, the ideas and proposals are by no means new; on the contrary, they have been around a long time. In broad essentials they were the focus of the 1964 United Nations Conference on Trade and Development (UNCTAD I), held in Geneva; and specifically they emerged in the background document for that conference, *Towards a New Trade Policy for Development*, prepared by the secretary general of the conference, Dr. Raúl Prebisch. Individually, the ideas had been around for much longer. On the one hand, the idea that international trade is a zero-sum game by which the rich benefit at the expense of the poor goes back to the Marxist view of "imperialism," and before that to the mercantilist idea that foreign trade is a means of transferring wealth from one's customers to oneself—the belief that Adam Smith's *Wealth of Nations* and classical economics aimed to refute. On the other hand, the idea that exporters of food and raw materials necessarily and inevitably lose in trade with exporters of industrial products was Prebisch's own Latin American interpretation and overgeneralization of the Latin American experience of the 1930s' depression.

The elevation of these ideas to a policy theory of the problem of economic underdevelopment, incidentally, represents a transfer of intellectual leadership, of a sort, or a shift of stereotype or ideal case. The first, early post–World War II phase of development theory was concerned with the case of India and had as its model Russian economic planning; UNCTAD I had the Latin American case in mind and had as its model industrialization, on what are often thought of as German protectionist lines; the more recent demands for a new international economic order have brought into the picture African and (largely Mediterranean) oil-producing countries—with an emphasis on exploiting monopolies over scarce natural resources—and have as a model the presumed policies of the large international oil companies.

UNCTAD I was concerned—apart from the general purpose of calling advanced-country attention to the grievances of less-developed countries against developed countries— with four major policy demands. One was for an increase in the amount of development aid provided by the advanced to the less-developed countries and, in that framework, for an increase in the proportion of that aid provided through the multilateral agencies of the United Nations rather than bilaterally. Little success was achieved on that score, beyond promises, since the advanced countries' legislatures have had more pressing preoccupations and have also become disillusioned with the results of the aid-giving process itself. The second demand was for a unilateral preference system for manufactured exports of less-developed countries in the markets of the developed countries; this was eventually conceded but has taken a form yielding relatively little benefit to the developing countries capable of taking advantage of it—for the reason that it has tended to give to the less-developed producers of industrial products carefully circumscribed monopoly positions rather than free competitive access to world trade. A subordinate aspect of this demand was for acceptance of preferential trading arrangements among groups of less-developed countries; acquiescence to this imposed relatively little cost on the advanced countries, but little has come of it, owing to the inability of the developing countries to negotiate agreements among themselves. The third demand was for international commodity agreements to raise and stabilize the prices of primary products exported by the developing countries; little has come of that demand either, for reasons to be discussed in more detail later. The fourth demand evolved into the so-called link proposal for coupling the creation of new international reserves, or "liquidity," with distribution of a substantial part of the new money, in one way or another, as aid to the less-developed countries. So attractive is the idea that the creation of money involves creation of something for nothing, that it has both excited a great deal of expert discussion and become a general operating principle of International Monetary Fund thinking about world monetary reform. Nevertheless, the benefits to the developing countries are likely to be small, since the subsequent emergence of world inflation is a symptom of the fact that the world has too much international liquidity, not too little.

The idea of international commodity agreements, crystallized at UNCTAD I into the concept of "an integrated programme for commodities," is the core of the current demands for a new international economic order. Nothing much came of it, however, in the decade or so after the first conference. (There has, incidentally, been a conference every four years since, the sequence happening to coincide with that of U.S. presidential elections. The meetings have thus been minimally capable of achieving anything that requires influencing American foreign policy.) The "integrated programme for commodities" got nowhere, in spite of apparently intensive, sustained work on the question by the Secretariat, for a very simple reason: it is not possible to integrate a program designed to secure a multitude of quite inconsistent economic objectives. All a Secretariat can do is to draft a weasel-worded first chapter listing all the objectives and asserting baldly, but intellectually dishonestly, that they are consistent and then go on to other chapters discussing concrete schemes for doing something, without asking whether it is a good thing to do and, if so, whether it can be done. What gave the program fresh life was not fresh thinking but the demonstration by the countries of the OPEC—the oil-producing and -exporting countries—that, in the case of oil, concerted monopolistic action could extract a greatly higher price from the consuming countries. This demonstration naturally, but mostly wrongly, suggested that the producers of other commodities had a similar monopoly power and could use it in the same way for the same agreeable results.

A Divisive System

The demand for a new international economic order is therefore not new; nor are the proposals themselves new; what is new, if anything, is the idea of trying to make a "system" or "order" out of a collection of monopolistic and discriminating policies.

It is for this reason that the "new" order is not "interna-

tional" either. It is not envisioned as a system of arrangements among nations, each of which participates by virtue
of its being a nation. Instead, it proposes a system of international political confrontation between two groups of
nations, a numerical minority of successfully developed
nations and a preponderant majority of developing or less-
developed nations. Moreover, the "developing country"
group is based on no clear-cut criteria; certain poor countries, most notably Israel, are excluded—a case of blatant
discrimination. In this proposed system, the minority are
expected to yield to the majority partly on the basis of a
false parallel with democratic procedures and partly on
the basis of presumed guilt, past and present, for the underdeveloped state of the underdeveloped.

Uneconomic Transfers

Nor is the proposed new order economic, at least if "economic" means more than the truism that any international
arrangement has economic effects. Economics as defined
by the vast majority of its practitioners is concerned with
the rationale and effects of trade through markets—including, by extension, the rationale and effects of the replacement of competitive markets by central planning. Central
planning entails replacing multifarious private decision
takers by a centralized social decision-taking process but
does not alter the principle of using rational allocation
procedures to maximize the extent to which planning
objectives can be fulfilled. Where the market process of
exchange is replaced or modified by transfers of income or
resources from one party to another, economics is concerned
with the criteria for selecting the benefactors and beneficiaries in such a process and with the best method of
achieving the desired objectives of the transfer. Put simply,
economic considerations usually point to taking away
resources from those most able to pay and giving them to
those most in need, according to some agreed definitions
of ability to pay and of need.

By these standards, there is nothing economic about a
system in which transfers would be extorted by those less-
developed countries that have and can use monopoly power
in world markets. On the one side, it conveniently ignores
the fact that, both domestically and internationally, monop-

oly power tends to be enjoyed by the rich at the expense of the poor—the countries that have suffered most from the rise in the price of oil have been, not the majority of developed countries, least of all the United States, but the non-oil-producing poor countries, whose hopes of economic development had been based on the assumption of continuing supplies of cheap power. Further, there is little reason to believe that the possession of monopoly power leads its holders voluntarily to redistribute their monopoly profits to their workers—the folklore of monopoly typically depicts the monopolist as exploiting his workers as well as his customers; and there is, if anything, less reason to think that the government of a country deriving monopoly profits from exploitation of a collective monopoly of a primary-product export will redistribute those profits to the poor farmers and miners who do the work of producing the product in question. On the other side, such a system relies on the ability to create and enlist feelings of guilt sufficiently strong to support regular payments of blackmail, made in the particular form of artificially high commodity prices. Economists have, it is true, been working on the economics of crime, bribery, and (so far as I know) hush money and blackmail as well; but no one has yet suggested that these phenomena have ever been, or are likely to be, the basis of a viable economic system.

Chaos, Not Order

Finally, the system that would result—namely, one of developed-country toleration and support of developing-country exploitation of every devisable monopolistic opportunity— would not be an "order," but an experiment in the rule of the jungle—a rule modified by the hope that the largest and most savage carnivores will be so ashamed of their present existence, secured by the killing and eating successes of their ancestors, that they will offer themselves up as willing sacrifices to the hunger of the smaller fry. No amount of repetition of the rhetoric of "an integrated commodity policy" can convert the rule of the jungle into a rule of law. For the purpose of the rule of law is precisely, by restraining everyone equally to abide by the law, to prevent the domination of a free-for-all contest by those who have sufficient power or finance or both. (To give a concrete example, consider the case of Patty Hearst.) It is, of course, easy enough to find violations of the rule of law in any country; but in such cases, if they occur frequently, the remedy is generally found in tightening up the law, not in abandoning it altogether.

This discussion has been focused on one of the more specific and continuing proposals for change in international economic relations, the so-called integrated program for commodities. (Incidentally, the only "integration" involved in the proposals actually made is the establishment of a common fund, to be subscribed by the developed countries, to finance experiments with individual commodity agreements.) But the discussion applies equally, though with more difficulty of explanation, to another major item on the agenda at Nairobi, the demand for nations' "full permanent sovereignty" over their natural resources and their economic activities in general. The phrase "full permanent sovereignty" has a ringing note to it; but realization of its meaning—that the price of anything I agree to sell you can be changed unilaterally by me at any time I choose, and you have no right to protest—reveals that it amounts to an assertion of the law of the jungle, or, more accurately, to a demand for the rights of the law of the jungle for me (the less-developed) and the obligations of the rule of law for you (the developed).

Sorting Out the Issues

The demand for a new international economic order can be discussed at different levels. One is the level of economic analysis of the issues involved. In fact, I treated these issues fairly exhaustively in a monograph published ten years ago about UNCTAD I (*Economic Policies toward Less Developed Countries* [New York: Praeger; Washington, D.C.: Brookings Institution, 1967]), and my main conclusions still stand, in my judgment.

Economic Issues

These conclusions were, first, that the possible gains in economic development from changes in international trade policy are quantitatively relatively small and peripheral: economic development is primarily a process of domestic

economic and social transformation of a society or nation
into one that seeks economic improvement and is organized
to allow and encourage its citizens to undertake the investments in material, human, and intellectual capital that are
required for steady accumulation. An important part of this
transformation, incidentally, is the establishment of political stability and of greater certainty about the policies likely
to be followed by governments. Second, while there are
strong grounds for complaint about some of the trade policy
and other international economic policies and practices of
the various developed countries, the policies in question
involve the use of monopoly power or government interference in international competition, and the proper remedy
on the part of the developing countries is to insist on freedom
of trade and the solution of domestic political problems by
more efficient methods than protection against foreign
competition. (Another part of the response, incidentally,
should be for developing countries to reduce their own
obstacles to freedom of international competition, since
their protectionist attempts to promote economic growth
through industrialization have typically produced extremes
of inefficiency in the use of the scarce available resources
—and also extremes of inequality in the distribution of income—without engendering a viable process of economic
growth.) Third, while UN proposals for reform might
possibly be followed as a sort of "third best" method of
achieving some international redistribution of income
toward the developing countries, international commodity
agreements raise virtually insuperable difficulties, in terms
both of implementation and of the logic and ethics of the
resulting international transfers from consuming to producing countries.

Unfortunately, this level of discussion—the scientific
economic level—is quite beside the main point of the issues
involved in the demand for reforming the international
economic order (as indicated, among other things, by the
fact that my book has had a lot of readers but no influence
whatsoever on subsequent discussion of the issues). There
are, in fact, three issues involved that are more fundamental
—and, in a sense, more fundamentally questions of social
science—than the narrowly economic questions raised by
commodity buffer stocks and price-raising agreements,

controlling exploitation of depletable natural resources, and the international operations of business corporations —to restate the main economic issues upon which discussion and controversy have focused. To these other questions I now turn.

Prices and Incomes

The first, and the most closely related to economics, is why public discussion is so prone to, even insistent on, focusing on prices as proxies for incomes and wealth. One major contribution of economic analysis, especially in this century, has been to distinguish carefully between prices and their consequences in terms of distribution of income among groups of producers and consumers, including those not directly concerned with the commodity whose price is being considered. It has become a commonplace among economists that, for example, a minimum-wage law may create poverty by pricing low-skilled workers, or juvenile or aged workers, out of potential employment—the standard example in the United States being the chronic high rate of unemployment among young adult black males; or that the main benefit from agricultural price supports goes to the owners of land, not the farm workers, who may be made even worse-off if supports are reinforced by quotas or acreage restrictions. Yet the public and politicians continue happily to talk about prices, and propose both price supports and price controls, as if prices were synonymous with incomes; and in the international sphere, UN politicians and their supposedly professional advisers and staff continue— not happily, but bitterly in this case—to talk about prices of traded goods, and the terms of trade, as if these were synonymous with income and its distribution.

The best hypothesis I have been able to come up with on this question is that, appearances to the contrary, the skills of the economist are difficult to acquire, precisely because they require looking at systems and at the system repercussions of changes. The ordinary man lives in and is familiar with one small part of the system, which part he knows as his environment and considers subject to control by himself or by others. Thus it seems to make obvious sense, for example, to argue that if wages in an industry are thought to be too low for decency, the employers should be forced to pay more—it being beyond the imagination that the effect could be to wipe out the industry and turn all the workers into worse-off unemployables. Similarly, it is apparently obvious that if primary-commodity producers are poor, higher prices for the product would enable those who produce the product to earn more; but not at all obvious that raising prices will reduce consumption demand, reduce the number of producers needed or allowable, give the extra income to those who have control over the right to produce (the government, or the landowners with quota rights, but almost certainly not the farm workers), and create a problem of what to do with the workers displaced from production by the price-increase-induced decrease in demand.

There is an alternative, but not necessarily conflicting, hypothesis to explain the concentration on the prices of primary commodities and, more generally, on policies of discrimination promising higher prices for exports of all kinds from developing to developed countries. This hypothesis is that national political thinking about international affairs is largely a matter of imitation rather than analysis, and the assertion of "national independence" is the assertion of the right to do whatever is done by other countries— especially richer countries—whether or not it is a good thing. This hypothesis, to my mind, is a necessary part of explaining why so much of developing-country international economic policy has been concerned with asserting the right to use tariff protection to promote development and with demanding that the protection provided by advanced countries to their own industries should be inverted, with preferential advantages for developing-country exporters in the markets of the developed countries.

Present Status and Past Action

The second social science question I would raise is why the notion of retribution for past wrongs should lead developed countries to accept the demands for a new international economic order. There are in fact two aspects of this question: why the developing countries believe that their "less-developed" status is attributable to past policies of the developed countries, usually encapsulated in the rhetoric of "colonialism" and "imperialism" and, more recently, "dependence"; and why so many intellectuals in the developed countries seem so ready to feel and express guilt for the presumed past wrongdoings of their ancestors.

At one level—political convenience—the explanation of the first aspect is fairly simple: to assert that one ought to be rich but is poor because one had to contend with bad luck and the malevolence of enemies, is far easier, and more consistent with self-respect, than to face the fact that one is poor because one's parents were feckless and selfish and never taught one the necessity of hard work or the importance of taking education seriously. The study of "the poverty culture" popular domestically some years ago demonstrated the correlation between poverty (or its opposite) and belief-systems about the rewards of economic activity; and it is understandable that politicians of the developing countries should transfer the blame for poverty away from the shortcomings of their societies, as producers of goods and investors for economic growth, to other societies whose lack of those shortcomings can be interpreted as unfair exploitation of others rather than as deserved success due to superior performance.

At a somewhat deeper level, both aspects of the question seem related to a fundamental problem in economic philosophy, the rights of property and the justification for them. The problem was a difficult one for the early modern political philosophers, largely because it has been from the beginning a fundamental problem in Christian philosophy; and it remains a difficult one for the Western tradition for the same essentially religious reasons, even though most intellectuals in this tradition tend to regard themselves as nonreligious. The important point is that there is a great difference between the traditional society and economy from which it sprang—an economy of known and static technology in which the ownership of property was associated with status and carried no obvious personal productive contribution—and the modern economy of growth and change, in which the management and accumulation of property is a means of increasing output, efficiency, and the general standard of living. Property, very crudely, is the outcome of productive contribution, rather than an alternative freeing its owner from the obligation to make a productive contribution. Yet the old idea of property—as an entitlement to enjoy income without working for it—continues to hold sway in the public and political mind.

The reasons are obviously complex. To my mind, however, they owe a great deal to the fact that, to the ordinary politician and the ordinary person, the world in which he currently lives is the environment, a fixed point in time; property, then, is something that people have for no obvious reason and that they can and should be deprived of, so far as is possible, for the benefit of others with better current social claims to it. More concretely, it is easy for the politician and his public in the developing country to disregard the centuries of effort, educational improvement, and accumulation that have gone into the creation of the high incomes of advanced Western societies and to claim that, as living human beings, they should have the same high living standards as the heirs of those centuries of effort. And it is equally easy for their Western intellectual counterparts to be as forgetful of the past and to feel guilt that they are so much better off than the descendants of a different set of ancestors.

International Bureaucracies

The third and final question concerns the identification of establishing a new international economic order with shifting political power from the governments and civil services of national states to the UN apparatus and its flock of international civil servants, professional experts, and so forth. In one respect, the explanation is obvious and in accordance with widely observed phenomena. In international politics as in economics, systems tend to converge on an equilibrium—in political terms, a "balance of power"—in which the scope and limits of power of the individual participants become clearly defined. For those who are acutely dissatisfied with the amount of power they have within the system, there is an incentive to try to acquire more, not by increasing their power within the existing system, but by changing the system in the hope of either confusing the others into giving away some of their power or changing the basis on which power depends. This explains, for example, the lengthy political battles over the past century or so for the extension of the franchise; and it is also the motive force for the American governmental habit of piling new agencies on top of old ones, in the (usually vain) hope of giving purposive direction to government policies and priorities. What is perhaps less obvious, but of at least equal importance, is that the growth of the United Nations has created a very strong vested interest in the extension of its bureaucracy, quite apart from any concern with the welfare of the citizens of the less-developed countries and any claims they may legitimately have or be thought to have for income redistributions, but obviously favorable to any measures—such as international commodity agreements and increased aid-giving through multilateral agencies—that will incidentally increase the numbers, self-importance, and salaries of the international bureaucrats. The growth of the United Nations has meant the creation of job opportunities for university and technical school graduates, opportunities far better and more comfortable and pleasant than anything they could hope for from their native lands and governments, paid for by taxes on their fellow citizens and the civilian taxpayers of richer countries, notably the United States. The demand for a new international economic order is to an important extent a demand for greater power for these international bureaucrats, disguised as a demand for more justice for the ordinary people of the developing countries; and it is important, especially for American foreign economic policy, to recognize the reality before committing ourselves too heavily to acceptance of the rhetoric.

Harry G. Johnson

The North-South Issue

"The North-South issue," as a means of focusing discussions about development of the less-developed majority of the world's population, is a convenient, sloganeering half-truth, more misleading than useful. Geographically, the existence, on the one hand, of Australia and New Zealand—despite Australia's persistent efforts to get itself treated as "under-developed" or "developing"—and, on the other hand, of Portugal and various Mediterranean and Caribbean countries, makes nonsense of the distinction between North and South. So does the exclusion of the Communist countries from "the North," though some of these countries—including both Eastern European countries and mainland China—should certainly be classed as underdeveloped. Still more important, the group of "developing countries," as it is represented by political organization within the United Nations framework, is a self-selected and in some significant ways politically discriminatory grouping. Certainly in its official utterances the group provides an extremely biased source of opinion on the causes and nature of "underdevelopment" and on recommendations for overcoming it.

It is, in my view, of fundamental importance to recognize the (broadly) political element in current thinking about

Prepared for "In Search of New Prosperity," International Symposium on The World Economy, in commemoration of the centennial of the *Nihon Keizai Shimbun* *(Japan Economic Journal)*, Tokyo, October 26–28, 1976. Printed by permission of the author.

development—both among the political leaders of the developing countries and their civil servants and domestic intellectuals and among the intellectual groups that tend to form, or at least influence, public opinion in the advanced countries. Otherwise, one is in danger of assuming about the debate, quite wrongly, that its protagonists, which include some quite eminent people in the economics profession, understand and accept economic logic and the scientific method of testing hypotheses against facts. Consequently, one may devote considerable time in economic theory and research that will be disregarded, misrepresented, or even officially suppressed for calling attention to the clay feet of the idols of political mythology.

Attribution and Retribution

Anything like a satisfactory exploration and explanation of the reasons for prevailing ideas on development and development policy is far beyond the scope of the present paper. One can, however, suggest some broad explanations of two salient features of what may be termed the UNCTAD approach to development policy. One is the conviction that underdevelopment is the fault, not of the people currently underdeveloped or of their ancestors, but of "the system" of international organization and particularly of international competition, specifically, free enterprise or capitalist competition. The other is the belief that the solution is to reform the system and, in particular, to transfer income and wealth from the "undeserving" rich to the "deserving" poor: both directly, through explicit transfers of money and resources (of course without "strings"); and indirectly, through the organization of cartels, monopolies, discriminatory market-entry privileges, and so forth for the benefit of producers (assumed poor) at the expense of consumers (assumed rich). Both features, in my view, reflect the fact and the political implications of the fundamental characteristics of men as individual intelligences incorporated in virtually identical physical forms, endowed with the ability to communicate with each other.

Take first the question of attributing blame for present economic differences to "the system" or to historical bad fortune or victimization rather than to the incompetence or erroneous choices of contemporary people. It is natural and understandable, but mythical rather than rational, to assume that because we are both men, both of a similar age, and both able to communicate by talking, we ought to be equal in economic position. Further, if I am not as economically well-off as you, I must have been deprived of my natural rights either by the wickedness of your ancestors or by the inequitable operation of "the system." If you have property and I have not, it is not because I and my ancestors did not choose to accumulate property whereas you and yours did but because there is something wrong with the system of property ownership and accumulation, for which I deserve recompense by wealth and income transfers from you to me.

This way of looking at the results of economic growth and its absence is particularly easily translated into the stuff of political activity, since those in politics seek to influence and manipulate other people in order to control the use of other people's property. It necessarily appeals to and promotes the belief that the exercise of social control over the use of existing property is much more important than the establishment of conditions favorable to the further accumulation of property. Indeed, the political process, by the short-run nature of its concern with the present electorate, is biased toward concentrating on existing property and its distribution, to the neglect of considerations of accumulating new property through investment. The politicians, the civil service, and the intellectuals are, because of their daily preoccupations, virtually forced to conceive of the world in terms of existing accumulations of property, of the "power" of the owners and controllers of that property, and of the role of politics and government in forcing, inducing, and cajoling those controllers to surrender as much as possible of both the income from and the power of control over property. This conception of economics, in terms of property and power over it, and the use of political power to obtain control over economic power, is both necessitated by the nature of government and reinforced by the shortness of active human life in relation to the slow pace of social and economic change. It is further reinforced by the "specialization and division of labor" characteristic of modern social, political, and economic life, as a result of which—in contrast to earlier phases of social and economic organization—politics, the civil service, and intellectual activity are careers divorced from, ignorant of, and often contemptuous toward the grubby business of producing goods and services and the often grubbier and nastier business of increasing efficiency by changing the social and economic organization in microeconomic respects. The obvious consequence is to lay the blame for inferiority of economic performance, not on the social and especially the political side of the economic interaction between man and his environment, but on an unjust deprivation of the society in question of the economic wherewithal to which it feels itself entitled: if another society has cumulatively done better than ours, it is not our fault but the fault of "the system" or, more humanly and hatefully, the result of the wickedness of the people of the other society.

The other salient feature of "the UNCTAD approach" is the belief that the remedy is to be found in the inversion of the monopolistic practices of the developed countries, which are assumed to be the essence of the system of competition, in favor of the less-developed countries. A rational economic approach would involve condemnation of the practices in question, whoever is the monopolistic beneficiary, and establishment of a "rule of law" whereby such practices would be prohibited and penalized. It would also suggest that the possibilities of monopoly profit are likely to be quantitatively small, when contrasted with the many alternative ways of producing an income, and to be progressively undermined by the competitive process, including competition between monopolists. A rational approach also suggests that the rich rather than the poor are likely to win in any real test of the ability to monopolize.

The inversion of monopoly demanded for the benefit of the developing countries depends on enlisting the moral approval and acquiescence of the governments of the developed countries—a requirement whose voluntary fulfillment by countries accused of being rich by virtue only of pervasive antisocial monopoly practices is extremely doubtful. The continuing reliance on this demand can only be understood in the context of the political process. At a general level, there is the belief that individuals who indulge in antisocial activities not only should be discriminatorily taxed but ought to agree that they should be so taxed. At least, there is the belief that all right-thinking people would agree that such taxation is eminently fair, and there is a corollary that poor people should be forgiven for minor thefts and dishonesties. (Caesar's wife should be above suspicion, but Lazarus's wife should be entitled to get a living in any way she can.) At a more specific level, there is a strong tendency in the political process to prefer transfers of income to "deserving" groups by policies that raise the prices of the products they produce and lower the prices of the goods they consume. Regardless of the economic inefficiency, wastefulness, and often complete ineffectiveness of such policies in achieving their stated objectives, they are preferred simply because direct subsidies and transfers seem to make the beneficiary economically incompetent and dependent on public charity, whereas price fixing can be regarded by the beneficiaries as only giving them a "fair" chance to demonstrate their competence as economic producers.

The argument so far has been concerned with the reasons for the popularity of "the UNCTAD approach" among the governments and intellectual elites of the less-developed countries. There remains the question of its popularity among intellectuals and academics in the developed countries themselves. Here again, only a few thoughts may be offered. To begin with, there are obvious and strongly surviving elements of the Christian religious tradition that are both hostile to the possession of existing wealth and disdainful of the idea that present wealth is the result of past sacrifice and effort. This uneasiness, which largely reflects failure to draw a distinction between the accumulation of wealth and the right to enjoy the product of wealth once accumulated, persistently troubled the English classical economists and still troubles their successors, with results varying from unwillingness to make clear statements about the economic nature and source of interest and profits, to denial of any economic justification for the receipt of income from property. The extreme, and uniquely influential, case was Marx. On the one hand, he attributed property income to "exploitation" rather than to scarcity (conveniently ignoring the problem of scarcity of land, which was the centerpiece of the Ricardian economic system). On the other hand, Marx made the accumulation of property by capitalists a matter of nonmeritorious necessity rather than an act of choice requiring an incentive return.

Apart from this fundamentally religious bias against admitting the importance of saving and investment and of opportunities and incentives for them in the form of freedom of economic choice and returns on successful choices, there is the fact that the intellectual's role in Western society involves little or no firsthand experience and understanding of the processes of social and economic modernization. His role is, instead, that of the owner of a certain kind of property (intellectual and cultural), the income from which is derived largely by criticizing the behavior of the less vocal and literate owners of other kinds of property, with the reward paid by politicians and private citizens who approve of that kind of criticism. And, for at least some purposes, both the moral fervor of criticism and the credibility of the allegation of evildoing are generated more easily with reference to the (necessarily foreign) less-developed countries than with reference to the domestic economy.

Finally, it is not stretching the influence of history too far to recall that universities were originally religious establishments whose purpose was to conduct discussion of and research into theological issues and to turn out priests to provide religious ceremonies and advice to the working rank and file. Consequently, some part of the output of the contemporary university shares the traditional conceptions of its social role and is attracted by missionary work, not among, but for the benefit of, the heathen.

These remarks have been directed, not at the development issue itself, but at the level below that: the question of why the issue is seen in terms of a confrontation between two groups of nations, in which the less-developed group provides both an accusatory philosophy of the reasons for its inferior economic position and a retributive philosophy of remedies based on the inversion of monopolistic practices. The most important implication is that "the North-South issue" is very unlikely to be resolved by any sort of compromise by the advanced countries involving some degree of acceptance of, and cooperation in the implementation of, the kinds of reform of the international economic system "demanded" by the less-developed countries. For this there are two major reasons. One is political; concessions along those lines imply partial acceptance of the charge of willful responsibility for the condition of economic underdevelopment, which in turn will be interpreted as justification for still more demands. The other is practical; significant success with the proposed kinds of intervention in and regulation of international trade—particularly the organization of a series of international commodity agreements integrated solely through the provision of a massive common fund to finance the necessary investment in large stocks of commodities—would require a quantity and quality of commercial, managerial, and econometric forecasting talent that is most unlikely to be available even at vast expense. But, as is common with schemes of this kind, the result of failure is likely to be a demand for still more finance and still more expenditure on high-priced talent, not recognition that it is the concept itself that has failed and needs to be reconsidered.

Toward Rational Development Policies

What positive suggestions can be made, then, about the amelioration of the North-South issue? First is a point that rarely is made publicly or officially, thanks to the old tradition of respect for national sovereignty and national governments (whether democratic or totalitarian) and the new diplomatic practice of never offending the governments of less-developed countries (no matter how they came to power or how long they may last). It is that economic development is primarily a domestic matter, issues of international trade and investment being peripheral to the problem. This point can be made by the familiar simple arithmetic of income redistribution: because the rich are necessarily few in number, confiscation and sharing of their wealth or income among the poor would yield negligible per capita gains. The same conclusion can be arrived at by a more sophisticated route, through the recently developed technique of growth accounting and through consideration of the magnitude of the investments in material and human capital required to create and maintain an affluent society. Since development is overwhelmingly the result of domestic accumulation of capital in its manifold forms, and accumulation is the result of an interaction between the size and certainty of returns on investments and the capacity of and incentives for individuals and groups to save and invest resources, it follows that governments claiming to seek development ought to pay prime attention to policies encouraging private accumulation. Many such governments in fact do not do so but instead create political and economic uncertainty; penalize the saver and enterpriser; and attempt to subject private initiative to bureaucratic central control, to confine opportunities to politically or socially privileged groups, and to extract a high proportion of the returns from accumulation for government expenditure in the pursuit of its own objectives and in the maintenance of its army of bureaucrats. It would, at least in the longer run, help to resolve the North-South issue if the developed countries moved toward criticizing development-inhibiting policies in the less-developed countries as freely as they criticize one another's economic policies and as freely as the less-developed countries, with far less circumspection and respect for national sovereignty, censure the developed countries.

The second point is that, while international trade and investment policies are not central to the process of economic development, their influence is not negligible, particularly when one turns from the macroeconomics to the microeconomics of growth and the opportunities for gains through international specialization and division of labor. Here there are two main sets of issues: trade in industrial products, particularly standard-technology low-skilled-labor-intensive industrial products; and trade in primary commodities and foodstuffs.

As regards labor-intensive industry, there is no question that the dynamics of comparative advantage point to both the desirability and the inevitability of a shift of location from the advanced to the less-developed countries. Nor is there any doubt that political considerations and pressures in the developed countries lead their governments to impede the process of transference by the commonly recognized device of retention of high tariffs in a general process of negotiated tariff liberalization, reinforced by quotas and "voluntary" export-limitation agreements. Governments also impede the process by more subtle methods, partially disguised as regional policies or as subsidies for modernization of capital and technology. Where the disagreement emerges is, first, at the conceptual level, with the conviction of "the UNCTAD approach" that the indicated changes in the international division of labor can only be secured by deliberate intergovernmental agreement on the need for a new international division of labor and by international enforcement of the trade patterns so decided on, rather than by occurring naturally, through the automatic workings of free international competition—with far greater likelihood of increasing efficiency and raising standards of living. Second, at the practical level of domestic and international politics, it is only too easy for less-developed countries' spokesmen and sympathizers to ignore the fact that the human adjustments required by the loss of erstwhile comparative advantage are real and are far more difficult than the opposite adjustment of transferring people and resources into an expanding new export industry. It is easy for them to argue or assume that the citizens and governments of the advanced countries should simply absorb these costs without complaint, in the interests of expanding the exports of the developing countries. The hard issue here is for the governments of the advanced countries to develop politically acceptable policies that cushion adjustments but do not in fact result in providing additional protection against the need for adjustment.

In the area of trade in primary products and foodstuffs, it is equally indisputable that the severity of the problems of instability and chronic overproduction can, to an important extent, be blamed on the agricultural protection policies of the advanced countries. In this connection, mention should also be made of the chronic tendency toward underfulfillment of agricultural production targets in Russia and China, which, combined with grossly inadequate storage arrangements, make these countries on occasion an important source of instability of demand and prices in world markets. The most paradoxical feature of the chaos of advanced-country agricultural support policies is that there are no desirable results, in terms of their announced objectives, to set against the damage they do to world agricultural trade and to the incomes and agricultural trade prospects of the developing countries. In the United States, it has been conclusively demonstrated that the main effect of farm policy is to raise the price of land; for the Common Agricultural Policy in Europe, the beneficiaries of all the expense are unknown—with the possible exception of the cows whose survival on a diet of their own reprocessed butter is one of the minor technical triumphs of the policy. It would be an important step both toward a rational economic policy and toward economic development in the less-developed countries if the developed countries could bring themselves to cease regarding agricultural policy as a special case, sacrosanct and not subject to rational examination because agriculture is "a difficult social problem," and would instead devise policies aimed directly at the rural poverty that farm policy is intended to, but does not, alleviate.

To make this point, however, is to confine attention to only half of the story; for agricultural policy in most of the less-developed countries discourages agriculture by taxation at least as strongly as agricultural policy in the advanced countries encourages it by subsidization. The contrast between policies is presumably one of the main reasons why agricultural production has been consistently growing faster than population in the advanced countries, while barely keeping abreast of population growth in the less-developed countries. Incentives for increased agricultural production in the less-developed countries could be quickly changed by governmental policy, unlike the other variable in the equation—the rate of population growth—changes in which, to be macroeconomically significant, would take a very long time indeed.

Nevertheless, the more one thinks about the economics of the development problem and "the North-South issue," the more crucial becomes the problem of the control of population growth. The reason is not simply the Malthusian one, or the "Club of Rome" doomsday prediction. If human populations are to be raised generally to the level of affluence, distributed according to some broad notions of equity, population growth must be restrained. This would not merely free investible resources for the deepening, as distinct from the widening, of the capital stock (again broadly defined), but would make human beings scarce enough relative to cooperating resources to motivate conscious efforts and policies to improve the productive and income-generating capacities of the average citizen.

Daniel Patrick Moynihan

The United States in Opposition

"We are far from living in a single world community," writes Edward Shils, "but the rudiments of a world society do exist." Among those rudiments, perhaps the most conspicuous, if least remarked, are the emerging views as to what kind of society it is. A measure of self-awareness has appeared, much as it did for smaller polities in earlier times. These assessments tend at the international level to be as diverse as those commonly encountered concerning national societies, or local ones. Some will think the society is good and getting better; others will see it as bad and getting worse. Some want change; some fear it. Where one sees justice, another sees wrong.

The notion of a world society is nothing new to Americans. It dominated the rhetoric of World War II, of the founding of the United Nations, of much of the cold war. It is now a received idea, and its impress may be measured by the success with which advocates have found audiences for issues defined in international terms: the world environmental problem; the world population problem; the world food problem. Not a generation ago, these were national issues at most.

Much of this internationalist rhetoric is based on things real enough. There *is* a world ecology; there *is* a world

Reprinted by permission of the author and *Commentary*, from *Commentary*, March 1975. Copyright 1975 by the American Jewish Committee.

economy; and some measures important to individual countries can only be obtained through international accord. Thus the concept of interdependence has become perhaps the main element of the new consciousness of a world society. This is a valid basis on which to posit the existence of a society; it is almost a precondition of a society's coming into being.

Yet societies rarely stop at the acknowledgment of the need for cooperation which is implied by the term interdependence. The image of a society as a family is a common one, and with reason; for in both cases the idea of cooperation is frequently supplemented or even supplanted by the idea of obligation. What does one member *owe* another? This is something new in international pronouncements. If one were to characterize the discomfiture and distress with which Americans responded to the events of the 29th General Assembly of the United Nations in 1974, some measure would have to be attributed to the discovery that a vast majority of the nations of the world feel there are claims which can be made on the wealth of individual nations that are both considerable and threatening—in any event threatening to countries such as the United States, which regularly finds itself in a minority (often a minority of one or two or at most a half-dozen) in an assembly of 138 members.

The tyranny of the United Nations' "new majority" has accordingly been deplored, and there has been much comment that whereas opposition to the United Nations was once a position of "conservatives" in the United States, it is increasingly one of "liberals" also. Yet while there have been some calls to boycott the General Assembly, or not to vote in it, there have been but few calls for withdrawal from the United Nations. It is almost as if American opinion now acknowledged that there was no escaping involvement in the emergent world society. All the more reason, then, for seeking to understand what has been going on.

An Ideological Revolution

Now, of course, a lot is going on, and no single element dominates. Yet it may be argued that what happened in the early 1970s is that for the first time the world felt the impact of what for lack of a better term I shall call the British revolution. That is the revolution which began in 1947 with the granting by socialist Britain of independence to socialist India. In slow, then rapid, order the great empires of the world—with the single major exception of the Czarist empire—broke up into independent states; the original membership of the United Nations of 51 grew to 138. These new nations naturally varied in terms of size, population, and resources. But in one respect they hardly varied at all. To a quite astonishing degree they were ideologically uniform, having fashioned their polities in terms derived from the general corpus of British socialist opinion as it developed in the period roughly 1890–1950. The Englishmen and Irishmen, Scotsmen and Welsh, who created this body of doctrine and espoused it with such enterprise—nay, genius—thought they were making a social revolution in Britain. And they were. But the spread of their ideology to the furthest reaches of the globe, with its ascent to dominance in the highest national councils everywhere, gives to the British revolution the kind of worldwide significance which the American and French, and then the Russian, revolutions possessed in earlier times.[1]

From the perspective of their impact on others, the American and French revolutions can be treated as a single event. They were not of course identical in themselves, and profoundly important distinctions can be made between them. But these distinctions were little noted in the political rhetoric of the century that followed, or in the forms of government fashioned in the likeness of this rhetoric, or in

---

1 The term British revolution is open to objection as seeming to exclude the influence of continental socialism on the new nations, and indeed a good case could be made for calling the phenomenon I am trying to describe the revolution of the Second International. But the term "British" can be justified by the fact that of the 87 states to have joined the United Nations since its founding, more than half —47—had been part of the British Empire. Even apart from the Empire, British culture was in the first half of this century incomparably the most influential in the world, and that culture was increasingly suffused with socialist ideas and attitudes. I anticipate and hope for a rigorous critique of the arguments of this paper, but I also hope it will not be too much distracted by the difficulties of finding a concise term to describe what was on the whole a concise phenomenon: the development of socialist doctrine and the formation of socialist parties in Western Europe at this time. I should also note that the political ideology in the new states of the Third World of which I will be speaking was best described by the late George Lichtheim as "national socialism." This term has, of course, acquired an altogether unacceptable connotation.

the goals of governments so fashioned. Men sought a constitutional regime which disestablished ancient privilege, guaranteed liberties, and promoted the general welfare through what came to be known as liberal social policies. Liberalism was at first characterized by the opposition to state intervention in economic affairs, and later by the advocacy of such intervention, but the intervention in question was a fairly mild business, it being no liberal's view that the state was an especially trustworthy servant of the citizen. The citizen, as liberals viewed the world, was a very important person, especially perhaps if he tended to clean linen.

The Russian revolution of 1917 brought into existence a regime even more dramatically different from its predecessors than had the liberal regimes of a century earlier been from theirs. Everything, it was understood, had changed. Those who would change everything, or who believed that, like it or not, everything was going to change, rallied to this rhetoric. As for the rest of the world, it came soon enough to know that a wholly extraordinary event had occurred, even that the future had occurred. For three decades, culminating in the triumph of Communist arms in China in 1948, this was quite the most vivid, and the most attended to, movement in the world.

The British revolution of the second quarter of the 20th century attracted no such attention. Everyone certainly recognized that new states were coming into existence out of former European, and indeed mostly British, colonies; but the tendency was to see them as candidates for incorporation into one or the other of the older revolutionary traditions then dominant elsewhere in the world. It was not generally perceived that they were in a sense already spoken for—that they came to independence with a pre-existing, coherent, and surprisingly stable ideological base which, while related to both the earlier traditions, was distinct from both. This most likely accounts for the almost incurious initial reaction in what would soon be known as the First and Second Worlds. In the Republic of India the United States could see democracy; the Soviets could see socialism. In truth, a certain Hegelian synthesis had occurred. On the one hand, the Minimal State of the American revolution; in response, the Total State of the Russian revolution; in synthesis, the Welfare State of the British revolution.

Samuel H. Beer describes the doctrine of British socialism as follows:

> it is especially the socialist's commitment to "fellowship" that fundamentally distinguishes his approach.... For private ownership he would substitute public ownership; for production for profit, production for use; for competition, cooperation. A cultural and ethical revolution would also take place, and motives that had aimed at individual benefit would now aim at common benefits. Industry, which had been governed by individual decisions within the competitive system, would be subject to collective and democratic control.... Government would consist in comprehensive and continuous planning and administration.

Two general points may be made about this British doctrine. First, it contained a suspicion of, almost a bias against, economic development which carried over into those parts of the world where British culture held sway. The fundamental assertion of the age of the Diamond Jubilee was that there was plenty of wealth to go 'round if only it were fairly distributed. No matter what more thoughtful socialist analysts might urge, redistribution, not production, remained central to the ethos of British socialism. Profit became synonymous with exploitation. That profit might be something conceptually elegant—least-cost production—made scarcely any impress. "Production for profit" became a formulation for all that was wrong in the old ways, and Tories half agreed. (For it was the Liberals and the Radicals who were being repudiated by such doctrine, and it was the Liberal party that went under.) This, too, was passed on. When Sir Arthur Lewis in 1974 gave the Tata lectures in India and found himself pleading, as a socialist and as a man of the Third World, but also as an economist, that profit was not a concept public-sector enterprise could afford to ignore, no less a personage than the head of the Indian Planning Commission felt called upon to rebut him.

To be sure, much of this redistributionist bias was simply innocent. British socialists, for example, proved in office to know almost nothing about how actually to redistribute income, and British income has not been significantly redistributed. Coming to power just after World War II, the socialists appeared to think they had abolished wealth by imposing a top income-tax rate of nineteen shillings six pence in the twenty-shilling pound, which is to say, confiscating the rich man's pay envelope. Few seemed to note that capital gains remained exempt from income tax altogether, so that in large measure thereafter only those with property could acquire property: the very antithesis of the social condition socialism sought. (This detail perhaps did not escape the well-to-do of the developing nations when the prospect of socialism on the British model first appeared there.)

The second general point about socialist doctrine as it developed in Britain was that it was anti-American. More anti-American, surely, than it was ever anti-Soviet. The reasons for this are not that obscure. The British were not overmuch admiring of Americans in that era, nor we of them. In part their attitude began as aristocratical disdain. (An intimate of Pandit Nehru's describes once asking India's first prime minister why he was so anti-American. This was in 1961. Nehru's first reaction was a rather huffy denial of any such predisposition, but he then became reflective and after a moment admitted that, yes, it was true, and that probably it all dated back to his days at Harrow. There was one American boy there at the time: filthy rich, and much too pushy.) But more importantly, of course, America was seen as quintessentially capitalist.

With the Russian revolution, and then especially with the world depression of the 1930s and the onset of popular-front movements in Europe, a considerable number of British socialists, despite their party's fundamental and central attachment to democratic processes, became supporters of the Soviet regime. Russia was the future. America was the past. With the coming of the cold war this attitude became institutionalized and almost compulsory on the British Left. The *New Statesman*, a journal which tended to follow Asian and African graduates after they had left Britain and returned home, became near Stalinist in its attachment to Soviet ways with the world and its pervasive antagonism to things American.

And yet the *New Statesman* was never communist, and neither, save in small proportion, were its readers. They were British socialists, part of a movement of opinion which spread in the course of the first half of the 20th century to the whole of the British Empire, a domain which covered one-quarter of the earth's surface and which an inspired cartographic convention had long ago decreed be colored pink. It was British civil servants who took the doctrine to the colonies. (How curious, in retrospect, are the agonizings of Harold Laski and others as to whether the civil service would carry out the policies of a socialist government. What more congenial task for persons whose status comes from the power and prestige of government? But in the Britain of that era it could be thought that class origin would somehow overcome occupational interest.)

What the civil service began, British education completed. Has there ever been a conversion as complete as that of the Malay, the Ibo, the Gujarati, the Jamaican, the Australian, the Cypriot, the Guyanan, the Yemenite, the Yoruban, the sabra, the felaheen to this distant creed? The London School of Economics, Shils notes, was often said to be the most important institution of higher education in Asia and Africa. In her autobiography, Beatrice Webb wrote that she and her husband felt "assured that with the School [LSE] as the teaching body, the Fabian Society as a propagandist organization, the LCC [London County Council] as object lesson in electoral success, our books as the only elaborate original work in economic fact and theory, no young man or woman who is anxious to study or to work in public affairs can fail to come under our influence." For reasons that are understandable, this was true most particularly for young men and women coming from abroad in that long and incongruously optimistic intellectual age that began amid late Victorian plumpness and ended with the austerity of postwar Britain. In 1950 the conservative Michael Oakeshott succeeded to the Fabian Harold Laski's chair in political theory at LSE and in a sense *that* party was over. But by then not communists but Fabians could claim that the largest portion of the world's population lived in regimes of their fashioning. Before very long, the arithmetical majority and the ideological coherence of those new nations brought them to dominance in the United Nations and, indeed, in any world forum characterized by universal membership.

But if the new nations absorbed ideas about others from the doctrines of British socialism, they also absorbed ideas about themselves. The master concept, of course, is that they had the right to independence. This idea goes back to the American revolution and even beyond, to the Glorious Revolution in 17th-century Britain, but British socialism readily incorporated and even appropriated it. As the 20th century wore on and the issue of independence arose with respect to these specific peoples and places, it was most often the socialists who became the principal *political* sponsors of independence. It was a Labour government which in 1947 granted independence to India and formally commenced the vast, peaceful revolution that followed. The Indian Congress party had been founded in 1883 by a British civil servant, Alan Octavian Hume, whose politics were essentially Liberal. But by the time of independence, it was a matter to be taken for granted that the Congress was socialist and that its leaders, Gandhi and then Nehru, were socialists too.

Two further concepts triangulate and fix the imported political culture of these new nations. The first is the belief —often, of course, justified—that they have been subject to economic exploitation, exactly as the working class is said in socialist theory to have been exploited under capitalism. The second is the belief—also, of course, often justified—that they have been subject to ethnic discrimination corresponding to class distinctions in industrial society. As with the belief in the right to independence, these concepts, which now seem wholly natural, rarely occur in nature. They are learned ideas, and they were learned by the new nations mostly where they mostly originated, in the intellectual and political circles of Britain of the late 19th and early 20th century. Gandhi greatly elucidated the moral dimensions of exploitation and discrimination, but he did so in the context of a worldwide political movement that was more than receptive to his ideas, a political movement of which he was a part. At root, the ideas of exploitation and discrimination represent a transfer to colonial populations of the fundamental socialist assertions with respect to the condition of the European working class, just as the idea of independence parallels the demand that the working class break out of bondage and rise to power.

Now it is possible to imagine a country, or collection of countries, with a background similar to that of the British colonies, attaining independence and then letting bygones be bygones. The Americans did that: our political culture did not suggest any alternative. International life was thought to operate in Wordsworth's terms:

> The good old rule
> ...The simple plan
> That they should take, who have the power.
> And they should keep who can.

So in their own terms might Marxists judge the aftermath of Marxist triumph: history was working its ineluctable way; there would be no point, no logic, in holding the past to account. Not so the heirs of the British revolution. British socialism is, was, and remains a highly moral creed. It is not a politics of revenge; it is too civil for that. But reparations? Yes: reparations. This idea was fundamental to the social hope of a movement which, it must ever be recalled, rested on the assumption that there existed vast stores of unethically accumulated wealth. On the edges of the movement there were those who saw the future not just in terms of redistribution, but of something ominously close to looting. In any event, the past was by no means to be judged over and done with. There were scores to be settled. Internally and internationally.

A final distinctive character of the British revolution concerns procedure. Wrongs are to be righted by legislation. The movement was fundamentally parliamentarian. The Labour party came to power through the ballot and proceeded to change society by statute. This was dramatically so with respect to the Empire. For the first time in the history of mankind, a vast empire dismantled itself, piece by piece, of its own systematic accord. A third of the nations of the world today owe their existence to a statute of Westminister. What more profound experience could there be of the potency of parliamentary majorities in distant places, and of their enactments?

Plainly, not all the new nations of the postwar world were formerly British. There were French colonies. Belgian. Dutch. Portuguese. Political traditions in each case were different from the British. But only *slightly* different: viewed from *Mars*, London, Paris, and The Hague are not widely separated or disparate places. By the time of the granting of independence, all were democratic with a socialist intelligentsia and, often as not, a socialist government.

With the exception of Algeria—which is marked by the exception—the former French and Dutch colonies came into being in very much the manner the British had laid down. For a prolonged initial period the former British possessions had pride of place in the ex-colonial world—they speak English at the United Nations, not American—and pretty much set the style of politics which has become steadily more conspicuous in international affairs.

Not everyone has noticed this. Indeed, there is scarcely yet a vocabulary in which to describe it. In part, this is because the event is recent, but also because it was incomplete. As with the liberal revolution which came out of America, and the communist revolution which came out of Russia, this socialist revolution coming mainly out of Britain carried only so much of the world in its initial period of expansion. The liberal revolution of America was not exactly a spent force by the mid-20th century, but (*pace* the Mekong Delta Development Plan) there was never any great prospect of its expanding to new territories. On the other hand, the heirs of the Russian revolution did capture China, the greatest of all the prizes, in 1948, and at least part of Indochina a bit later. But in the main the communist revolution stopped right there, and the two older revolutions now hold sway within fairly well defined boundaries. Since 1950 it has been not they but the heirs of the British revolution who have been expanding.

Almost the first international political act of the new states was to form the nonaligned bloc, distinguishing themselves—partially—from the two blocs into which the immediate postwar world had formed. From politics, the emphasis shifted to economic affairs. In 1968 these countries, meeting at Algiers, formed the Group of 77 as a formal economic bloc. Their joint statement described the group as "comprising the vast majority of the human race"—and indeed it did. The B's in the list of members gave a sense of the range of nations and peoples involved: Bahrain, Barbados, Bhutan, Bolivia, Botswana, Brazil, Burma, Burundi. And yet there was—now somewhat hidden—unity to the list. Of these eight countries, five were formerly British-governed or British-directed. At its second ministerial meeting in Lima in 1971, the group (now numbering 96) drew up an Action Program which stated, *inter alia,* that developing countries should

> encourage and promote appropriate commodity action and, particularly, the protection of the interests of primary producers of the region through intensive consultations among producer countries in order to encourage appropriate policies, leading to the establishment of producers' associations and understandings....

This was represented in the press as a major gain for the black African states, who carried the point over objections from Latin Americans accustomed to working out raw-material and commodity arrangements with the United States. But the idea was fundamentally a heritage of the British revolution, and if the black Africans took the lead in proclaiming it, there is no reason to think it was any less familiar to Arabs. They had all gone to the same schools. Was it not right for those who have only their labor to sell, or only the products of their soil, to organize to confront capital? Had they not been exploited?

U.S. Acquiescence

How has the United States dealt with these new nations and their distinctive ideology? Clearly, we have not dealt very successfully. This past year, in the 29th General Assembly, we were frequently reduced to a voting bloc which, with variations, consisted of ourselves, Chile, and the Dominican Republic. As this "historic session" closed, the permanent representative of India to the United Nations declared: "The activities of the Soviet delegation at the session showed once again that the Soviet Union deeply understands and shares the aspirations of the Third World." This was not Krishna Menon, but a balanced and considerate Asian diplomat. If no equivalent pronouncement on China comes immediately to hand, this may be because the Chinese feel free to identify themselves as members of the Third World. As such, at the end of 1974 they declared that the new majority had written a "brilliant chapter" during the twelve months previous, that it was "sweeping ahead full sail as the boat of imperialism [the United States] and hegemonism [the Soviet Union] founders." "These days," the Chinese statement continued, "the United Nations often takes on the appearance of an international court with the Third World pressing the charges and conducting the trial." A statement to which many could subscribe. But no such statement could come from an American statesman, no such praise would be accorded American policy. Clearly at some level—we all but *started* the United Nations—there has been a massive failure of American diplomacy.

But why? Why has the United States dealt so unsuccessfully with these nations and their distinct ideology? A first thought is that we have not seen the ideology as distinctive. Not recognizing it, we have made no sustained effort to relate ourselves to it. The totalitarian states, from their point of view, did. They recognize ideologies. By 1971 it was clear enough that the Third World—a few exceptions here and there—was not going communist. But it was nevertheless possible to encourage it in directions that veered very considerably from any tendency the bloc might have to establish fruitful relations with the West; and this was done. It was done, moreover, with the blind acquiescence and even agreement of the United States which kept endorsing principles for whose logical outcome it was wholly unprepared and with which it could never actually go along.

A relatively small but revealing example of this process may be seen in the development of the World Social Report, a document of the Economic and Social Council. The first volume, covering the year 1963, was directed almost exclusively to problems of the developing countries, and the United States took its advent as a promising event. The 1965 report, concentrating on "practical methods of promoting social change," might have caused some to take note, but American officials were entirely unwary; this was, after all, a report designed to help the developing world. In actual fact, it was becoming a document based on the veritably totalitarian idea that social justice means social stability and that social stability means the absence of social protest. Thus by 1970, the Soviet Union—not much social protest there!—emerges as the very embodiment of the just state, while the United States is a nation in near turmoil from the injustices it wreaks upon the poor and the protests these injustices have provoked. And Western Europe hardly comes off any better.

What happened here was that a "Finlandized" Secretariat

(the official in charge of preparing the document was indeed a Finn) found that the developing countries and the Communist countries had an easy common interest in portraying their own progress, justifying the effective suppression of dissent, and in the process deprecating and indicting the seeming progress of Western societies. It is easy enough to see that this would be in the interest of the Soviet bloc. (The Chinese did not participate in the debate.) But why the developing world? First, the developing nations could ally with the totalitarians in depicting social reality in this way, in part because so many, having edged toward authoritarian regimes, faced the same problems the Communists would have encountered with a liberal analysis of civil liberties. Secondly, the developing nations had an interest in deprecating the economic achievements of capitalism, since almost none of their own managed economies was doing well. To deplore, to deride, the social effects of affluence in the United States is scarcely a recent invention. For a generation, the British Left has held the patent. Further, there is an almost automatic interest on the Left in delegitimating wealth—prior to redistributing it—much as the opposite interest exists on the Right.

Small wonder that officials could describe the Social Report as the most popular document in the UN series, a statement intended as more than faint praise. Yet it has been more representative than otherwise. There are hundreds like it, suffused with a neototalitarian, anti-American bias.

American protests at the 26th General Assembly have evidently influenced the most recent Social Report, submitted to the 29th, but here the significant fact is that this protest—entered at the very last moment, when the document was being presented for pro forma approval—was the first of its kind, or one of the first. In fact the United States until then did not protest. To the contrary, the United States actively participated in preparing this sustained assault on American institutions. The 1970 Social Report had been three years in the making. During those three years it made its way through layers of bureaucracies, all manner of meetings. Americans were always present, and Americans always approved. This was, after all, a Third World document; it was to be treated with tolerance and understanding. Complacency of this order could only arise from the failure to perceive that a distinctive ideology was at work, and that skill and intelligence were required to deal with it successfully.

The blindness of American diplomacy to the process persists. Two large events occurred in 1971, and a series of smaller ones were set in motion. China entered the United Nations, an event the Third World representatives saw as a decisive shift of power to their camp. In that same year the Lima conference established the nonaligned as an economic bloc intent on producer cartels. Less noticed, but perhaps no less important in its implications, a distinctive radicalization began in what might as well be termed world social policy.

This radicalization was first clearly evidenced at the United Nations Conference on the Human Environment, held at Stockholm in 1972, or more precisely at the 26th General Assembly, which was finally to authorize the conference. The conference was in considerable measure an American initiative, and while American negotiators were primarily concerned with ways to get the Russians to join (which in the end they did not), the Brazilians suddenly stormed onto the scene to denounce the whole enterprise as a conspiracy of the haves to keep the have-nots down and out. The argument was that the rich had got rich by polluting their environments and now proposed to stay that way by preventing anyone else from polluting theirs. This, among other things, would insure that the rich would continue their monopoly on the use of the raw materials of the poor. Thus was it asserted that matters originally put forward as soluble in the context of existing economic and political relations were nothing of the sort. To the contrary, they were symptomatic of economic and political exploitation and injustice which could only be resolved by the most profound transformation: to expropriate the expropriators.

At Stockholm itself, this quickly became the dominant theme—espoused by a dominant majority. "Are not poverty and need the greatest pollutors?" Prime Minister Indira Gandhi of India asked. "There are grave misgivings," she continued, "that the discussion of ecology may be designed to distract attention from the problems of war and poverty."

She was wrong in this. They were not so designed. But at Stockholm the nations who feared they might be took control of the agenda. The conference declared as its first principle:

Man has the fundamental right to freedom, equality, and adequate conditions of life, in an environment of a quality which permits a life of dignity and well being, and bears a solemn responsibility to protect and improve the environment for present and future generations. In this respect, policies promoting or perpetuating apartheid, racial segregation, discrimination, colonial and other forms of oppression and foreign domination stand condemned and must be eliminated.

The American delegates routinely voted for this resolution. It was, after all, language the new countries wanted. What wholly unwelcome meanings might be attached to "other forms of oppression and foreign domination" which stood "condemned" and had to be "eliminated," was a thought scarcely in keeping with the spirit of the occasion.

The Stockholm conference had been turbulent. The United Nations World Population Conference, held nearly two years later, in August 1974, had an air of insurrection. This conference too was largely an American initiative, the culmination of years of State Department effort to put population on the agenda of world social policy. The secretary general of the United Nations proclaimed the gathering would be "a turning point in the history of mankind." The centerpiece was a Draft World Population Plan of Action, which in essence set 1985 as the year crude birth rates in developing countries would be reduced to 30 per thousand (as against an anticipated 34) and when "the necessary information and education about family planning and means to practice family planning" would be available "to all persons who so desire." There can be no doubt of the social change implicit in such a conference's even meeting: in most industrialized countries, family planning has only just achieved the status of an accepted social value deserving of public support. Yet neither should there be any doubt that a disaster overtook the American position in the course of the conference, and that this disaster was wholly predictable.

To begin with, the conference was thought up by Americans to deal with a problem we consider that other people have. (In fairness, not long ago the United States itself was

thought to have a problem of population size, while the provision of family-planning services is an issue of social equity
as well as of population growth.) Specifically, it was considered a problem of the developing countries: countries, that
is, of the British revolution who are animated by the liveliest
sense that their troubles originate in capitalist and imperialist systems of which the United States all but offered itself
as an exemplar. Further, the conference met in Bucharest,
capital of a Communist country. At one level no great imagination would have been required to anticipate the outcome. President Nicolae Ceausescu opened the conference by
declaring that "The division of the world into developed and
underdeveloped countries is a result of historical evolution,
and is a direct consequence of the imperialist, colonialist,
and neo-colonialist policies of exploitation of many peoples."
He called for "a new international economic order" and condemned "a pessimistic outlook" on population growth.

But if this was to be expected, few could have anticipated
the wild energy of the Chinese assault on the Western position. China has the strictest of all population-control programs. Yet the Chinese arrived in Rumania to assail with
unprecedented fury and devastating zeal the very idea of
population control as fundamentally subversive of the
future of the Third World. The future, the Chinese proclaimed, is infinitely bright. Only the imperialists and the
hegemonists could spoil it, and population control was to
be their wrecking device. A theory of "consumerism"
emerged: it was excessive consumption in the developed
economies which was the true source of the problems of the
underdeveloped nations and not the size of the latter's population. None dared oppose the thesis. The Indians, who are
thought to have a population problem, went to the conference rather disposed to endorse a plan of action. But they did
nothing of the sort. Instead, the Maharaja of Jammu and
Kashmir, who headed the Indian delegation, found himself
denouncing "colonial denudation" of the East, and the "vul-
gar affluence" of the West. The scene grew orgiastic.

In the end, a doctrine emerged which is almost certainly
more true than otherwise, namely that social and economic
change is the fundamental determinant of fertility change,
compared with which family planning as such has at most
a residual role. There need be no difficulty with this asser-

tion. The difficulty comes with the conclusion said to follow: that economic growth in the West should cease and the wealth of the world be redistributed. We are back to Keir Hardie, expropriating the expropriators. Not to produce wealth, but to redistribute it. As with the environment conference, the population conference turned into another occasion for reminding the West of its alleged crimes and unresolved obligations.

This tone attained to manic proportions in Population Tribune, an unofficial, American-financed parallel conference of a form that first appeared in Stockholm. Ritual recantation became the order of the day as one notable after another confessed to a class-bound past which had blinded him to the infinitely bright future. Most of the recanters were American, but it was Professor René Dumont of France who epitomized the argument in a statement, "Population and Cannibals," which was subsequently given the full front page of *Development Forum*, an official, five-language, UN publication. Professor Dumont—blaming the "Plunderers of the Third World" for world conditions— "They... 'under-pay' for the rare raw materials of the Third World and then squander them"—put the case with some vivacity:

> *Eating little children.* I have already had occasion to show that the rich white man, with his overconsumption of meat and his lack of generosity toward poor populations, acts like a true cannibal, albeit indirect. Last year, in overconsuming meat which wasted the cereals which could have saved them, we ate the little children of the Sahel, of Ethiopia, and of Bangladesh. And this year, we are continuing to do the same thing, with the same appetite.

Dr. Han Suyin, a sympathetic commentator on Chinese Communist affairs, summed up for others:

> You cannot cut off any talk about population, about people, from economics and politics. You cannot put in a vacuum any talk about population and world resources without relation to the present as it exists. I admire people who can talk about a noble future where there will be an equal society and where resources will be controlled by all. But, forgive me for saying so, if this is to be done, then we have to begin by sharing now everything and that would mean that a lot of people who have a lot of private property, for instance, should divest themselves immediately of it in favor of the poor. It means

that at this very moment we should start to implement a very simple thing—something which we heard...at the United Nations at the sixth special session of the United Nations where the voice of the Third World—the majority of the world—at last formulated their demand for more equitable terms of trade, and for an end to exploitation, for an end to the real cause of poverty and backwardness, which is not population, but which is injustice and exploitation. The Third World has a word for it, it calls it imperialism and hegemony.

And the American delegation? The official view, flashed to diplomatic posts around the world, was as uncomplicated at the end as it had been at the outset: "ALL BASIC U.S. OBJECTIVES WERE ACHIEVED AND U.S. ACCOMPLISHMENTS WERE MANY....U.S. DELEGATION UNANIMOUSLY PLEASED WITH FINAL RESULT."

The World Food Conference which followed in Rome in November was even more explicitly an American initiative. Yet as the American delegation somewhat sadly noted, the plenary forum was used to the fullest by less-developed countries to excoriate the United States and other developed nations as responsible for the current food crisis and the generally depressed state of their part of the world, calling for "radical adjustment in the current economic order and, in effect, reparations from developed countries" to the less-developed. Such negotiations as took place were somewhat more sober, since something immediately of value—wheat—was at stake and obviously only the United States and a few such countries were prepared to part with any. Even so, by the time the conference was concluded, one of the great, and truly liberal, innovations of world social policy—the American-led assertion that the hungry of the world should be fed by transfers of resources—had been utterly deprecated. Thus the Indian food minister's statement with respect to the needs of the developing countries:

It is obvious that the developed nations can be held responsible for their [the developing nations'] present plight. Developed nations, therefore, have a duty to help them. Whatever help is rendered to them now should not be regarded as charity but deferred compensation for what has been done to them in the past by the developed countries.

The UN General Assembly pursued this theme with notable persistence throughout 1974, commencing with a special session in the spring which dealt with the economic crises of the underdeveloped in just such terms. Occasioned as much as anything by the devastating impact of oil price increases, the special session dwelt on every conceivable abuse of economic power save that one. At the end of the regular autumn session, the General Assembly solemnly adopted a Charter of Economic Rights and Duties of States which accords to each state the right freely to exercise full permanent sovereignty over its wealth and natural resources, to regulate and exercise authority over foreign investments, and to nationalize, expropriate, or transfer ownership of foreign property pretty much at will. The vote was 120 to 6—the United States, Belgium, Denmark, West Germany, Luxembourg, and the United Kingdom. What was being asserted was a radical discontinuity with the original, essentially liberal vision of the United Nations as a regime of international law and practice which acknowledges all manner of claims, but claims that move in all directions. Now they moved in one direction only.

In general a rhetoric of expropriation became routine. At year's end, Prime Minister Indira Gandhi, opening the 56th Conference of the International Law Association meeting in New Delhi, declared:

> Laws designed to protect the political or economic power of a few against the rights of the many, must...yield place to laws which enlarge the area of equality, and...law itself should be an ally and instrument of change.

She spoke a now-common language of resentment over population issues:

> Is it not a new form of arrogance for affluent nations to regard the poorer nations as an improvident species whose numbers are a threat to their own standard of living?

She suggested a reversal of roles had taken place between the new nations and the old:

> An obligation rests on the haves to generate confidence among the have-nots....A new approach to foreign investments is indicated, in which investments abroad are regarded more as a service to the recipient community than as an enterprise where profits and their repatriation must be secured at all cost.

Now there is nothing unfamiliar in this language: only the

setting is new. It is the language of British socialism applied to the international scene. American diplomacy has yet to recognize this fact and, failing to recognize it, has failed even to begin dealing intelligently with it.

Enter Totalitarianism?

But if the beginning of wisdom in dealing with the nations of the Third World is to recognize their essential ideological coherence, the next step is to recognize that there is every reason to welcome this ideology and to welcome the coherence also. Because of the British revolution and its heritage, the prospect now is that the world will not go totalitarian. In the Christian sense, has there been such political "good news" in our time? But there is bad news also. The great darkness could yet consume us. The potential for absorption of these states into the totalitarian camp is there and will continue to be there. This is perhaps especially true where one-party states have been established, but even where multiparty democracy flourishes the tug of the "socialist countries," to use the UN term, persists.

The outcome will almost certainly turn on whether or not these nations, individually and in groups, succeed in establishing sufficiently productive economies. If they do not, if instead they become permanently dependent on outside assistance, that assistance is likely more and more to come from the totalitarian nations, and with it the price of internal political influence from the totalitarian camp through the local pro-Moscow, or pro-Peking, Communist party. For everywhere there are such parties. They appear able to go on indefinitely in a dormant state, and can be awakened pretty much at will. India, with a population equal to that of the whole of Africa and South America combined, is the best current example. Parliamentary democracy is vigorous enough there, but economic incompetence on its part and diplomatic blunders on ours have led to an increasing dependence on Soviet support, which in the space of three years has brought about an open electoral alliance between the Congress party and the Moscow-oriented Communists, an alliance we would have thought worth fighting a war to prevent two decades ago, but which we scarcely notice today. This alliance would not have come about save for the failure of the Indian economy to prosper and the success—typical—of the argument that the cure for the damage done by leftist policies is even more leftist policies, which in practice translates into dependence on the Soviets and alliances with their internal allies. And here is the nub of the bad news: for all the attractions of this variety of socialist politics, it has proved, in almost all its versions, almost the world over, to be a distinctly poor means of producing wealth. Sharing wealth—perhaps. But not producing wealth. Who, having read British political journals over the past quarter century, would be surprised to find that during this period (1950–73) the United Kingdom's share of the "Planetary Product" has been reduced from 5.8 to 3.1 percent? Why then be surprised that those who have made British socialism their model have trouble taking off in the opposite direction? Yet even so, one must be surprised at the decline of economies such as those of Burma and Sri Lanka: immensely productive places not a generation ago. Sri Lanka, for example, having first got to the point where it was importing potatoes from Poland, has now got to the further point where it can no longer afford to do so. A recent survey of the Ceylonese economy in the *Far Eastern Economic Review* was entitled: "Conspiracy or Catastrophe?" For what else could explain such failure?

What else, that is, to those experiencing it (with all that implies for political instability)? The outsider can indulge a more relaxed view. The fault lies in ideas, not persons. Americans—Westerners—do not have any claim to superior wisdom on the subject of these economies. Starting in the 1950s, a large number of first-rate economists began working on theories of economic growth designed to get the less-developed countries on a path of self-sustained growth. "To be perfectly brutal about it," Jesse Burkhead recently stated, "it hasn't worked." And yet there is no need to stand mute. Two assertions may be reasonably put forth of which the first is that to say these economies haven't worked as well as hoped is not to say that none has worked at all. There *has* been growth. In the main, things are better than they were. For every Argentina—that "miracle" of economic non-growth—there is a Brazil. For Ghana, Nigeria. For Calcutta, Singapore. The second assertion is that relative failure is particularly to be encountered in economies most heavily influenced by that version of late Fabian economics which compounded the Edwardian view that there was plenty to go around if justly distributed with the 1930s' view that capitalism could never produce enough to go around regardless of distributive principles.[2]

Still, there are gains in the relative loss of income associated with the managed economies of the Third World which need to be appreciated. An Asian economist has said of his own country, plaintively yet not without a certain defiance: "We are socialists, so we do not believe in capitalism. We are democrats, so we do not believe in terror. What, then, is our alternative save one per cent a year?" There *is* a welfare state of sorts; there is protection of industrial labor; and in some countries, at least, there is freedom to protest.

But the most distinctive gain and the least noted is that in the course of its outward journey, the managed economy was transmuted from an instrument of economic rationality to an instrument of political rationality. It is sometimes difficult to recall, but early socialist theory expounded the greater *efficiency* of production for use rather than for capital, and put much stress on capitalist wastefulness. In practice, however, the real attraction of the managed economy has been the means it provides to collect enough political power at the center to maintain national unity—almost everywhere a chancy thing in these generally multiethnic states.

One must still conclude, however, that these political gains are purchased at the expense of even more conspicuous economic losses. India will serve for a final example. In the year of its independence, 1947, India produced 1.2 million tons of steel and Japan only 900,000 tons. A quarter century later, in 1972, India produced 6.8 million tons and Japan 106.8. These outcomes are the result of decisions made by the ruling party of each nation, and only an innocent could continue to accept Indian protestations that the results were unexpected. The break in Indian growth came

---

2 This latter idea is very much alive. On leaving my post as United States ambassador to India, I gave a press conference in which, *inter alia*, I touched upon the failure of India to achieve a productive economy. The *National Herald*, the Nehru family newspaper, commented in an editorial: "Mr. Moynihan may be justified in some of his criticism of the state of the Indian economy, but what he is trying to sell is the capitalist system which can only impoverish India's millions further."

precisely in 1962 when the United States, which had been about to finance its largest aid project ever, a steel complex at Bokharo in eastern India, insisted that it be managed privately. India insisted on a public-sector plant, for which read: a plant that would do what the prime minister of India wanted done. In the manner of the Aswan Dam (and with as much political impact), the Russians stepped in to finance the public-sector plant. By 1974 this plant had yet to produce sheet steel. For the period 1962–72 Indian steel production grew by a bare 1.8 percent, while Japanese grew 13.4 percent.

There is no serious way to deny that India has in a very real sense desired this outcome, just as there is no way to deny that high living standards in the modern world are associated with relatively free market economies and with liberalist international trade policies. Granted that much economic policy does not have high living standards as its true objective, but is rather concerned with political stability, and granted that such a concern may be wholly legitimate in a new nation—in any event it is not anyone else's business —it nevertheless remains the case that the relative economic failure accompanying political success in regimes such as that of India sooner or later begins to undermine that very success. Promises are made and political stability, especially in the more democratic regimes, requires some measure of performance. When it is not forthcoming, regimes change. They become less democratic. They become less independent.

Neither of these developments can be welcomed by the United States. The United States in the past may have cared about the course of political events in these nations, but only in the most abstract terms. (Consider the casualness with which we armed Pakistan and incurred the bitter and enduring hostility of India, the second most populous nation in the world.) But India has now exploded a nuclear device. *That* may well prove the most important event of the turbulent year 1974. Other Third World nations are likely to follow. Hence political stability in the Third World acquires a meaning it simply has never in the past had for American strategic thinking, as well as our general view of world politics.

Minority Opposition

What then is to be done? We are witnessing the emergence
of a world order dominated arithmetically by the countries of
the Third World. This order is already much too developed for the United States or any other nation to think of
opting out. It can't be done. One may become a delinquent
in this nascent world society. An outcast in it. But one remains
"in" it. There is no escape from a definition of nationhood
which derives primarily from the new international reality.
Nor does this reality respond much to the kind of painfully
impotent threats which are sometimes heard of America's
"pulling out." Anyone who doubts that Dubai can pay for
UNESCO, knows little of UNESCO, less of what the United
States pays, and nothing whatever of Dubai.

In any event, matters of this sort aside, world society and
world organization have evolved to the point where palpable
interests are disposed in international forums to a degree
without precedent. Witness, as an instance, the decisions of
the World Court allocating the oil fields of the North Sea
among the various littoral states in distinctly weighted (but
no doubt proper) manner. Witness the current negotiations
at the Law of the Sea Conference. Two-thirds of the world
is covered by the sea, and the United Nations claims the
seabed. That seabed, especially in the region around Ha-
waii, is rich in so-called "manganese nodules"—concentra-
tions of ore which American technology is now able to exploit, or will be sooner than anyone else. At this moment we
have, arguably, complete and perfect freedom to commence
industrial use of the high seas. This freedom is being chal-
lenged, however, and almost certainly some form of international regime is about to be established. It can be a regime
that permits American technology to go forward on some
kind of license-and-royalties basis. Or it can assert exclusive
"internationalized" rights to exploitation in an international
public corporation. The stakes are considerable. They are
enormous.

And then, of course, there remains the overriding interest,
a true international interest, in arms control; and here true
international government has emerged in a most impressive
manner. If we were to ask who is the most important international official, a persuasive case could be made for choos-

ing the inspector general of the International Atomic Energy Authority, the man who supervises the safeguard agreements of the world's atomic reactors. Few would know the name of this unobtrusive Swiss chemist; few, perhaps, need to. But more than a few do need to know that the post is there and that its viability derives ultimately from the international system of which it is a part. For the moment, American security derives primarily from our own armaments, and our stategic agreements with the Soviet Union and a few other powers. But the international regime of arms control is already important and certain to become more so.

If, that is, it does not go down in the general wreckage of the world system embodied now in the United Nations. But assuming that the new majority will not destroy the regime through actions that drive nations like the United States away, is it not reasonable to anticipate a quasi-parliamentary situation at the international level—the General Assembly and a dozen such forums—in which a nominally radical majority sets about legislating its presumed advantage in a world which has just come into its hands? The qualification "quasi-parliamentary" is necessary, for in fact the pronouncements of these assemblies have but limited force. So did the pronouncements of the Continental Congress. They are not on that ground to be ignored. What then does the United States do?

The United States goes into opposition. This is our circumstance. We are a minority. We are outvoted. This is neither an unprecedented nor an intolerable situation. The question is what do we make of it. So far we have made little—nothing—of what is in fact an opportunity. We go about dazed that the world has changed. We toy with the idea of stopping it and getting off. We rebound with the thought that if only we are more reasonable perhaps "they" will be. (Almost to the end, dominant opinion in the U.S. Mission to the United Nations was that the United States could not vote against the "have-nots" by opposing the Charter on the Rights and Duties of States—all rights for the Group of 77 and no duties.) But "they" do not grow reasonable. Instead, we grow unreasonable. A sterile enterprise which awaits total redefinition.

Going into opposition requires first of all that we recognize that there is a distinctive ideology at work in the Third World, and that it has a distinctive history and logic. To repeat the point once again, we have not done this, tending to see these new political cultures in our own image, or in that of the totalitarians, with a steady shift in the general perception from the former to the latter. But once we perceive the coherence in the majority, we will be in a position to reach for a certain coherence of opposition.

Three central issues commend themselves as points of systematic attack: first, the condition of international liberalism; second, the world economy; third, the state of political and civil liberties and of the general welfare. The rudiments of these arguments need only be sketched.

It is the peculiar function of "radical" political demands, such as those most recently heard in the international forums, that they bring about an exceptional deprecation of the achievements of liberal processes. Even when the radicalism is ultimately rejected, this is rarely from a sense that established processes do better and promise more. American liberalism experienced this deprecation in the 1960s; international liberalism is undergoing it in the 1970s. But the truth is that international liberalism and its processes have enormous recent achievements to their credit. It is time for the United States to start saying so.

One example is the multinational corporation, which, combining modern management with liberal trade policies, is arguably the most creative international institution of the 20th century. A less controversial example is the World Health Organization. In 1966 it set out to abolish smallpox, and by the time this article is read, the job will more than likely have been successfully completed—in very significant measure with the techniques and participation of American epidemiologists. While not many Americans have been getting smallpox of late, the United States has been spending $140 million a year to keep it that way. Savings in that proportion and more will immediately follow. Here, as in a very long list, a liberal world policy has made national sense.

We should resist the temptation to designate agreeable policies as liberal merely on grounds of agreeableness. There are harder criteria. Liberal policies are limited in their undertakings, concrete in their means, representative in their mode of adoption, and definable in terms of results. These are surely the techniques appropriate to a still tentative, still emergent world society. It is time for the United States, as the new society's loyal opposition, to say this directly, loudly, forcefully.

The economic argument—which will appear inconsistent only to those who have never been much in politics—is that the world economy is not nearly bad enough to justify the measures proposed by the majority, and yet is much worse than it would otherwise be in consequence of measures the majority has already taken. The first half of this formulation will require a considerable shift in the government mind, and possibly even some movement in American elite opinion also, for we have become great producers and distributors of crisis. The world environment crisis, the world population crisis, the world food crisis, are in the main American discoveries—or inventions—opinions differ. Yet the simple and direct fact is that any crisis the United States takes to an international forum in the foreseeable future will be decided to the disadvantage of the United States. (Let us hope arms control is an exception.) Ergo: skepticism, challenge.

The world economy is the most inviting case for skepticism, although it will be difficult to persuade many Americans of this during an American recession, and although the rise in oil prices is now creating a crisis in the Third World which is neither of American contrivance nor of American discovery nor of American invention. But until the dislocations caused by OPEC, things were simply not as bad as they were typically portrayed. *Things were better than they had been.* Almost everywhere. In many places things were very good indeed. Sir Arthur Lewis summed up the evidence admirably:

> We have now had nearly three decades of rapid economic growth....Output per head has been growing in the developed world twice as fast as at any time within the preceding century. In the [less-developed] world, output per head is not growing as fast as in the developed world, but is growing faster than the developed world used to grow.

The data can be quite startling. In 1973, as Sir Arthur was speaking, the "Planetary Product," as estimated by the Bureau of Intelligence and Research of the Department of

State, grew at a real rate of 6.8 percent, an astonishing figure. The Third World product expanded by 5.75 percent, no less astonishing.

Simultaneously it is to be asserted that these economies do less well than they ought: that the difference is of their own making and no one else's, and no claim on anyone else arises in consequence. This will be hard for us to do, but it is time we did it. It is time we commenced citing men such as Jagdish N. Bhagwati, professor of economics at MIT, an Indian by birth, who stated in the Lal Bahadur Shastri lectures in India in 1973:

> In the 1950's our economic programs were considered by the progressive and democratic opinion abroad to be a model of what other developing countries might aspire to and emulate. Today, many of us spend our time trying desperately to convince others that *somehow* all the success stories elsewhere are special cases and that our performance is not as unsatisfactory as it appears. And yet, we must confront the fact that, in the ultimate analysis, despite our socialist patter and our planning efforts, we have managed to show neither rapid growth nor significant reduction of income inequality and poverty.

It is time we asserted, with Sir Arthur—a socialist, a man of the Third World—that economic growth is governed not by Western or American conspiracies, but by its own laws and that it "is not an egalitarian process. It is bound to be more vigorous in some professions, or sectors, or geographical regions than in others, and even to cause some impoverishment."

A commentator in *The Statesman*, Calcutta's century-old and most prestigious journal, recently warned:

> It would be unwise for policy planners in the developing world to dismiss too easily...the basic premise of a society that worships success: if you are poor, you have only yourself to blame. Development is a matter of hard work and discipline. So if you are not developing fast, it is not because the rules of the game are stacked against you or that structural changes are never easy to bring about, but because you are lazy and indisciplined. The general disenchantment with economic aid flows from this. It is difficult for Americans to understand why such substantial flows of food and money have made so little impact.

Well, the time may have come when it is necessary for

Americans to say, "Yes, it *is* difficult to understand that." Not least because some Third World economies have done so very well. For if Calcutta has the lowest urban standard of living in the world, Singapore has in some ways the highest. It is time we asserted that inequalities in the world may be not so much a matter of condition as of performance. The Brazilians do well. The Israelis. The Nigerians. The Taiwanese. It is a good argument. Far better, surely, than the repeated plea of *nolo contendere* which we have entered, standing accused and abased before the Tribune of the People.

Cataloguing the economic failings of other countries is something to be done out of necessity, not choice. But speaking for political and civil liberty, and doing so in detail and in concrete particulars, is something that can surely be undertaken by Americans with enthusiasm and zeal. Surely it is not beyond us, when the next Social Report comes along, to ask about conditions and events in many countries of the Third World of which almost everyone knows, but few have thought it politic to speak. The AFL-CIO does it. Freedom House does it. Amnesty International does it. *American* socialists do it. The time has come for the spokesmen of the United States to do it too.

It is time, that is, that the American spokesman came to be feared in international forums for the truths he might tell. Mexico, which has grown increasingly competitive in Third World affairs, which took the lead in the Declaration of the Economic Rights and Duties, preaches international equity. Yet it preaches domestic equity also. It could not without some cost expose itself to a repeated inquiry as to the extent of equity within its own borders. Nor would a good many other Third World countries welcome a sustained comparison between the liberties they provide their own peoples with those which are common and taken for granted in the United States.

For the United States to go into opposition in this manner not only requires a recognition of the ideology of the Third World, but a reversal of roles for American spokesmen as well. As if to compensate for its aggressiveness about what might be termed Security Council affairs, the United States has chosen at the United Nations to be extraordinarily passive, even compliant, about the endless goings-on in the commissions and divisions and centers and suchlike elusive enterprises associated with the Economic and Social Council. Men and women were assigned to these missions, but have rarely been given much support, or even much scrutiny. Rather, the scrutiny has been of just the wrong kind, ever alert to deviation from the formula platitudes of UN debate, and hopelessly insensitive to the history of political struggles of the 20th century.

In Washington, three decades of habit and incentive have created patterns of appeasement so profound as to seem wholly normal. Delegations to international conferences return from devastating defeats proclaiming victory. In truth, these have never been thought especially important. Taking seriously a Third World speech about, say, the right of commodity producers to market their products in concert and to raise their prices in the process, would have been the mark of the quixotic or the failed. To consider the intellectual antecedents of such propositions would not have occurred to anyone, for they were not thought to have any.

And yet how interesting the results might be. The results, say, of observing the occasion of an Algerian's assuming the presidency of the General Assembly with an informed tribute to the career of the liberator Ben Bella, still presumedly rotting in an Algerian prison cell. The results of a discourse on the disparities between the (1973) per capita GNP in Abu Dhabi of $43,000 and that of its neighbor, the Democratic People's Republic of Yemen, with one-thousandth that. Again, this need not be a uniformly scornful exercise; anything but. The Third World has more than its share of attractive regimes, and some attractive indeed—Costa Rica, Gambia, Malaysia, to name but three. Half the people in the world who live under a regime of civil liberties live in India. The point is to differentiate, and to turn their own standards against regimes for the moment too much preoccupied with causing difficulties for others, mainly the United States. If this has been in order for some time, the oil price increase—devastating to the development hopes of half-a-hundred Asian and African and Latin American countries—makes it urgent and opportune in a way it has never been.

A Common Cause

Such a reversal of roles would be painful to American spokesmen, but it could be liberating also. It is past time we ceased to apologize for an imperfect democracy. Find its equal. It is time we grew out of our initial—not a little condescending —supersensitivity about the feelings of new nations. It is time we commenced to treat them as equals, a respect to which they are entitled.

The case is formidable that there is nothing the Third World needs less—especially now that the United States has so much withdrawn—than to lapse into a kind of cargo cult designed to bring about our return through imprecation and threat rather than the usual invocations. The Third World has achieved independence, and it needs to assert it in a genuine manner. The condition of the developing countries is in significant measure an imported condition. In the main, a distinctive body of European ideas has taken hold, not everywhere in the same measure. Sri Lanka will be more cerebrate in its socialism than will, say, Iraq, Brazil more given to actual economic expansion than Syria or Egypt, Algeria considerably less libertarian than Nigeria. Still, there is a recognizable pattern to the economic and political postures of these countries, of which the central reality is that their anticapitalist, anti-imperialist ideologies are in fact themselves the last stage of colonialism. These are imported ideas every bit as much as the capitalist and imperialist ideas to which they are opposed. The sooner they are succeeded by truly indigenous ideas, the better off all the former colonies will be, the United States included.

The Third World must feed itself, for example, and this will not be done by suggesting that Americans eat too much. It is one thing to stress what is consumed in the West, another to note what is produced there. In 1973, 17.8 percent of the world's population produced 64.3 percent of its product—and not just from taking advantage of cheap raw materials.

In the same way, the Third World has almost everywhere a constitutional heritage of individual liberty, and it needs to be as jealous of that heritage as of the heritage of national independence. It should be a source of renown that India, for one, has done that, and of infamy that so many others have not.

Not long ago, Alexander Solzhenitsyn, speaking of the case of a Soviet dissident who had been detained in a mental hospital, asked whether world opinion would ever permit South Africa to detain a black African leader in this fashion. Answering his own question, he said, "The storm of world-wide rage would have long ago swept the roof from that prison!" His point is very like the one Stephen Spender came to in the course of the Spanish Civil War. Visiting Spain, he encountered atrocities of the Right, and atrocities of the Left. But only those of the Right were being written about, and it came to him, as he later put it, that if one did not care about every murdered child indiscriminately, one did not really care about children being murdered at all. Very well. But nothing we finally know about the countries of the Third World (only in part the object of the Solzhenitsyn charge) warrants the conclusion that they will be concerned only for wrongdoing that directly affects *them*. Ethnic solidarity is not the automatic enemy of civil liberties. It has been the foundation of many. If there are any who can blow off the roof of any such prison—then all credit to them. If you can be against the wrongful imprisonment of a person anywhere, then you can be against wrongful imprisonment everywhere.

It is in precisely such terms that we seek common cause with the new nations: granted that they, no more than we, are likely ever wholly to live up to either of our protestations. Yet there exists the strongest possibility of an accommodating relationship at the level of principle—a possibility that does not exist at all with the totalitarian powers as they are now constituted. To contemplate an oppositional role to the Soviet bloc, or the Chinese, in, say, the General Assembly would be self-deceptive. One may negotiate there as between separate political communities, but to participate as in a single community—even in opposition—would simply not be possible. We can, however, have such a relation with most Third World nations. And we can do so while speaking for and in the name of political and civil liberty.

And equality, what of it? Here an act of historical faith is required: What is the record? The record was stated most succinctly by an Israeli socialist who told William F. Buckley, Jr., that those nations which have put liberty ahead of equality have ended up doing better by equality than those with the reverse priority. This is so, and being so, it is something to be shouted to the heavens in the years now upon us. *This is our case.* We *are* of the liberty party, and it might surprise us what energies might be released were we to unfurl those banners.

In the spring of 1973, in his first address as director-designate of the London School of Economics—where Harold Laski once molded the minds of so many future leaders of the "new majority"—Ralf Dahrendorf sounded this theme. The equality party, he said, has had its day. The liberty party's time has come once more. It is a time to be shared with the new nations, and those not so new, shaped from the old European empires, and especially the British—and is the United States not one such?—whose heritage this is also. To have halted the great totalitarian advance only to be undone by the politics of resentment and the economics of envy would be a poor outcome to the promise of a world society. At the level of world affairs we have learned to deal with communism. Our task is now to learn to deal with socialism. It will not be less difficult a task. It ought to be a profoundly more pleasant one.

Peter T. Bauer

Letter to *Commentary* on Moynihan Article

The Third World

To the Editor of Commentary:

Daniel P. Moynihan's distinction and stature and the major insights of his article, "The United States in Opposition," ensure that its considerable impact will be more than ephemeral. Much of what he says is both welcome and long overdue: the neglect by the United States and the West generally of the political significance of ideas, and its perception by the Communist powers; the failure of Western diplomacy in dealing with the Third World (to accept reluctantly this infelicitous term); the benefits the Third World derives from multinational corporations. But I believe that Mr. Moynihan's essay incorporates major and potentially very damaging misconceptions.

1) It is fanciful to envisage the Third World as a community of nation states that have undergone a moderate, gradualist, reformist British revolution of Fabian inspiration. The distinctive features of the official ideology of the Third World are: pronounced and often bitter hostility to the West, the market system, and liberal economic order

Reprinted, with some changes, by permission of the author and *Commentary*, from *Commentary*, August 1975. Copyright © 1975 by the American Jewish Committee.

(expressed on platforms supported or even provided by the West); virulent allegations of Western exploitation as the cause of Third World poverty; and insistence on large-scale international redistribution of income and on the right to expropriate politically powerless groups. These components of Third World ideology are reflected in Mr. Moynihan's citations and even more so in the activities of Third World governments.

2) The *Washington Post* (a newspaper notably friendly toward the Third World, especially Africa) reported on May 6, 1975, that $310 million in aid, said to be indispensable to the government, had gone from the World Bank to Tanzania, Robert S. McNamara's favorite African country. The same dispatch reported the largest-ever population movement in Africa, the enforced herding of several million people into collective or quasi-collective villages in Tanzania. (This process, largely unreported in the West, has been going on since about 1967.) It also reported the introduction of "scientific socialism" in Somalia, a country largely made up of nomadic tribesmen, and similar developments elsewhere in Africa. And in the same month the President of Zambia announced the nationalization of the vestiges of private commerce in that country.

Large-scale maltreatment of many millions of politically ineffective or defenseless people is commonplace in the Third World. The maltreatment includes expropriation, expulsion, or even massacre and is tolerated, encouraged, or supported by governments prominent and articulate in the United Nations.

Many, perhaps most, Third World countries are not communities or nation-states in the accepted sense of these terms, but collections of radically diverse or even hostile groups with deep-seated ethnic, cultural, and linguistic differences. This heterogeneity casts further doubts on the meaning of democracy or majority rule, questionable in any case in countries where the vast majority know little about politics beyond the village or district level. The diversity is even more pronounced internationally. The mutual enmity of many Third World countries is bitter and patent. What they share mainly is politically and materially profitable hostility to the West.

The internal heterogeneity of many Third World countries is often reflected in wide group differences in economic performance (e.g., the Chinese, Indian, and more nearly indigenous populations of Southeast Asia; Asians and Africans of east Africa; Levantines, Ibo, and others in Nigeria). And again, these differences are magnified internationally: the Third World comprises such widely different societies as the Chinese communities of Southeast Asia, the peasantry of south Asia, the Muslim Middle East, the tribal societies of Africa, the millions of aborigines, desert people, and many others. The internal heterogeneity of many Third World countries is pertinent to the general tendency to establish state-controlled economies in the Third World. The consequent politicization of life greatly enhances the prizes and significance of political power, thereby provoking or exacerbating political and social tensions, especially so in racially heterogeneous societies. The Third World is scarcely a brotherhood of gradually evolving Fabians.

Mr. Moynihan cites Nigeria as relatively libertarian. This is so only by the standards of the Third World. In Nigeria, the export of all major agricultural products is handled by state monopolies which effectively limit the incomes of producers; the government is a military dictatorship; there is extensive and avowed discrimination against minorities; and a few years ago there were large-scale tribal massacres, followed by a murderous civil war.

The disregard of these patent realities in Mr. Moynihan's essay is disturbing.

3) Tracing the intellectual origins of ideologies and policies is always speculative. In the context of the contemporary Third World, the distinction between a Fabian-inspired British revolution and a Marxist-Leninist-inspired stance is not so significant as Mr. Moynihan suggests. The Leninist idea of imperialism owes much to British writings, especially to Hobson's *Imperialism*, which directly inspired the central notions of Lenin's tract, *Imperialism: the Highest Stage of Capitalism*. This book has been enormously influential both in the West and in the Third World, especially among the millions of vicarious readers who know of its contents only by hearsay. Some of the most influential Third World leaders in recent times have been explicit and avowed Marxist-Leninists, notably Nkrumah, perhaps the single most influential black African politician since World

War II. And the policies currently pursued in many Third World countries are obviously not Fabian-inspired. Fabianism has contributed primarily by promoting the politicization of economic life and also by reinforcing widespread feelings of guilt in the West. Even in India the priorities of the Second Five-Year Plan and the pronouncements of many of the leading academics (including Mahalonobis, the principal architect of that plan) were plainly Soviet-inspired and owed little to Fabianism.

Many Third World countries are indeed mixed economies and not totalitarian societies. This is not because the leaders reject totalitarian ideas or methods; it reflects mainly the limitations of the official administrative machinery. The present state controls of many Third World countries rely heavily on expatriate personnel; still more would be needed to run a full-fledged totalitarian system. A totalitarian system may also often be uncongenial to the traditional culture. But if the rulers have the political will and the required administrative apparatus, the traditional culture is unlikely to offer effective resistance. And the traditional culture in most of Africa and Asia is not individualistic and libertarian (as Mr. Moynihan suggests) but authoritarian, though not totalitarian. It upholds authority but does not favor all-embracing politicization of life.

4) Mr. Moynihan's conciliatory remarks toward the Third World on the alleged damage to it by Western exploitation and ethnic discrimination are inappropriate.

Contacts established by the West have been the principal instruments of material progress throughout the Third World. For instance, all the foundations and ingredients of modern social and economic life were brought to sub-Saharan Africa by Westerners, mostly during the colonial period. The allegations of exploitation are not only unfounded but also harmful to the peoples of the Third World. They divert attention from the personal and social determinants of material progress and thus from the possibilities of influencing these determinants favorably. Indeed, these allegations facilitate damaging policies, such as restrictions on external economic relations that are potent instruments of material advance. Finally, allegations of exploitation both reflect and encourage the notion that incomes are extracted rather than generated. Besides provoking international tension, this notion often spills into domestic discussion, where it encourages expropriation of groups who are economically productive but politically weak.

Ethnic discrimination need not impede material progress —witness the Chinese in Southeast Asia or the Asians in Africa. Nor is it substantially imported from the West. Discrimination on the basis of color pervades the Third World, notably so in India. And in Africa discrimination against Asians is far more vicious and virulent than was ever practiced by Europeans. These matters are rarely publicized in the West.

5) The official ideology of the Third World is Western-inspired: Marxism-Leninism, state socialism, and Fabianism are all of Western origin. So is the notion of a Third World broadly uniform, homogeneous, and exploited by the West. The spokesmen and staff members of the international organizations have helped to spread these notions. They frequently consider themselves as agents of the Third World and derive major material and political advantages from such a stance. They have both promoted the familiar standard ideology and helped to put it into practice.

There are also other groups in the West engaged in promoting this ideology, such as churchmen or professional humanitarians, who derive emotional and material benefits from the image of the peoples of the Third World as helpless victims of Western misdeeds in need of their ministrations. Finally, there are the disaffected groups in the West who welcome any ideology with which to assail their own societies and especially the market system and who consider the governments of the Third World, the official ideology of the Third World, and indeed the very concept of the Third World, as useful instruments in a conflict within the West. Altogether, it is the West which supplies both the arguments and the financial resources with which it is assailed by the Third World.

6) The hope that the substantial economic growth rates registered in the Third World in recent years will diminish its antagonism toward the West is also misplaced. To begin with, much of the less-developed world was already progressing rapidly long before the 1950s. Again, the optimistic liberal assumption that economic improvement and reduction in economic differences probably or even necessarily

diminish or avert political conflict is unfounded. Two world wars should have taught us better. And as has often been observed, when economic differences are diminished, those still remaining often appear especially intolerable. Moreover, the dominant ideology and policies of the Third World are unlikely to promote a rise in mass living standards, though they may produce misleading statistical growth rates unrelated to it.

7) One contention of Third World spokesmen is more substantial than Mr. Moynihan recognizes. This is their criticism of the advocacy of birth control for raising living standards. Even extensive adoption of birth control would not by itself greatly affect Third World living standards. Here are some reasons why. Most of Africa and Latin America, and much of Asia, is very sparsely populated. Some of the poorest groups live in largely empty areas (even where the land is not particularly infertile), as for instance Borneo, Sumatra, and much of Latin America. Indeed, the population is often too sparse for the construction of transport facilities. Conversely, some of the most advanced areas of the Third World are very densely populated, as witness Hong Kong, Singapore, parts of Malaysia, and west Africa. The relation between population density and living standards cannot be examined usefully without noting people's aptitudes and attitudes. This is obvious from the wide differences in economic performance between different ethnic and religious groups in the same country or region with the same physical resources—Chinese, Indians, and Malays in Malaysia; Punjabis and Bengalis in India; Asians and Africans in east Africa; Ibo and others in Nigeria; Jews, Armenians, Greeks, and Arabs in the Levant; and Chinese, Lebanese, and West Indians in the Caribbean.

The relation between the size and rate of growth of population and general living standards is far more complex than is recognized in Western-inspired discussions, including Mr. Moynihan's article. To begin with, the standard approach ignores that the generation and possession of children, or a reduction in mortality with a resulting longer life expectation, are significant benefits. Moreover, reduction in population growth could not by itself raise living standards appreciably; the prime determinants of the level of income and the rate of progress are not the level of physical resources but personal, social, and political factors. (The unwarranted contemporary preoccupation with numbers and physical resources, including the view that the higher cost of oil has blighted the development prospects of many Third World countries, is notable in much of Mr. Moynihan's essay.) Reduction in birth rates has indeed often coincided with substantial economic improvement: both reflect a change in outlook and motivation, notably, an increased interest in material living standards. Unless a decline in population growth is accompanied by other changes, it cannot bring about significant improvement in the level of living standards over a few years or even decades. These considerations do not add up to a conclusive argument against birth control, but exaggerated claims about its economic potentialities understandably arouse suspicions.

8) Mr. Moynihan argues that the United States cannot withdraw from a new world order in which there is a large measure of majority rule, interpreted apparently in the sense of the acceptance of majority decisions based on the number of member states in the United Nations. He envisages the appropriate role for the United States as that of a loyal opposition, engaged in a potentially pleasant and fruitful dialogue with the majority, a role made possible by the British, Fabian character of the official Third World ideology. There are wide, unwarranted, and unstated assumptions behind this approach; it is also shot through with major paradoxes and fraught with peril.

Neither the official ideology of the Third World nor the practices of most Third World governments conform to Western social democracy and Fabian reformism. As I have already suggested, a distinctive characteristic of this ideology is hostility to the West and to a liberal social and economic order; and the policies inspired by this ideology are all too often radical and even brutal.

Majority rule in the accepted sense of uncoerced compliance with the decisions of the representatives of the majority presupposes a community with a large measure of shared experiences of culture, history, living conditions, and purpose, as well as comparatively limited objectives on the part of the majority. These prerequisites of a genuine community and of acceptable majority rule are not present in most of the Third World. The worldwide aggregation implied in the idea of a new world order based on majority rule is therefore inappropriate. This inappropriateness is made even more glaring by the primary thrust of the Third World ideology, namely, hostility to the West and its institutions. And the politicization of life advocated by the standard ideology is likely to exacerbate political tensions both within the Third World countries and on the international level.

Mr. Moynihan's essay does not convey the extent and depth of the heterogeneity of the Third World nor the paucity of the human, material, and military resources of most Third World countries. For instance, most east and central African countries are very sparsely populated. A few decades ago they were virtually empty. They have been developed almost entirely by Asians and Europeans. It is paradoxical that people whose numbers are small and whose resources are so meager (and indeed even negligible) should be so influential in world affairs as are the spokesmen of African countries. Much the same applies to the great majority of Third World countries—that is, the majority in the new world order. Mr. Moynihan does not consider this paradox. It is explicable largely by the unfounded but widespread feeling of guilt in the West, by the operation of various articulate and politically effective interest groups in the West, and by various repercussions of internal discontent and conflict. A discussion that does not take note of the paradox misleads about the power and resources of the Third World.

The idea of a loyal opposition within a world order in any serious sense implies an appreciable measure of world government and administration. I wish to note here only one major implication of this far-reaching and far-fetched notion. Contemporary governments try almost of necessity to equalize and standardize material conditions in the area under their control, by redistributive taxation, direct controls, and other forcible means. This tendency is reinforced by the familiar official ideology of the Third World and of the international organizations, with its emphasis on international income redistribution. Because of the diversity of social and physical living conditions in the world, the wide differences in economic attainment, and, what is more important, the deep-seated causes behind these differences,

attempts substantially to reduce international income differences would require large-scale and far-reaching powers
of coercion. Such measures would provoke pronounced
political tensions, likely to become increasingly severe, until
the concept of a world order based on majority rule is
abandoned or opposition is forcibly suppressed.

P. T. BAUER

Department of Economics
The London School of Economics and Political Science
London, England

Peter T. Bauer

Western Guilt and Third World Poverty

Come, fix upon me that accusing eye.
I thirst for accusation.

—W. B. Yeats

The feeling of guilt has aptly been termed one of America's few remaining surplus commodities. Ubiquitous and repeated allegations that the West is responsible for the poverty of the so-called Third World both reflect and strengthen this feeling of guilt. Yet while such allegations have come to be widely accepted, often as axiomatic, they are not only untrue but are more nearly the opposite of the truth. Their acceptance has nevertheless paralyzed Western diplomacy, both toward the Soviet bloc and toward the Third World, where the West has abased itself before countries which have negligible resources and no real power.

The feeling of guilt toward the Third World has been reinforced by political, emotional, and financial interests. It often goes together with condescension and contempt toward the people of the Third World. On the other hand, it is unaccompanied by a sense of responsibility for the results of the policies it itself inspires—policies which have ironically obstructed development in the Third World and have contributed to intense and widespread suffering in many parts of it.

Reprinted, with some changes, by permission of the author and *Commentary*, from *Commentary*, January 1976. Copyright © 1976 by the American Jewish Committee.

Allegations of Western responsibility are usually expressed vaguely, and their ostensible grounds shift. But the general thrust is unequivocal. It is a persistent theme in the United Nations and its numerous affiliates. It is expressed virulently by spokesmen from the Third World and the Communist bloc and is often endorsed by representatives of the West, especially of the United States. It is sounded continually in the universities, in the churches, and in the media.

Peter Townsend, for example, perhaps the most prominent British writer on poverty, asserts in his much-acclaimed book, *The Concept of Poverty:*

> I argued that the poverty of deprived nations is comprehensible only if we attribute it substantially to the existence of a system of international social stratification, a hierarchy of societies with vastly different resources in which the wealth of some is linked historically and contemporaneously to the poverty of others. This system operated crudely in the era of colonial domination, and continues to operate today, though more subtly, through systems of trade, education, political relations, military alliances, and industrial corporations.[1]

So too, the late Paul A. Baran of Stanford argues in another widely-used text, *The Political Economy of Growth:*

> To the dead weight of stagnation characteristic of pre-industrial society was added the entire restrictive impact of monopoly capitalism. The economic surplus appropriated in lavish amounts by monopolistic concerns in backward countries is not employed for productive purposes. It is neither plowed back into their own enterprises nor does it serve to develop others.[2]

And finally—though of course examples could easily be multiplied[3]—we have the late Dr. Nkrumah, Prime Minister and President of Ghana, perhaps one of the most influential African politicians since World War II, who declares in *Africa Must Unite:*

> Thus all the imperialists, without exception, evolved the means, their colonial policies, to satisfy the ends, the exploi-

---

1 Townsend, *The Concept of Poverty* (London: Heinemann, 1970), pp. 41–42.

2 Baran, *The Political Economy of Growth* (New York: Monthly Review Press, 1957, p. 177.

3 Several remarkable ones were cited by Daniel P. Moynihan in his celebrated *Commentary* article, "The United States in Opposition," March 1975.

tation of the subject territories, for the aggrandizement of the metropolitan countries. They were all rapacious; they all subserved the needs of the subject lands to their own demands; they all circumscribed human rights and liberties; they all repressed and despoiled, degraded and oppressed. They took our lands, our lives, our resources and our dignity. Without exception, they left us nothing but our resentment. It was when they had gone and we were faced with the stark realities, as in Ghana on the morrow of our independence, that the destitution of the land after long years of colonial rule was brought sharply home to us.[4]

All these allegations are either misleading or untrue. Thus Professor Townsend cannot be right in saying that the backwardness of poor countries is explicable only in terms of an international social stratification or of colonial domination: the poorest and most backward countries have until recently had no external economic contacts and often have never been Western colonies. Baran's statement is again obviously and wholly untrue since throughout the Third World large agricultural, commercial, and industrial complexes have been built up through profits reinvested locally. Nor does Nkrumah's statement bear much relation to reality. For example, before colonial rule there was not a single cocoa tree in the Gold Coast (Ghana); when colonial rule ended, cocoa exports, entirely from African-owned and -operated farms, totaled hundreds of thousands of tons annually—and this was the case with external trade in general.

Western Sources of Third World Progress

Far from the West having caused the poverty of the Third World, contact with the West has been the principal agent of material progress there. Indeed, the very idea of material progress is Western, especially in the sense of a constant and steadily increasing control over man's environment. People in the Third World did not think in these terms until the arrival of Western man. The materially most advanced societies and regions of the Third World are those with which the West established the most numerous, diversified,

4 Nkrumah, *Africa Must Unite.*

and extensive contacts: the cash-crop-producing areas and *entrepôt* ports of Southeast Asia, west Africa, and Latin America; the mineral-producing areas of Africa and the Middle East; and cities and ports throughout Asia, Africa, the Caribbean, and Latin America. The level of material achievement usually diminishes as one moves away from the foci of Western impact: the poorest and most backward are the populations with few or no external contacts, the aborigines being the limiting case.

All this is neither new nor surprising. The spread of material progress from more to less advanced regions is familiar from economic history. This process is especially evident in Black Africa. All the foundations and ingredients of modern social and economic life present there today were brought by Westerners, almost entirely during the colonial era. This is true of such fundamentals as public security and law and order; wheeled traffic (the wheel was never invented in sub-Saharan Africa); mechanized transport (transport powered by steam or gasoline instead of muscle— almost entirely human muscle in Black Africa); roads, railways, and man-made ports; modern forms of money (instead of barter or commodity money, such as cowrie shells, iron bars, or bottles of gin); the application of science and technology to economic activity; towns with substantial buildings, water, and sewerage; public health and hospitals and the control of endemic and epidemic diseases; and formal education.[5]

In short, over the last hundred years or so, contact with the West has transformed large parts of the Third World for the better. Southeast Asia and West Africa provide well-documented examples. For instance, in the 1890s Malaya was a sparsely populated area of hamlets and fishing villages. By the 1930s it had become a country with populous cities, thriving commerce, and an excellent system

5 On the other hand, of course, there was the Atlantic slave trade. But horrible and destructive as this trade was, it cannot legitimately be claimed as a cause of African backwardness. Indeed, the slave trade to what is now the Middle East began before the Atlantic slave trade and far outlasted it. (It was also even more brutal because the young males were usually castrated, often with fatal results.) And, as it happens, the most backward parts of the continent, such as the interior of Central and Southern Africa and most of East Africa, were relatively unaffected by Western slavery, while the currently most advanced areas, notably' West Africa, were much affected by it. (Asia was, of course, altogether untouched.)

of roads, primarily thanks to the rubber industry brought there and developed by the British. Again, before the 1890s there was no cocoa production in what is now Ghana and Nigeria, no exports of peanuts or cotton, and relatively small exports of palm oil and palm kernels. These are by now staples of world commerce, all produced by Africans but originally made possible by European activities. Imports, both of capital goods and of mass consumer goods designed for African use, also rose from negligible amounts at the end of the 19th century to huge volumes by the 1950s. These far-reaching changes are reflected in statistics of government revenues, literacy rates, school attendance, public health, infant mortality, and many other indicators, such as the ownership of automobiles and other consumer durables.

Western activities—supplemented at times by the activities of non-Western immigrants, notably Chinese, Indians, and Levantines, whose large-scale migration was, however, made possible by Western initiative—have thus led to major improvements in the material conditions of life in many parts of the Third World. This is not to suggest that there has been significant material progress everywhere in the Third World. Over large areas there have been few contacts with the West. And even where such contacts have been established, the personal, social, and political determinants of economic performance have often proved unfavorable to material advance. But wherever local conditions permitted, contact with the West most often resulted in the elimination of the worst epidemic and endemic diseases, the mitigation or disappearance of famines, and a general improvement in the material standard of living for all.

Western Exploitation?

Many of the assertions concerning Western responsibility for poverty in the Third World express or reflect the belief that the prosperity of relatively well-to-do persons, groups, and societies is always achieved at the expense of the less well off—i.e., that incomes are not generated by those who earn them but are somehow extracted from others, so that economic activity is akin to a zero-sum game, in which the gains of some are always balanced by the losses of others.

In fact, incomes (other than subsidies) are earned by the recipients for resources and services supplied and are not acquired by depriving others of what they had.

The notion that incomes are extracted rather than earned has been among the most disastrous of popular economic misconceptions or delusions. It has, however, served the purposes of those who expect to benefit from the maltreatment of other people—through, for example, the expropriation or even destruction of relatively prosperous minorities. The notion has been used by medieval rulers and modern demagogues alike, and their victims range from medieval Jewish communities to the ethnic minorities of contemporary Asia and Africa. In Asia and Africa it is widely regarded as axiomatic that poverty reflects exploitation by foreigners, including ethnic minorities who have risen from poverty to prosperity. This belief is encouraged assiduously by local politicians, especially those who promised that political independence under their auspices would herald material prosperity, and is often propagated as well by other influential local groups who expect to benefit from policies inspired by these ideas.

In recent decades the effectiveness of the notion that incomes are extracted rather than generated has been extended and reinforced by two streams of influence whose operation in this area has been cumulative. The first is Marxist-Leninist ideology, and the second is the spurious belief that the capacities and motivations of people are the same the world over.

In Marxist-Leninist ideology, any return on private capital implies exploitation, and service industries are regarded as unproductive. Thus, earnings of foreign capital and the incomes of foreigners or ethnic minorities in the service industries become forms of exploitation. Further, neo-Marxist literature has extended the concept of the proletariat—which in this scheme of things is poor because it is exploited—to the peoples of the Third World (most of whom are in fact small-scale cultivators).

The notion that all individuals and societies are basically alike has also promoted the belief that Western prosperity has been achieved at the expense of the Third World. For if human aptitudes and motivations are substantially the same everywhere and yet some societies are richer than others, then the more prosperous must have oppressed and exploited the rest.

There are several variants or derivations of the theme that incomes and property are extracted rather than earned. Perhaps the leading such variant is the argument that the poverty of Asia and Africa can be attributed to colonialism. This idea is axiomatic in much of the Third World and in publications of the UN and its affiliates, and it has great appeal in the United States.

According to General Principle XIV of the first United Nations Conference for Trade and Development (UNCTAD): "The liquidation of the remnants of colonialism in all its forms is a necessary condition of economic development." This passage (which would not have been acceptable to Marx) reflects the Leninist doctrine under which colonialism is by definition exploitative. Leninist doctrine is reflected also in the phrase, "colonialism in all its forms"—a covert reference to foreign investment, which in Leninist ideology is itself a species of external exploitation.

Whatever one thinks of colonialism, however, it is certainly not incompatible with economic development. Some of the richest countries were formerly colonies and were even as colonies already very prosperous (North America, Australasia). As I have already stressed, many of the African and Asian colonies of the European powers progressed very rapidly during colonial rule, usually much more so than the independent countries in the same area. And at present one of the few remaining European colonies is Hong Kong. Conversely, some of the materially most backward countries in the world never were colonies: Afghanistan, Tibet, Nepal, Liberia. Ethiopia is perhaps an even more telling example, though it was an Italian colony for a very brief period (six years) in its long history.

The manifest untruth that colonial status must imply poverty, stagnation, and exploitation is sometimes camouflaged by suggestions that without colonialism the peoples of the colonial territories would have created nation states, developed their own industries, or undertaken economic planning. Yet it is purely fanciful to imagine that such policies would or could have been pursued by the tribal chiefs or local rajahs or sultans who were replaced by colonial governments. And even if they had, such policies would not necessarily have made for progress. Indeed, state subsidies to particular activities or centralized control of economic activity are more likely to perpetuate poverty than to relieve it.

The terms "economic colonialism" and "neo-colonialism" have sprung up recently to describe almost any form of economic relation between relatively rich and poor countries, regions, or groups. This terminology confuses poverty with colonial status, a concept which has always been understood to mean lack of political sovereignty. Since the late 1960s, the usage has been extended to cover the activities of multinational corporations in the Third World. In fact, these activities have promoted progress in poor countries by expanding opportunities and raising incomes and government revenues. Thus, the new terminology not only reflects a debasement of language; it also distorts the truth.

External Trade

According to another set of allegations, the West damages the Third World by manipulating the terms of trade so that these are unfavorable to the latter and also deteriorate persistently. This is alleged to have contributed to a decline in the share of the Third World in international trade. A related form of damage is said to be the indebtedness inflicted on the Third World by the West. These allegations are again fictitious, untrue, or irrelevant.

To begin with, the diversity of trading patterns within the Third World renders the aggregation of their terms of trade largely meaningless. The terms of trade of particular Third World countries and groups can move differently and even in opposite directions (the experience of the OPEC countries against other Third World countries is only a recent and familiar example). And, except over very short periods, changes in the terms of trade as conventionally measured are of little welfare significance without reference to changes in the cost of production of exports, the range and quality of imports, and the volume of trade.

Insofar as changes in the terms of trade do affect development and welfare, what matters is the amount of imports which can be purchased with a unit of domestic resources, and this cannot be inferred from the ratio of import and

export prices. (In technical language, the comparisons relevant to economic welfare and development are the factoral
terms of trade and not the crude commodity terms.) Further, expressions such as "unfavorable terms of trade" are
meaningless except by reference to a base period. In recent
decades, however, even the crude commodity terms of trade
of Third World countries have been exceptionally favorable.
When changes in the cost of production, the great improvement in the range and quality of imports, and the huge increase in the volume of trade are taken into account, the
external purchasing power of the exports of the Third World
in the aggregate is now very favorable, probably more so
than ever before. This in turn has made it easier for governments to retain a larger proportion of export earnings
through major increases in royalty rates, export taxes, and
corporation taxes.[6]

But the terms of trade are in any case irrelevant to the
basic causes of Third World poverty. This is obvious, for
instance, from the material backwardness of societies and
countries with little or no external trade. Changes in the
share of the Third World in international trade are also
irrelevant to its poverty. A reduction in the share of a country or group of countries in global trade has by itself no adverse economic implications because it often reflects the
expansion of economic activity and trade elsewhere, which
normally does not damage but benefits those whose relative
share has declined. For instance, since the 1950s the large
increase in the foreign trade of Japan, the reconstruction
of Europe, and the liberalization of intra-European trade
have brought about a decline in the share of other groups
in world trade, including that of the United States and the
United Kingdom. Furthermore, domestic developments and
policies unrelated to external circumstances—such as increased domestic use of previously exported products, or

6 Although these observations differ radically from the ideas reaching the public
in the West, they should not come as a surprise. Some years ago, Sir Arthur Lewis
noted in an important address that in the 1950s the terms of trade of primary
producers were more favorable than at any time in the preceding eighty years
(see "A Review of Economic Development," *American Economic Review*, May
1965). Sir Arthur wrote before the subsequent upsurge in the prices of primary
products and without reference to the favorable factors noted in the text. The
exporters of primary products are far from the same as Third World exporters,
but they are often so identified in discussions of Third World poverty.

domestic inflation, or special taxation of exporters, or the intensification of protectionist policies—frequently reduce the share of a country or group of countries in world trade. (As an aside, I may note that in recent decades the share of the Third World in total world trade has increased and not decreased, notably so since before World War I.)

So far as indebtedness is concerned, the external debts of the Third World reflect resources supplied to it. Indeed, the bulk of the current indebtedness of Third World governments consists of soft loans, often very soft loans, under various aid agreements, frequently supplemented by outright grants. With the worldwide rise in prices, including those of exports of Third World countries, the cost even of these soft loans has diminished greatly. If governments cannot service such soft loans, this reflects either wasteful use of the capital supplied or inappropriate monetary or fiscal policies. It is worth remembering that in the course of their development many rich countries relied extensively on external loans, and hard loans at that.

Nor do persistent deficits in the balance of payments of many Third World countries mean that they are being impoverished by the West. Such deficits are inevitable if the government of a country, whether rich or poor, advancing or stagnating, lives beyond its resources and pursues inflationary policies while attempting to maintain overvalued exchange rates.

It is paradoxical to suggest that external economic relations are damaging to development. They normally benefit people by opening up markets for exports, providing a large and diverse source of imports, and acting as channels for the flow of human and financial resources and for new ideas, methods, and crops. Because of the vast expansion of world trade in recent decades and the development of technology in the West, the material advantages from external contacts are now greater than ever before. The suggestion that these relations are detrimental is not only unfounded but also damaging, because it serves as a specious justification for official restrictions on their extent or diversity.

Harmful Western Examples?

Another batch of arguments has it that the mere presence of the West and the day-to-day activities of its peoples are in themselves harmful to the Third World. One form of such damage is said to derive from the so-called international demonstration effect, brought about by the new availability of cheap consumer goods supplied by the West. This availability supposedly obstructs the material progress of the Third World by encouraging spending there, an argument which of course completely disregards the fact that the level of consumption and the extension of choice are what economic development is about. The notion of a damaging international demonstration effect also ignores the role of external contacts as an instrument of development; it overlooks the fact that the new consumer goods have to be paid for, which usually requires improved economic performance, such as more work, additional saving and investment, and readiness to produce for sale. In short, it overlooks the obvious consideration that a higher and more varied level of consumption is both the principal justification (or even the meaning) of material progress and an inducement to further economic advance.[7]

An updated version of the international demonstration effect proposes that the eager acceptance of Western consumer goods in the Third World is a form of cultural dependence engendered by Western business. (Rather paradoxically, this charge is often accompanied by allegations of the damage to the Third World done by Western patents, which are said to obstruct the spread of technology.) The implication here is that the peoples of the Third World have no independent minds, that they are manipulated at will by foreigners. In fact, however, Western goods have been selectively and not indiscriminately accepted in the Third World and have been of massive benefit to millions of people there.

As was to be expected, allegedly lavish consumption habits and the pollution of the environment in the West

---

7 At an official level, a damaging international demonstration effect may indeed encourage the adoption of show projects and unsuitable technologies financed with public funds. But this is not usually what the exponents of the international demonstration effect have in mind. Nor is it appropriate to blame the West for the policies of Third World governments in adopting unsuitable external models.

have also been pressed into ideological service. A standard formulation is that per capita consumption of food and energy in the United States is many times that in India, so that the American consumer despoils his Indian opposite number on a large scale—or even, according to Professor René Dumont, is guilty of a kind of cannibalism (for "in over-consuming meat which wasted the cereals which could have saved them, we ate the little children of the Sahel, of Ethiopia, and of Bangladesh").[8] Apart from everything else, such formulations fail to note that per capita production in America exceeds production in India by more than the difference in consumption, allowing it not only to pay for this consumption but also to finance domestic and foreign investment, as well as foreign aid.

The so-called brain drain, the migration of qualified personnel from the Third World to the West, is again influentially canvassed as an instance of Western responsibility for poverty in the less-developed countries. This is a somewhat more complex issue, but it certainly does not substantiate the charge it is meant to support. As an adverse factor in Third World development, the voluntary departure of formally trained people seeking to improve their condition is almost certainly less important than the enforced exodus of highly educated people and of others with commercial and administrative skills, or the discrimination of Third World governments against ethnic minorities who remain, or their refusal to employ foreigners. Indeed, many voluntary emigrants leave because their own governments cannot or will not use their services—and not only when they belong to ethnic minorities. Thus their departure does not deprive the society of resources which are productive at present or in the foreseeable future.

Finally, there is the allegation that the West has damaged the Third World by ethnic discrimination. Yet the very countries in which such discrimination occurred were those where material progress was initiated or promoted by contact with the West. The most backward groups in the Third World (aborigines, desert peoples, nomads, and other tribesfolk) were quite unaffected by ethnic discrimination

8 Cited in Moynihan, "The United States in Opposition," *Commentary*, March 1975; reprinted in this volume.

on the part of Europeans, whereas many communities against which discrimination was often practiced—Chinese in Southeast Asia, Indians in parts of Southeast Asia, Asians in Africa, and others—made great material strides forward. In any case, discrimination on the basis of color or race is not a European invention but has been endemic in much of Africa and Asia, notably so in India, for many centuries or even millennia.

Politicization

The West may indeed be said to have contributed to the poverty of the Third World in two senses. But these differ radically from the familiar arguments.

The changes which have come about in much of the Third World through contact with the West have resulted in a significant decline in mortality and a corresponding increase in life expectation. Many more people survive in the Third World as a result of Western contacts and activities, which means that many more poor people are alive. But this Western contribution to poverty reflects an improvement, not a deterioration, since people prefer to survive and to see their children survive. This improvement is obscured in conventional national income statistics, as these do not register health, life expectation, and the possession of children as components of welfare.

A second sense in which the West may be said to have contributed to the poverty of the Third World is through the politicization of social and economic life—that is, through the tendency to make everything a matter of politics. Thus, the terminal years of British colonial rule saw the introduction of extensive and pervasive state economic controls, such as widespread licensing of economic activity and state trading monopolies, including state monopolies over agricultural exports. This last measure was particularly important because it enabled the government to exert direct control over the livelihood of producers, and it has also served as a major source of government finance and patronage. In most British colonies, the ready-made framework of a *dirigiste* was handed over to the incoming independent governments.

Inefficient allocation of resources is a familiar result of

state controls. Less familiar but more important results of these controls are restrictions on the movement of people between jobs and places and on the volume, diversity, and local dispersion of external contacts, which are of special significance for the progress of poor countries. Still more important is the exacerbation of social and political tensions. The question of who runs the government has become paramount in many Third World countries and is often a matter of life and death for millions of people. This is especially so in multiracial societies, like those of much of Asia and Africa. In such a situation the energies and resources of people, particularly the most ambitious and energetic, are diverted from economic activity to political life, partly from choice and partly from necessity. Foreign aid has contributed substantially to the politicization of life in the Third World. It augments the resources of governments as compared to the private sector, and the criteria of allocation tend to favor governments trying to establish state controls.

Many Third World governments would presumably have attempted such policies even without colonial rule or foreign aid, probably with the help of international organizations. But they could hardly have succeeded without the examples set by colonial governments or the personnel and money provided by Western aid or by international organizations, which in turn are financed largely by the West. Yet, far from deploring these policies, the most vocal and influential critics of colonial rule and Western influence, both in the West itself and in the Third World, have usually urged their adoption and extension and have blamed Western governments for not having pursued them sooner and more vigorously.

Guilt and Contempt

I have already indicated my belief that it is the feeling of guilt over material prosperity which accounts for the widespread promotion and acceptance of the bizarre and insubstantial arguments behind allegations of Western responsibility for poverty in the Third World. A striking example of much Anglo-Saxon sentiment in this area is an article by the late Cyril Connolly, published several years ago in the

London *Sunday Times* under the title "Black Man's Burden." Connolly wrote:

> There is not a single country of which we can truthfully say that its occupation by a European power did it more good than harm....It is a wonder that the white man is not more thoroughly detested than he is....In our dealings with every single country, greed, masked by hypocrisy, led to unscrupulous coercion of the native inhabitants and worse, the culture and civilization which we brought was rotten to the core.... Cruelty, greed, uncertainty, and arrogance—the affectation of superiority exemplified by the color bar characterized what can be summed up in one word: exploitation....We are to blame (I say we for nearly everyone has had some family connection with India, Africa, or the Far East).

This statement by a prominent intellectual is both ludicrous and characteristic. Actually, only a tiny fraction of the British population ever had such contacts, and only a fraction of that fraction in any way misconducted itself toward the Third World. The article regards the population of Africa and Asia as much of a muchness ("the black man"), a treatment which is repugnant to millions of people both in the Third World and in the West, and especially so to the great majority of Indians, Chinese, and Arabs. The passage also suggests that incomes are extracted and not earned. And it well expresses the conception of collective guilt which has replaced individual sin in these discussions, thereby exonerating any single identifiable person of responsibility for immoral behavior.

Such feelings help to explain why Western governments support and endorse nonsensical, groundless, and offensive statements by leading Third World politicians and why the West so often abases itself before governments (usually unrepresentative governments) whose countries are often sparsely populated by relatively small numbers of materially very backward people. It is sometimes suggested that such postures are necessary to keep the Third World outside the Soviet orbit. But with very few and rather doubtful exceptions, these stances have been counterproductive and have not served the interests of Western political or military strategy (assuming that such a strategy exists). The references to political objectives are unconvincing ex post facto rationalizations of anomalous and baffling policies.

But it is not only an unfounded sense of guilt which is reflected in these policies. There is also condescension or even contempt. Economic conditions in the Third World are thought to reflect Western exploitation, compounded by current Western consumption habits, while its economic future supposedly depends on Western aid. Thus it is we and not they who, it is assumed, will largely determine what happens to these societies.

The image of the Third World as a uniform, stagnant mass devoid of distinctive character is another aspect of the same condescension or contempt. The stereotype denies identity, character, personality, and responsibility to the societies and individuals of the so-called Third World. When a distinct independent culture and set of values are recognized, they are often condemned, and their enforced removal is proposed on the ground that they obstruct material progress. For instance, compulsory transformation of man and society is a major theme of Gunnar Myrdal's *Asian Drama*.

The most brutal maltreatment of minorities and the most extensive official discrimination on the basis of color, race, or religion in the Third World are often excused by saying that they have been inspired by the West. This allegation is altogether unfounded and implies again that the peoples of the Third World have no will or identity of their own and are simply creatures of the West.

Toleration or even support of the brutal policies of many Third World governments, then, seems to reflect a curious mixture of guilt feelings and condescension. Third World governments are not really guilty because they only follow examples set by the West. Moreover, like children, they are not altogether responsible for what they do. In any case, we must support them to atone for alleged wrongs, which our supposed ancestors perpetrated on their supposed ancestors. And economic aid is also necessary to help the children grow up. Similarly, the most offensive and baseless utterances of Third World spokesmen need not be taken seriously, because they are only Third World statements (a license which has been extended to their supporters in the West).

The truth, however, is that the so-called Third World is a vast and diverse collection of societies differing widely in religion, culture, social institutions, personal characteristics and motivations, political arrangements, economic attitudes, material achievement, rates of progress, and many other respects. It is a travesty and not a useful simplification to lump together Chinese merchants of Southeast Asia, Indonesian peasants, Indian villagers, tribal societies of Africa, oil-rich Arabs of the Middle East, aborigines and desert peoples, inhabitants of huge cities in India, Africa, and Latin America—to envisage them all as a low-level uniform mass, a collectivity which moreover is regarded as no more than a copy of Western man, only poorer, and with even this difference the result only of Western responsibility.

The adoption of this stereotype and of the misleading terminology has been made easier by the lack of first-hand public knowledge of conditions in the Third World. Few people in the West know these countries, let alone the diverse policies pursued in them.

Yet had this travesty not suited certain influential interests in the West, it might never have succeeded in establishing itself. These interests have ranged from the churches seeking a new role for themselves to exporters seeking sheltered markets. Two categories may have been specially effective: the personnel and associates of the international organizations, and various disaffected groups who have come to dislike or even hate Western society.

Since World War II the people who work in one way or another for international organizations have come increasingly to consider themselves as agents and representatives of the Third World, a stance which has often suited their political, professional, and personal interests. They have helped to weld together at least superficially the representatives of extremely diverse, conflicting, or even bitterly hostile societies and countries into a bloc united only by politically and materially profitable enmity to the West. This was achieved by preparing briefs for Third World spokesmen, by organizing meetings for the formulation of positions at international gatherings, and by other similar measures. The ideologies of the Third World and of the United Nations and its associated agencies have become largely interchangeable.

As to the second group—made up of people in the West who are sufficiently disillusioned with their own society to have become disaffected from or even hostile to it—some of them see the Third World as a useful instrument for promoting their cause in what is in essence a civil conflict in the West. This usefulness is enhanced if Third World countries are regarded as a homogeneous, undifferentiated mass or brotherhood united in opposition to the West.

Anomalous Policies

Policies and activities engendered by a sense of guilt and by attitudes and interests related to it do not usually promote the welfare of the people they are supposed to help. Appeasement of guilt has nothing to do with a sense of responsibility. In the present context this is evident in the lack of concern with the conduct of governments which receive economic aid or with the results of policies ostensibly inspired by humanitarian motives.

Thus the West supports governments whose domestic policies impoverish their own peoples and often inflict extreme hardship both on ethnic minorities and on the indigenous population. President Amin's massive and explicit persecution and expulsion of Asians is only one of many instances. Another is Tanzania (Mr. McNamara's favorite African country, as it has rightly been called) which receives large-scale Western aid while it forcibly herds millions of people into collectivized villages, often destroying their households to make them move.[9] Western aid has conferred respectability on governments like these and helped them conceal temporarily from their own people the economic consequences of their policies.

Commodity agreements for primary products present another anomaly. They are proposed and implemented ostensibly to relieve Third World poverty. Yet these arrangements raise the cost of living in an inflationary world; they benefit the most prosperous countries and groups in the Third World, including expatriates living there; they often benefit Western exporters of the same products or their close substitutes (many rich countries are net exporters of primary products); they provoke political tensions within the exporting countries as well as between them; and they

---

9 See the *Washington Post*, May 6, 1975, for a report on this process.

greatly damage some of the poorest groups in many Third World countries, especially people who are barred from producing the controlled products in order to raise their prices. Yet commodity agreements continue to be advocated and established because any measure which appears to represent a transfer of resources to Third World governments automatically finds favor.

It would be a delusion to believe that the reasoning and evidence produced here, even if accepted as valid, could substantially influence prevalent attitudes, let alone modify the policies they inspire. Argument and evidence will not affect conduct and measures which are rooted in emotion, often reinforced by the play of personal and political interests. Moreover, the costs and sacrifices of policies inspired by such feelings are rarely borne by those who so warmly advocate their imposition. They are borne instead by ordinary people, mostly of the Third World, who will go on being harmed so long as such feelings, ideas, and policies continue to hold sway.

Peter T. Bauer

Hostility to the Market in Less-Developed Countries

Virulent hostility to the market, as a system and as an outcome of voluntary transactions, dominates the literature on the position of less-developed countries and on the domestic and international policies appropriate for their material progress. The sources of this hostility bear examination.[1]

The validity of arguments can be assessed conclusively on the basis of evidence and logic. The motives or reasons that lead people to accept arguments, hold ideas, or adopt certain stances cannot be established so firmly; their examination, therefore, must involve some conjecture. This does not detract from the importance of the subject. Indeed, because ideas have consequences (in Richard Weaver's

This essay is a revised version of a paper read at a conference on *Hostility to the Market System* held at the Homestead, Hot Springs, West Virginia, in March 1975 under the auspices of the Liberty Fund. Permission to reprint this paper is gratefully acknowledged.

1 In recent and current parlance, most of Africa, Asia, and Latin America have come to be lumped together, on the basis of a low level of conventionally measured incomes, as less-developed countries, the less-developed world, or the Third World. This terminology and the worldwide aggregation of profoundly diverse components is misleading and objectionable. I cannot avoid this infelicitous terminology on the present occasion. Its shortcomings do not affect the substantive argument.

   I shall use the term "source of hostility to the market" to denote both certain ideas, attitudes, and conditions, and also organizations and institutions promoting this hostility. I hope it will be clear from the specific context what kind of influence is under discussion.

words) their provenance is a matter of real interest. Nor is one explanation as good as another. Even when formal testing is not possible, observation and analysis can establish significant connections.

Location of sources of hostility to the market presents a special problem, or at any rate, a problem especially pronounced in our context. The activities of Western politicians and intellectuals and of staff members and spokesmen of the official international organizations are a principal factor behind hostility to the market in less-developed countries.[2] Further, some of the most influential exponents of this hostility in the Third World are Westernized or Western-educated people. Thus, much of the hostility to the market that *emanates* from the Third World *originates* in the West.

A qualification may be appropriate here. In emphasizing the Western sources and the role of the international organizations in hostility to the market in the Third World, I do not suggest that spiritual and material attainment there depends on the West. What I do mean is that, in the generation and maintenance of hostility to the market, the role of the West and of individuals, groups, and organizations supported by the West has been highly significant and possibly decisive.

Western Origin of Third World Hostility

Expert Advice

Some passages from prominent academics will illustrate the Western origin of hostility to the market in less-developed countries and the close links between this Western origin and its local expression. Professor Gunnar Myrdal, a Nobel Laureate, is a prominent advocate of the necessity for development of comprehensive planning and socialism. After noting in a much-quoted publication that Third World governments now accept and adopt such policies as indispensable for emergence from poverty and misery, he adds that "Positive and urgent advice to do so is given to them by all scholars and statesmen in the advanced countries."[3]

---

2 Throughout this paper, reference to international organizations is to official intergovernmental organizations.

3 *Development and Underdevelopment* (Cairo: National Bank of Egypt, 1956), p. 63.

Elsewhere he writes, "The special advisers to underdeveloped countries who have taken the time and trouble to acquaint themselves with the problem, no matter who they are, . . . all recommend central planning as the first condition of progress."[4]

The merits of central planning for development are not the key issue in the present context. I am concerned with the contention that governments and experts in advanced countries are unanimous in advising governments of less-developed countries to pursue these policies. Indeed, many economists—and some of the most vocal, articulate, and influential groups with close contacts with governments, international organizations, the press, and large foundations—express these views and endorse these policies. More to the point, only those who support central planning are classed as experts by the media and these institutions. Although prominent academic economists insist that comprehensive planning is demonstrably unnecessary for economic development and is much more likely to retard than to promote it, by Professor Myrdal's definition, they cannot be experts whatever their technical qualifications, academic position, or field of study.

The acceptance of Myrdal's definition is confirmed by Professor John P. Lewis of Princeton University, former Director of the U.S. Agency for International Development in India:

> It has been decided in India that it is the duty of government —and it cannot be delegated—to create and maintain that "growth perspective" which, Albert Hirschman has rightly insisted, is the one *sine qua non* for successful economic development.
>
> Outside supporters of the Indian development process who refuse to accept this proposition well-nigh disqualify themselves from the outset.[5]

---

4 *An International Economy* (London: Routledge & Kegan Paul, 1956), p. 201.

5 *Quiet Crisis in India* (Washington, D.C.: Brookings Institution, 1962), p. 28. The context of Professor Lewis's statement is development planning in India. The suggestion that the government's maintenance of a growth perspective, whatever that means, is the only indispensable condition of economic development cannot possibly be true. Professor Lewis, formerly Distinguished Service Professor of Economics at Indiana University and director of its International Development Research Center, established with the help of the Ford Foundation, subsequently became Dean of the Woodrow Wilson School at Princeton.

Consider also the concluding paragraph of Professor Jagdish Bhagwati's book, *The Economics of Underdeveloped Countries:*

> Indeed, for the idealists among us, the challenge of development represents today the kind of invigorating stimulus for sustained action that the Soviet revolution was for progressive opinion after continual, even though halting, transition to an international framework favorable to rapid economic growth in the underdeveloped world.[6]

Information

Since the Second World War, the effectiveness of the thrust for economic controls in the Third World has been enhanced by the preponderance of opponents of the market in contacts between the West and the Third World, especially in the international transmission of information. What the Third World learns from the West, or about it or about present and past economic relations between the West and Third World countries, comes from or is filtered through opponents of the market. They dominate international reporting, the wire services, documentary films, and entertainment. The academic contacts between the West and the Third World are also dominated by opponents of the market. This influence has been paramount in augmenting the financial and intellectual resources and in enhancing the prestige and effectiveness of Third World opponents of the market. The latter have a virtual monopoly in the local commissions and delegations of the United Nations and its specialized agencies and affiliates, in the research institutions financed by these organizations, in the local operations of the large Western foundations, in international academic exchanges, in the planning teams supplied to Third World governments by American and British universities.

The views of market supporters are so strange to Third World audiences that they sound eccentric, paradoxical, or bizarre, even when voiced by prominent persons, whether foreign or local, but especially when advanced by foreign

---

6 *The Economics of Underdeveloped Countries* (London: Weidenfeld & Nicholson, World University Library, London, 1966), p. 244. Professor Bhagwati, an economist of international standing, is a full professor of economics at the Massachusetts Institute of Technology. Formerly full professor at Delhi, he has been on a number of international missions. The book from which I quote was published in many countries.

academics. This is so even when what market supporters say is both simple and obvious. Visiting academics address a public soaked in antimarket ideas, derived from practically all Western visitors and the textbooks and other economic literature reaching these countries. What market supporters say is inconsistent with the material interests and the political and emotional inclinations of local academics, politicians, and civil servants. It is in conflict also with the opinions expressed or endorsed by the resident representatives of the international organizations and the Western foundations and governments, that is, by all major sources of money and patronage.[7] This situation puts great pressure on those local academics and businessmen who are promarket. Whatever their actual views, they have to operate in societies with a strong authoritarian tradition, where their professional and financial survival depends on the state or on Western academic, intellectual, or financial support. Thus, a market-oriented visitor has little chance of making a lasting impact on public opinion. Nonetheless, the visitor can help market-oriented local academics and businessmen to maintain their bearings, sanity, and self-respect.

An example will illustrate the situation. In 1970 I lectured at about a dozen of the leading Indian universities and economic research institutions. Everywhere it was taken for granted that socialist planning is indispensable to raise the standard of living. According to my various hosts (who, I may add, treated me with impeccable courtesy) the only choice was between what they called Chinese or Soviet models of development. The preponderance of opponents of the market in academic contacts between the West and the Third World has promoted, not only the notion that comprehensive central planning or a socialist economy are indispensable for development, but also the idea that such

---

7 These groups also disassociate themselves from local and visiting market-oriented academics, which affects the prestige and effectiveness even of academics of standing who are well prepared and who know the local scene. My own experience is that if the visitor is well prepared, this is often less important than might appear.

It happens, however, that market-oriented visitors are often insufficiently prepared. In particular, they do not know the local scene well, and this can be damaging. Market opponents can get away with shortcomings that are not forgiven to market supporters.

policies promote or even imply social and economic equality and that they command the overwhelming or even unanimous support of respected academics.[8] The opponents of the market have also travestied the history of prerevolutionary Russia and the subsequent history and present conditions in the Soviet Union. They also consistently transmit to the Third World those theoretical developments of contemporary economic analysis which emphasize imperfections of the market system. Unfortunately, they never examine the costs and consequences of alternatives to the market system, alternatives which are always presented in idealized form.

The Legacy of Colonialism

Throughout most of its history, British colonial rule was, on the whole, one of limited government—paternalistic and authoritarian, yet limited. But in the closing years of British colonialism, extensive and pervasive government economic controls came to be introduced throughout Africa and, to a lesser extent, elsewhere.[9] As a result, the ready-made framework of a *dirigiste* or even totalitarian state was handed over by the British to the incoming independent governments.

Many Third World governments would presumably have attempted to establish such institutions and introduce such policies even without colonial rule, or for that matter, foreign aid. But they could hardly have succeeded in organizing or administering them without the examples set by colonial governments or the personnel and money provided by external aid.

The establishment of tightly controlled economies, such as those handed over by the departing British colonial administrators and supported wherever possible by Western aid, reflected the operation of political, intellectual, administrative, and commercial interests and pressures and the vagaries of fashion and convenience. Some of these controls,

---

8 Witness the passages by Professor Myrdal quoted above.

9 Primary examples are widespread licensing of economic activity and government trading monopolies, including export monopolies for agricultural products. The latter were introduced virtually throughout British Africa and Burma and a number of other territories but did not have significant monopoly power in export markets. They had and still have monopoly of the purchase of crops subject to them, that is, monopsony power over the producers.

especially the export monopolies, have served as power bases for Third World politicians who became influential figures on the world scene. Yet such policies were not the necessary corollaries of colonialism. In British Africa until the late 1920s and in Southeast Asia until much later, British colonial administrators appreciated the role of the market and the functions of traders.[10] Official hostility came about largely as a result of an increase in the number of administrators and technicians, who were removed from the realities of economic life and found controls to be tidier than market forces; the growth of intellectual fashions and ideologies hostile to private trading; belief in the efficacy of closely controlled economies, allegedly in the interests of the population but in practice for the political, personal, and financial benefit of politicians and administrators and in some instances for the benefit of influential trading interests. Thus, the livelihood of the great majority of the local population came to depend on governments, often endowed with quasi-totalitarian powers by policies instituted in the closing years of British colonialism.

Groups Hostile to the Market

Third World Groups

In less-developed countries, hostility to the market is widespread among the most articulate, influential, and politically effective groups. Replacement of the market by government-imposed economic controls suits the political, emotional, and financial interests of these groups. Among the rural population—the overwhelming majority of the population in most undeveloped countries—there is little sustained hostility to the market. People at large evince little interest in political or public affairs beyond the tribal or village level: throughout the Third World the discrepancy in political effectiveness and in the ability to shape discussion between the urban population and the rural population, and between the vocal and articulate groups and the unorganized, inar-

---

10 Perceptive and explicit observations on this subject by early colonial administrators are quoted in my book *Dissent on Development* (Cambridge, Mass.: Harvard University Press, 1972), especially essay 14, "Background to Exodus."

ticulate groups, is very wide—far wider than in the West. We need, therefore, to focus on opinion- and policymakers: largely intellectuals and academics, writers, and media men; literate politicians and administrators, primarily civil servants and to a lesser extent other professional men; and urban businessmen. In some countries, religious leaders and priests are also important agents in our context. (Army officers often play a part in shaping the course of events, but they rarely serve as sources of general ideas.)

The intellectuals, politicians, and administrators are often closely associated. The relative importance of these groups as agents of hostility to the market is to some extent a matter of judgment and is partly arbitrary because the categories so often overlap. On the whole, intellectuals and civil servants, including the staffs and spokesmen of the international organizations, are more important than politicians, army officers, and businessmen. (In some regions, especially Latin America, the priesthood may be an intermediate category.) The latter groups have fewer international contacts and less interest in general issues. They are often ready to acquiesce in hostility to the market and may benefit from it; they are less able, however, to generate it systematically over a wide area of public concern. The close connection between intellectuals—especially academics—civil servants, and politicians is particularly significant in India.

The great distance of these groups from the rest of the population promotes a feeling of superiority, which suggests to them that they have a right, often rationalized as a duty, to control the economic conduct and the pattern of consumption of their fellow men. They favor the replacement of the market by state controls. Moreover, planned and socialized economies create positions of power and status for intellectuals, such as do not exist in a market system. Their ideas are also shared by the corresponding groups in the West, but they are much stronger in the Third World, where they can be translated into practice much more easily because of the discrepancy in political effectiveness.

This difference in political effectiveness is magnified by other factors. One of these is the more authoritarian character of the cultures of the Third World: the subjection of the individual to the authority both of rulers and of custom is more extensive and more unquestioned than in the West. Some effects of the authoritarian tradition were reinforced by the attitude of colonial civil servants, who tended to be hostile to the market and to its most active representatives. Civil servants frequently mistrusted traders, whose activities they found unintelligible and who were less susceptible than their subordinates to orders and commands.

International Organizations

The patently insubstantial idea that international trade damages the less-developed world has been generated and propagated by the staffs and associates of the international agencies, especially by the United Nations Secretariat and the Economic Commission of Latin America. These institutions have also assiduously alleged inadequacies of the market system and the consequent necessity of central planning for the development of poor countries. They have consistently favored Third World governments who try to establish state-controlled economies, and they have also often supplied to these governments the personnel for running state export monopolies, state trading companies, and state-run cooperatives, planning commissions, and so forth.

The United Nations and its affiliates have fostered hostility to the market in more significant ways. They have sponsored and promoted the concept of a broadly uniform less-developed world, or Third World, with substantially identical interests that conflict with those of the Western market economies. Many of the most influential, energetic, and purposeful staff members of the international organizations think of themselves as agents of such a Third World. These organizations have been the major, perhaps the dominant, factor in promoting the concept of the Third World as a united and loving brotherhood of countries exploited by the West.

The international organizations also systematically attempt to unite less-developed countries into a bloc in opposition to representatives of the market economy. They organize informal meetings of representatives of less-developed countries and present briefs for their spokesmen, almost always with an anti-Western thrust. For instance, such a series of meetings was organized by the regional commissions of the United Nations prior to the first UN Conference on Trade and Development (1964) to provide Third World countries with briefs (and, incidentally, also to unite them against the West).

Other Groups

There are many people in the West, including some influential groups, who have for various reasons come to dislike or even to hate their own society and some of its institutions, and especially the market system. They seem to be engaged in a civil conflict in which they regard the less-developed countries as allies. They see these countries as a homogeneous and largely united category whose governments and representatives can be relied on to assail both the West and the market system.[11]

Anthropologists and missionaries also constitute sources of hostility to the market in the Third World. They are apt to deplore the disruption of established ways. It is true that the impact of rapid and uneven change can set up severe strains and inflict hardship. But these types of strain or hardship require far more difficult decisions and choices than the imposition of monopolies or other economic controls.

In Western countries, missionaries and churches have become a vocal and articulate source of hostility to the market, chiefly by emphatic allegations of Western guilt for the poverty of the Third World. Such allegations may promote official foreign aid and also the liquidation of Western influence in the Third World—other than that of the international organizations, the churches, and professional humanitarians. These activities of the churches may reflect a desire to be in the swim, to show that they are "relevant." Perhaps more important, the churches now plainly seek a new role for themselves, namely, that of social welfare

---

11 It is a moot point whether in this context the less-developed countries are regarded more appropriately as allies or instruments. They are allies in that their spokesmen are articulate, especially when they express opinions derived from the West or when they are briefed from the West. But their resources are often so meager and so largely derived from the West that they may be regarded as instruments. But frequent and often evident lack of concern of their champions in the West for the consequences of many policies in the Third World supported by them also suggests that they look on the peoples of less-developed countries as instruments rather than as allies (see the concluding section of this paper).

agencies on behalf of distant peoples. Such sentiments may also be behind their uncritical acceptance of ideas of exploitation.

Ideas Hostile to the Market

Marxism-Leninism

The sense of superiority of the Westernized and partly Westernized groups in the Third World is often accompanied by a sense of isolation, which is a source of unhappiness. The intellectuals, while feeling much superior to their fellow men, insist that they represent their societies. They often wish that it were so but know that it is in fact not true.[12] Their sense of isolation compounds the strains arising from the erosion of traditional beliefs and values and from conflicts of loyalties brought about by the impact of comparatively recent contacts with radically different and materially more advanced societies. These situations predispose the intellectuals and the educated classes to an all-embracing creed, especially one that promises emotional integration or reintegration with their fellow men. Here is a major attraction of Marxism-Leninism.[13] It is imperative to remember the threefold character of Marxism-Leninism: first, it is an intellectual structure of method, analysis, and observation that claims to explain the operation and prospects of society; second, it is also an all-embracing messianic creed promising salvation on earth, at least in the indefinite future—salvation here, if not now; third, it is a program for political action.

The appeal of Marxism-Leninism in the Third World is unrelated either to its merits or defects as an intellectual structure. It derives from the all-embracing messianic creed and from the political program, from the promise of

---

12 In 1958 I asked a highly educated and very helpful Indian economist in Delhi about legislation that prohibited the slaughter of cows or even of all cattle in most major Indian States, including the largest. Although this legislation was common knowledge and widely publicized in the Indian press (but for many years not reported in the West) he first denied its existence and then his knowledge of it. On being questioned further, he virtually broke down and begged me not to remind him of his isolation from the vast majority of his countrymen.

13 This factor in the appeal of Marxism-Leninism is a theme of a penetrating study by Czeslaw Milosz, *The Captive Mind* (London: Secker & Warburg, 1953).

salvation on earth, and from the promise of a society in which the rulers enjoy enormous power over their fellow men while they are simultaneously emotionally integrated with them. The appeal is reinforced by the Marxist doctrine of exploitation, the idea that poverty is always the result of an exploitative social system; the presence of an intellectual structure that, however defective, confers intellectual respectability on a messianic creed; and the political and military successes of Communist parties and movements that have seized control of two of the largest and most powerful countries in the world. The socialist influence in the media and over the transmission lines ensures that the most is made of these successes and also that the social and economic costs of the domestic policies are understated or even ignored.

The influence of Marxism-Leninism in the Third World dates perhaps from Lenin's *Imperialism: The Highest Stage of Capitalism,* which has influenced many millions who have not read the book but have some hearsay knowledge of its contents. They know that the book has been widely acclaimed and has influenced countless politicians, writers, and publications, that its author had made himself master of a world power, and that he wrote that capitalism can continue only by exploiting the rest of the world. The insubstantial ideas of that book and of many of its successors continue to be extremely influential and to serve as a source of Third World hostility to the market.[14]

Exploitation

The doctrine of exploitation, especially of Western exploitation of the Third World, has been a significant factor in the appeal of Marxist-Leninist ideology in less-developed countries.[15] It derives from the wider notion that property incomes, business incomes, and trading incomes are extracted from other people rather than earned by the recipients. This long-standing misconception has gained wide

---

14 See, for example, the passages from the prominent academics Paul A. Baran and Peter Townsend cited in my "Western Guilt and Third World Poverty," *Commentary,* January 1976, reprinted in this volume.

15 In much current discussion, the people of less-developed countries have come to be regarded as a proletariat, which is by definition exploited. In fact, most people there are small-scale farmers, not workers employed by capitalists.

currency in the Third World and is often compounded with the doctrine of imperialism.[16] Many local politicians find it useful to insist that the prosperity of the West has been achieved at the expense of the Third World generally and their own country in particular. The suggestion helps to explain away a country's failure to meet political promises, such as prosperity, after decolonization.

To Marxists, property incomes imply exploitation, and service industries are regarded as unproductive. In many less-developed countries, the principal agents of material progress have been external contacts, ethnic minorities, expatriate personnel, and foreign investments. Ethnic minorities have often enjoyed above-average incomes, usually from trade and related activities. The emotional and political appeal of the notion that the incomes of the relatively well-to-do are somehow extracted rather than earned and produced is exceptionally strong when those who are well-to-do are members of an ethnic or religious minority.

The notion of external exploitation has particular appeal because it effectively stirs up guilt feelings in the West and results in significant political and financial benefits to Third World governments. If Western profits are produced by exploitation, the expropriation of foreign enterprises is not only justified but even necessary to protect the population from exploitation and to make the country truly independent.

Western Guilt

A widespread feeling of guilt led the West also to accept, often subconsciously, the idea of Western exploitation of the Third World. Especially in America, acceptance of the idea has been assisted by the belief in the natural equality of man and by an unhistorical approach to the study of economic and social situations. If we believe that all are inherently equal, and also that history is bunk, then we are likely to accept the notion that income differences are evidence that some malevolent force has perverted the natural course of events.

---

16 Thus, in the context of the Third World the idea of exploitation as a cause of backwardness is primarily Leninist rather than Marxist; Marx was rather explicit in recognizing the role of capitalism in promoting material progress in backward societies.

The media, the arts, and the academies direct a ceaseless flow of allegations about Western guilt to the less-developed world, thus encouraging hostility to the market. Quite apart from straight exploitation through foreign investment, the operation of the market allegedly thrusts unwanted Western goods on the Third World, destroys or inhibits local industries for the benefit of the West, pollutes the environment, depletes resources, promotes inequality, erodes tradition (or alternatively, helps traditional rulers to repress the population, if that serves as a more effective accusation in the context). External market forces supposedly also damage less-developed countries by inflicting on them unfavorable and persistently deteriorating terms of trade and also by bringing about wide fluctuations in their export prices and earnings. These ideas originate in the West and readily germinate and multiply in the Third World. They are altogether insubstantial: external contacts have been prime agents in the development of many poor countries.[17]

These allegations treat the Third World as if it were a uniform, homogeneous collectivity, the component parts of which have identical interests which are opposed only to those of the West. These allegations have also encouraged the practice of worldwide aggregation and averaging of incomes, terms of trade, and other concepts and magnitudes that obscure the enormous diversity of physical, social, and economic conditions within the less-developed world. The outlook it promotes is that both domestic and international differences in income and wealth are abnormal and reprehensible and reflect market inadequacies; therefore, large-scale, coercive reduction of income differences is both feasible and desirable.

Foreign Aid

Official foreign aid also serves as an independent source of hostility to the market.[18] Since the aid is given to governments, it strengthens the position of and enlarges the state

---

17 The role of external contacts in the development of many poor countries is discussed in my article "Western Guilt and Third World Poverty," *Commentary*, January 1976, reprinted in this volume.

18 All references to foreign aid are to official intergovernmental economic aid.

sector as compared to the private sector. It also serves as a source of money and patronage. In practice, the influence of foreign aid in promoting government-controlled economies is reinforced by the criteria of allocation, which favor governments trying to establish such economies. This accords with the prescriptions of academic economists, especially in the United States, for the determination of these criteria. They are reinforced further by the influence of opponents of the market in the administration and local distribution of aid.

Foreign aid also assists the politicization of life, that is, the tendency to make everything a matter of politics; and the politicization of life provokes and exacerbates political tension, which again arouses hostility to the market, especially in multiracial societies. Many recipient governments engaged in wholesale socialization have expelled ethnic minorities and other economically productive but politically ineffective groups. Altogether, official aid is, in practice, an important antimarket force.

Market Failures and Economic Controls

Poverty and Advance

Paradoxically, both the material poverty of less-developed countries and the frequent instances of rapid advance have been used to promote hostility to the market. Articulate groups both in the West and in the Third World often adduce the comparative poverty of less-developed countries as evidence of the failure of the market to secure development and prosperity, a failure said to be exacerbated by external exploitation. From these misdiagnoses, they infer the need for comprehensive planning, wholesale politicization of life, expropriation of foreign and domestic enterprises, or even enforced collectivization of farming.

As a further paradox, the rapid advances of recent decades in many Third World countries have often promoted a climate hostile to the market. There has been rapid advance in many parts of Asia, Africa, and Latin America, very largely as a result of contacts established with the West. But, though rapid, the advance has often been very uneven; it has affected some groups and regions sooner and more pervasively than others, causing considerable political and social strains. The tensions have been exacerbated by the greater ability of some groups and individuals to adapt to changing conditions and to seize the emerging economic opportunities. The causes of these various social and political tensions come to be attributed to the market system, which plays into the hands of its opponents.

Market Risks

Another source of hostility to the market is the belief that economic controls are necessary to shield people from the risks of the market, especially price fluctuations of export crops. Sometimes this belief is related to sentimental notions about the operation of a near-subsistence economy. Such an economy, although it operates at a low level, is thought to be secure or snug. This is a misconception. Famines and the worst epidemic and endemic diseases occur in subsistence economies, not in market economies, because the former are very poor, have no accumulated reserves, and have no access to external resources and reserves. But although the hazards of a subsistence economy are much more severe than those of a market economy, they are more readily accepted because they appear unavoidable and the causes seem obvious and certainly not man-made. On the other hand, the causes of economic reverses in a market economy—such as, say, a fall in export prices or a rise in retail prices—are more remote, more plausibly attributed to human malice and incompetence, and therefore more suspect. Thus, price fluctuations are more often thought to present a case for state control than are fluctuations in crops, even though the latter cause greater hardship.

The idea that the population needs to be shielded from the hardships of price fluctuations has served as justification for the establishment of state export monopolies with the sole right to buy the crops. In many Asian and African countries, these bodies have for many years paid the farmers a fraction of the market prices of the products, thereby taxing away the bulk of their incomes. This has retarded the expansion of the exchange economy and restricted the volume of private saving, thus inhibiting the emergence of a local capitalist class. At the same time, even the very modest incomes left in the hands of the farmers have often fluctuated widely as a result of the vagaries of official policy.

State controls have not secured stability in any meaningful sense for the farmers or other economic agents subject to them. Both controls and the consequent politicization of life involve hazards more severe and less predictable than those of the market. After all, if agricultural prices fluctuate, it is possible for producers (or, for that matter, governments) to set aside reserves. No such protection is available against the withdrawal of a trading license, the confiscation of income or property, or deportation.

The Unsystematic Market

References to planning often confuse or identify the idea of foresight in private or business conduct with government control of economic activity, that is, replacement of individual decisions by government decisions in economic activity. Actual or attempted state control of economic activity outside subsistence production has become the standard interpretation of planning in Third World development policy.

Planning thus interpreted has obvious appeal to politicians, administrators, and intellectuals, since it creates positions of power that members of these groups expect to fill, with resulting political, emotional, and financial advantages. A further source of appeal is the misconception that planning replaces an irrational and confused system by one based on method, reason, and science. This appeal is enhanced further if planning is linked to the all-embracing messianic creed of Marxism-Leninism. This linkage is especially important in the Third World, where the literati feel much superior to the rest of the population, while at the same time regretting their isolation. Economic controls do not solve either the very real emotional problems of the alienated intellectuals nor the real or alleged problems of market failure. But this does not detract from the ex ante appeal of planning, particularly because people are rarely informed about the political implications and the social and economic results of comprehensive planning.

Business Interests

Local and expatriate businessmen, too, have frequently

welcomed economic controls. People habitually and understandably wish to increase the scarcity value of their services by curbing actual or potential competitors. Academic economists often blame businessmen for supporting restrictions or seeking direct subsidies, thus enfeebling or even undermining the market system, supposedly against their own interests, especially their own long-term interests. These charges bypass the central problem. If people pursue their immediate interests, they must be expected to do so consistently. Support for restrictionism need not be short-sighted, since neither the immediate cost nor the ultimate consequences fall on those who support such measures. Indeed, it can be argued that directors or managers of businesses with outside shareholders fail in their duty if they do not support the restrictions advantageous to businesses they manage. As a result of the politicization of economic life, all too often under Western pressure, the prospects or even survival of businesses in less-developed countries often depends on political or administrative decisions. Vigorous or explicit resistance to restrictionism in the Third World is often economically damaging to businessmen and may even be economic suicide.

Analogous considerations apply to the failure of businessmen to resist academic and media hostility to the market. Effective action to influence the climate of opinion is difficult, expensive, complex, and often also requires reflection and some subtlety. It is in the nature of the market system that decision making is diffused, and in this sense the system is fragmented. The cost of attempts to influence opinion on a general issue falls on the particular business. Any benefit is conjectural, delayed, diffuse, and rarely compensates those who bear the cost. Moreover, in a market system, resources accrue to people who are efficient in the performance of specific functions, a capacity very different from the understanding of abstract ideas and concepts. A more valid charge against the conduct of businessmen in this area is their undiscriminating attitude toward ideas and their purveyors, which leads them to extend massive support to determined and effective opponents of the market.

Relevant to this discussion, one curious contrast between a market system and a socialist system deserves notice. The market system delivers the goods people want, but its supporters do not manage to explain why; the socialist system does not deliver the goods, but its supporters are very good at explaining why it does not, cannot, or even should not, do so. One system is long on desired goods and short on effective arguments; the other is short on desired goods but long on effective arguments.

Conclusion

A brief summary may be appropriate now.

1. In many less-developed countries the politicization of economic life has vastly increased the stakes in and the intensity of the fight for political power. Such a situation inevitably provokes political tension, especially in multiracial societies. As a result, communities that have co-existed for generations or even centuries have turned against each other. Moreover, the energies and activities of ambitious and resourceful men have come to be diverted from economic activity to politics and administration, sometimes from choice but quite often from necessity, since economic or even physical survival has come to depend on political developments and administrative decisions.

   In many less-developed countries, government controls have also restricted occupational and geographical mobility within the country. The results of the restrictions on external contacts and on domestic mobility are generally harmful to economic development. External contacts and the movement of people are prime agents in promoting peaceful, uncoerced change in ideas and mores, including the spread of new methods of production, new crops, new wants, and the attitudes, habits, and conduct congenial to material advance.

2. The preponderance of opponents of the market in the external intellectual, academic, and official contacts of the Third World with the West has been a major factor promoting hostility to the market. The international organizations have played a key role in this process.

3. The role of ideas and ideologies as a source of hostility to the market in the Third World has been compounded by misleading, loose, and loaded terminology. For in-

stance, less-developed countries are habitually described as "deprived" and "underprivileged." But people cannot be deprived of something they never had. The term serves to suggest that the West has caused the poverty of the Third World. "Underprivileged" is a nonsense expression. Privilege denotes officially conferred favors officially denied to others. All those not in receipt of such privilege can be described as underprivileged. Thus, this term is a self-contradiction, an expression akin to "under-overfed."

We have also accepted much too readily the term "distribution of income." Incomes (other than subsidies) are not distributed but earned, that is, produced. There is no world distribution of income: there are only incomes produced in the numerous different societies of the world.

Finally, in this context, as in others, we should talk about income *differences*, not *inequalities*. The former term is neutral, the latter implicitly prejudges the issue. This again stands out starkly on the international plane.

4. The military, political, and economic resources of most less-developed countries are meager or even negligible. Yet they yield considerable political power on the world scene. Indeed, the West often abases itself before countries with no resources to speak of. This loss of nerve largely reflects a widespread but unfounded guilt feeling in the West. The guilt derives chiefly from the idea that the prosperity of the West has been extracted from the Third World, an instance of the pernicious misconception that incomes of the relatively better-off have been achieved at the expense of the relatively poor, that is, that the economic process is a zero-sum game.

5. Hostility to the market is often closely allied to hostility to the West. Many people who insist that the West has caused the poverty of the Third World, whether through colonialism or the operation of the market, belong to disaffected and disenchanted groups in the West who treat less-developed countries as useful instruments to promote their own concerns in a civil conflict within the West. The abolition of the market system is their primary object. Though professing concern for the Third World, these people support policies that result in massive and acute hardship and suffering in the Third World, as shown, for instance, by the fate of the Asian minorities in Africa.

More generally, the Western support indispensable to governments who pursue brutal and inhuman policies—the principal victims of which are Third World people—is often spurred by a feeling of guilt, or at any rate accompanied by expressions of guilt. But the feeling of guilt is rarely matched by a sense of responsibility for the policies it inspires.

6. The West often supports the people opposed to it or dedicated to its destruction. A large volume of virulent anti-Western and anti-market literature on the Third World and on its external contacts emanates from politicians, academics, and publicists, heavily supported by Western governments, international organizations, or Western foundations. This literature includes travesties of history, evident economic misconceptions, and simple lapses. The extreme character of some of this literature and the extent of the dependence of the authors on Western support are apt to be ignored. Unfortunately, neither the political thrust not the patent shortcomings of these publications have diminished either the support enjoyed by their authors or the effectiveness of the publications in promoting hostility both to the West and to the market system.

Peter T. Bauer
Basil S. Yamey

World Wealth Redistribution:

Anatomy of the New Order

Proponents of the New International Economic Order (NIEO) demand massive official wealth transfers from the West to developing or less-developed countries (ldcs), often collectively termed the Third World, to reduce and eventually to eliminate international income differences. These demands and proposals are embodied in various formal United Nations statements and documents. In 1974 the Sixth Special Session of the UN General Assembly adopted a Declaration on the Establishment of a New International Economic Order. At its Seventh Special Session in 1975 the General Assembly resolved "to eliminate injustice and inequality which afflict vast sections of humanity and to accelerate the development of developing countries," and it reaffirmed the "fundamental purposes" of the 1974 Declaration, in particular, "the imperative need of redressing the economic imbalance between developed and developing countries." Indeed, the 1975 resolution envisaged elimination of this imbalance, that is, the equalization of per capita incomes between rich and poor countries.[1]

The 1974 Declaration proposes a wide range of instruments for establishing the NIEO, including not only direct wealth transfers but also, among other things, reform of the international monetary system, trade preferences for ldcs,

---

[1] Quotations not otherwise identified are from two official United Kingdom publications: *Report on the Sixth Special Session of the United Nations General Assembly*, Cmnd. 6031, 1975, and *Report on the Seventh Special Session of the United Nations General Assembly*, Cmnd. 6308, 1975.

commodity agreements, and debt cancellation. To achieve the NIEO, the developed countries (in practice the West) are urged to adopt various policies ranging from taxation to pay for aid, to controlling the production of synthetics competing with exports from developing countries. On the other hand, the only reasonably specific obligation put on the ldcs is to promote cooperation amongst themselves. But even here the developed countries must assist. At the Seventh Special Session it was agreed that developed countries and the "United Nations system" should "provide, as and when requested, support and assistance to developing countries in strengthening and enlarging their mutual cooperation at sub-regional, regional and inter-regional levels."

The Declaration explicitly states that the policies of the recipients of wealth transfers must not be questioned. "Every country has the right to adopt the economic and social system that it deems to be the most appropriate for its own development and not be subjected to discrimination of any kind as a result." Discrimination includes failure to provide aid. The various UN statements and the NIEO literature generally take it for granted that wealth transfers promote the progress of the recipients.

The NIEO Declaration is yet another stage in the advocacy of large-scale aid from the West to the less-developed world, the aid to be effected in a variety of ways.[2] What is new is the more explicit link between the alleged responsibility of the West for Third World poverty and the *duty* of the West to "correct inequalities and redress existing injustices." It appears from the British government's reports on these special sessions of the UN General Assembly that only one delegate denied responsibility for the "unfavoura-

---

2 Professor Martin Bronfenbrenner characterizes the NIEO in the following terms: "The unifying idea behind all these things is the desire to increase the bargaining power of ldcs against mdcs (more developed countries) over a broad range of international issues relative to trade, to aid, and to the international transfers of both capital and technology." He observes: "What seems to have developed is a collection of self-serving ldc theories of international economic relations, summarized under the glittering head of 'A New International Economic Order.' Of this collection..., UNCTAD (in concert with other ldc-dominated UN agencies) has become the leading world spokesman." "Predatory Poverty on the Offensive: The UNCTAD Record," in *Economic Development and Cultural Change*, July 1976, p. 829.

ble economic situation of the developing countries" while supporting them in "their just demands." Their situation, he said, is due to the "colonial system" and is "preserved, and in many cases even made worse, by neo-colonialist policies." This was the Czech delegate, who spoke for the Eastern bloc. The Western delegates either accepted responsibility by their silence or were unwilling to reject the charges even if they thought them unfounded—a notable instance of the inability of the West to conduct its ideological self-defense.

The NIEO demands are a signpost to disorder. They imply that everybody everywhere is entitled to a substantial income, regardless of economic performance. Attempts to enforce the NIEO would lead to a Hobbesian war of all against all, to a spread of totalitarian government, and to further erosion of the West.

Aid as a Right

The major strands in the advocacy of the NIEO are readily discernible. They are that the West is responsible for Third World poverty; that official wealth transfers are required as restitution for past wrongs and also as instruments for reducing economic inequality, relieving Third World poverty, and securing Third World development; and that unless its demands are met the Third World would resort to force.

These arguments are conveniently epitomized in a widely applauded address by President Nyerere of Tanzania during his state visit to Britain in November 1975.

> I am going to argue that the whole concept of aid is wrong. I am saying it is not right that the vast majority of the world's people should be forced into the position of beggars, without dignity. In one world, as in one state, when I am rich because you are poor, and I am poor because you are rich, the transfer of wealth from the rich to the poor is a matter of right; it is not an appropriate matter for charity....If the rich nations go on getting richer and richer at the expense of the poor, the poor of the world must demand a change, in the same way as the proletariat in the rich countries demanded change in the past. And we do demand change. The only question at issue is whether the change comes by dialogue or confrontation. ...At any one time there is a certain amount of wealth pro-

duced in the world. If one group of people grab an unfair share of it, there is less for the others.[3]

Dr. Nyerere's opinions are of considerable interest because he is among the African leaders most respected in the West. Moreover, Tanzania has been termed, we believe correctly, Mr. McNamara's favorite African country, and according to observers sympathetic both to the World Bank and to Tanzania, the Bank regards President Nyerere's policies as a model for other African countries.[4] The NIEO Declaration assumes that aid-recipient Third World governments are dedicated to the welfare of their peoples and insists that the policies of the recipient governments must not be questioned. Thus Dr. Nyerere's policies are pertinent in our context on several grounds.

Before the West established substantial economic contacts with it, Tanganyika, the largest part of the present Tanzania, was a largely empty, disease-ridden region. It is still very poor and sparsely populated. Such economic development as has taken place is the result of the activities of Asians and Europeans and of access to Western markets and Western enterprise, capital, and ideas. The poorest groups in Tanzania are tribal people who have had little or no contact with the West. Their poverty cannot conceivably be attributed to the West.

For about ten years now, under Dr. Nyerere's regime, millions of people have been herded into collectivized villages to create "a rural socialist society" consisting of "village communities of brotherhood." Powerful pressure, including the use of force and the destruction of existing homesteads, has been exerted to get people to move into the collectivized villages or often onto sites without dwellings.[5] Reluctant farmers have been "denied I.D. cards, forbidden to use communal transport, to enter official beer shops, participate in ceremonial dances or attend cattle

---

3 "The Economic Challenge—Dialogue or Confrontation," *African Affairs* (London), April 1976, pp. 242–50.

4 For instance, according to the *Washington Post*, May 6, 1975: " 'Somalia is one of McNamara's favorite countries,' Mr. Malone said. 'But the real African favorite of the World Bank is undoubtedly Tanzania.' "

5 "Some correspondents tell us of certain cases where people have been transplanted from villages into the bush...and left to fend for themselves under conditions in which even the most ardent would find it difficult to cope....

auctions; in other words, the farmer and his family are made outcasts and denied social intercourse."[6]

Apart from the brutality of these measures, the resulting dislocation, business uncertainties, and diversions of energy have damaged agricultural production for several years. Nor will enforced collectivization benefit future output, both because of the elimination of incentives for the individual and because, "by concentrating people in villages, poor African soils" may well be "over-cultivated and demand an ever-growing amount of expensive inputs such as fertilizers and mechanization."[7] An economist on the staff of the World Bank wrote recently:

> Despite the vital need for production increases, the government appears to be gauging the success of its program primarily on the rate of villagization. This is reflected in the paucity of data on the economic achievements of the *ujàmaa* policy in contrast with the data available on numbers of villages and people settled.[8]

Besides this enforced collectivization, there also has been large-scale confiscation of Asian and European enterprises and denial of economic opportunities to Asian and European businessmen, employees, and workers as well as European farmers, who have had to leave in large numbers. In Zanzibar, formally part of Tanzania, political mass-murder was frequent until a few years ago.

Western Wealth and Third World Poverty

In NIEO advocacy, the poverty of the Third World is ascribed to dependence on the West in international economic relations, an aspect of colonialism in the past and of "neocolonialism in all its forms" in the present. This explanation not only intensifies guilt feelings in the West but also provides a

---

There are even reports of property being destroyed...." Government-owned *Daily News* (Tanzania), quoted in the *Times* (London), November 17, 1975. See also "Tanzania's Collectives Reap Little Food, Much Hostility," *Washington Post,* February 7, 1977.

6 *Financial Times* (London), January 7, 1975.

7 *Times* (London), November 17, 1975.

8 Uma Lele, *The Design of Rural Development: Lessons from Africa* (Baltimore: Johns Hopkins University Press, 1975), p. 158.

scapegoat for failures of development planning and policies in the Third World. Yet the notion that the West is responsible for Third World poverty is false.

Advocates of the NIEO, as of other policies described as egalitarian, often suggest that the prosperity of the relatively well-off has been extracted somehow from the poor. This is not so. Incomes are normally earned, that is, produced by the recipients; they are not extracted from others.

The misconception that the West has caused the poverty of ldcs is most emphatically canvassed and most readily accepted when it is most obviously untrue. How else could Dr. Nyerere get away with his allegations that wealth transfers to the Third World, as reparations, are a matter of right when it is so evident that the wealth of, say, North America, Japan, Scandinavia, and Switzerland has nothing whatever to do with the poverty of Tanzania or of the Third World in general? And the extreme backwardness of, say, the aborigines, pygmies, nomads, or African tribesfolk can hardly be due to international transactions, as these groups have had few or no contacts with the rest of the world. The list of least-developed (so-called Fourth World) countries in UN agency documents consists predominantly of countries which do not spring to mind as being involved even moderately in international trade, investment, and the activities of multinational companies. The roll includes Burundi, Chad, Lesotho, Rwanda, Afghanistan, Bhutan, the Maldives, Nepal, Sikkim and Western Samoa. Conversely, throughout the Third World the most advanced regions and groups are those with the most extensive contacts with the West—Malaysia, Singapore, Mexico, Brazil.

The West was materially far more advanced than Asia, Africa, and Latin America when it established substantial commercial contacts with them. These contacts have enabled people in the Third World countries to improve their productivity by giving them access to markets, by making available to them a wide variety of goods, ideas, and information, and by supplying relatively scarce complementary resources such as enterprise, capital and specific skills.

Nineteenth-century Brazil is often instanced as a case of colonial or neocolonial dependence: the backwardness of Brazil is attributed to its dependence on the United States' market for its coffee and on Britain as the source of its capital. Recent studies have demonstrated the invalidity of the general thesis. In the period of the free coffee market, 1857–1906, the income terms of trade of the coffee economy of Brazil improved at an average compound rate of about 4.0 percent a year (and this ignores the steady improvement in the quality of imported goods). The coffee economy was the engine of growth which made possible the first transition to modernization and industrialization. "Great Britain contributed significantly entrepreneurship, capital, social overhead, and liberal ideas of industrialism and progress which were of importance in the development of Brazilian industry and other economic activities." Early industrialization was assisted by "the supply of skilled immigrant labour that flowed into Brazil in response to the high returns available in the coffee plantations."[9]

Of course, the West also benefits from commercial relations with Third World countries; but this is the normal situation in any uncoerced exchange relationship.

Thus, commercial contacts between the West and the Third World have promoted Third World development. This is not to say that certain Western policies and practices have been ideal in the sense that different policies and practices might have promoted Third World development even more, especially for those ldcs best able to make use of wider opportunities. But this is very different from the allegations that these commercial contacts have damaged poor countries or account for their backwardness. Moreover, the combined effect of the relevant policies and practices cannot be significant.[10]

Roots of Economic Differences

The world is not divided into two sharply distinct homogeneous collectivities with a wide gap between them reflecting

9 Carlos Manuel Peláez, "The Theory and Reality of Imperialism in the Coffee Economy of Nineteenth-Century Brazil," *Economic History Review*, May 1976, pp. 276–90.

10 Several of the specific policies and practices commonly referred to in current discussions are considered in our paper, "Against the New Economic Order," *Commentary*, April 1977. See also M. Bronfenbrenner. *op. cit.* The question of slavery and its relation to development are considered briefly in P. T. Bauer, "Western Guilt and Third World Poverty," *Commentary*, January 1976, reprinted in this volume.

the exploitation or oppression of one category by the other. The world comprises a very large number of societies and groups that have emerged in varying degrees from a base of material poverty. There is no reason why some groups' emergence from poverty sooner and to a greater degree than others' should in any way have retarded the progress of these others. Indeed, the rise of some has made it easier for others to follow.

Economic achievement and progress depend primarily on people's aptitudes, motivations, mores, and modes of thought and on social institutions and political arrangements. It is these combined factors which either foster or hinder the willingness to work, to save, and to take risks and which condition the perception and pursuit of economic opportunities. Individuals, groups, and societies differ greatly in these respects.

Familiar group differences in economic performance within ldcs include those between the Chinese, Indians, and Malays in Malaysia, between Indians and Singhalese in Sri Lanka (Ceylon), between different tribal and ethnic groups in West and East Africa, and between different ethnic groups in the West Indies. Substantial differences in economic achievement between Greeks and Turks are evident in Cyprus.

Familiar examples of social values that manifestly affect economic performance include refusal to allow women to work outside the home, treatment of cattle as inviolable, and reluctance to take animal life.

Yet it is still widely believed that people's aptitudes, motivations, and mores, including their economic capacities and inclinations, are somehow basically uniform. This belief in the natural equality of man as an economic performer underlies much of the advocacy of NIEO ideas. Everybody is basically the same. And if everyone and every society are basically the same in economic potential and yet there are differences in income and wealth (economic differences), then these differences must surely reflect some perversion of the natural and just course of events by some malevolent force, in particular, the power of the rich to impoverish the rest. It follows that the distribution of income and wealth should be reformed and that this can be achieved relatively easily and painlessly without reduction in the wealth and income of the world (mankind) as a whole. In this scheme of things, differences in income and wealth are in a curious way superficial and therefore readily tractable, and yet these differences are also somehow the only differences that matter among people, societies, and countries.

If economic activity were in fact a zero-sum game, then making rich countries poorer through wealth transfers *would* make poor countries correspondingly richer. If people everywhere could use resources equally effectively, then total economic performance would be unaffected by these transfers. But when it is recognized that economic differences reflect the operation of the determinants of economic performance, it follows that the political and economic repercussions of transfers such as those envisaged under the NIEO will be far-reaching and complex.

Adverse Third World Policies

Third World poverty cannot be attributed to the West. Moreover, it is evident that many Third World governments have contributed greatly to that poverty, for they pursue policies damaging to the economic welfare and development of their subjects. A conspicuous instance is the large-scale persecution or discriminatory treatment of highly productive groups, especially politically unpopular and powerless ethnic and tribal minorities.

The expulsion of Asians from East Africa, where their incomes were much above those of the Africans, promptly reduced per capita incomes and living standards and retarded development. This instance of maltreatment became familiar only because so many of the immediate victims had British passports. Since the Second World War, African and Asian countries have engaged in large-scale persecution of productive but distinctive and powerless groups—ranging from discrimination in employment and in the allocation of contracts, supplies, and licenses, to expulsion or even massacre. The persecution has taken place, alphabetically, from A to Z—that is, from Algeria to Zambia—and, geographically, from Morocco to Indonesia, including Burma, Burundi, Egypt, Ethiopia, Ghana, Indonesia, Iraq, Kenya, Malawi, Malaysia, Nigeria, Pakistan, Sri Lanka, Tanzania, Uganda, and Zaire. It has occurred in countries often thought of as quiet and tolerant, such as Burma, Malaysia, and Sri Lanka. Less conspicuous but also very damaging in its effects on the economic opportunities and prospects of the local population is the general policy of Third World governments in restricting the inflow and deployment of foreign capital and personnel.

There are other major categories of policy that damage economic performance and general living standards. They include enforced collectivization of farming and establishment of state export monopolies that pay farmers a small fraction of the market value of their produce and deny them access to other marketing opportunities and to Western economic contacts. Others are proliferation of costly state trading, transport, banking, and industrial enterprises and monopolies; expansion of wasteful and damaging public spending; confiscation of property; and heavy taxation of productive but politically powerless groups. Performance is also damaged by large-scale diversion of resources to support state-sponsored enterprises and projects and activities often based on inappropriate Western prototypes; suppression of private commercial activities in favor of state enterprises, including officially sponsored so-called cooperatives; widespread restrictive licensing of economic activity; and restrictions on the import or even local production of cheap consumer goods. This list could be greatly extended.

Some of these policies have brought about prompt and readily observable reverses or even collapse in large sectors of the economy in many countries, including reversion to subsistence production following the destruction of the trading system. Recent examples so conspicuous that they have been reported in Western media friendly to the Third World include the experiences of Burma, Ethiopia, Tanzania, Uganda, and Zaire. A report in the *Washington Post*, February 7, 1977, critical of forced collectivization in Tanzania, was headlined "Tanzania's Collectives Reap Little Food, Much Hostility."

The same paper reported on July 1, 1976, that in Zaire

> Mobutu completed the effect of natural neglect by forcing out the Greek, Portuguese and Pakistani traders who kept the bush marketing and distribution system functioning. Farmers no longer can get their produce to market over

washed-out roads and are no longer able to buy the textiles, kerosene, and other staples. Farmers have either stopped planting for want of incentives or taken to smuggling their produce abroad.[11]

The London *Times* reported (September 13, 1976) on Burma:

> Under General Né Win's direction year by year parcels of the economy were nationalized and promptly suffered thereby. The more that was nationalized the lower the production, the larger the black market, the greater the corruption. Year after year it went on because the motives were beyond criticism and surely success must be round the next corner.

Burma is now "an object lesson in the disaster that can follow the resolute application of western-conceived socialist policies."

Various detailed studies have shown how particular economic policies have wasted resources, reduced incomes, and retarded development. Thus a study of India's foreign-trade policy concludes:

> India's foreign trade regime, in conjunction with domestic licensing policies in the industrial sector, led to economic inefficiencies and impaired her economic performance.... The policy framework was detrimental, on balance, to the growth of the economy by adversely influencing export performance, by wasteful inter-industrial and inter-firm allocation of resources, by permitting and encouraging expansion of excess capacity and by blunting competition and hence the incentives for cost-consciousness and quality-improvement.[12]

A similar study for Ghana's first fifteen years of political independence reports:

---

11 Yet another very recent report refers to the results of the economic policies of Sékou Touré, president of Guinea, policies which "have largely succeeded in keeping Guinea poverty-stricken when it has the resources to be one of Africa's more prosperous nations. State organizations have mainly failed to collect or distribute many of the necessities of life, and the real business of the country is in the hands of the black market, efficiently run by the officially disbanded entrepreneurial class. That most important policy of all in a continent where 80 per cent of the population live on the land, agricultural policy, has been a story of continuous failure in Guinea, with each new disaster being met with a change of names, and little else." Anthony Delius, book review, *Times Literary Supplement*, February 18, 1977.

12 Jagdish N. Bhagwati and T. N. Srinivasan, *Foreign Trade Regimes and Economic Development: India* (New York: Columbia University Press, 1974), p. 245.

> The restrictive [foreign trade and exchange controls] regime contributed to the economic atrophy of the 1960s. The combination of inflation and massive discrimination between activities was too much for the economy to withstand without suffering.... There is a clear presumption that a significant share of the blame for reduced domestic savings rates, low productivity of investment, and poor export performance must fall on the control regime.

A combination of policies and measures affecting the production of cocoa, the most important export and source of foreign exchange, "led to a relative decline in the attractiveness of growing cocoa for export.... In 1964/65 new plantings ceased, and have apparently not been resumed since."[13]

The poor economic performance of many Third World countries, and their balance-of-payments problems, are manifestly not the result of sinister Western interests and their manipulation of markets, but in large measure the result of the policies of Third World governments. Much of the advocacy of aid is in terms of a constraint which inhibits growth because of a supposedly inevitable lack of foreign exchange. Yet it is obvious both from general reasoning and from our examples that export earnings are significantly affected by government policies.

Some of the wealth-reducing policies and measures may have been merely misguided. But the only reasonable explanation of many actions taken by Third World governments is that they are motivated by purposes other than the improvement of the living standards of the people. This is sometimes admitted by Third World rulers. A few years ago a Burmese cabinet minister assured a European visitor that he was well aware that the expulsion of foreigners harmed general living standards but that his primary objective was getting rid of foreigners.

Of course, even if Third World governments were genuinely concerned with the promotion of the material welfare of their peoples and also adopted appropriate policies, a high level of economic achievement would still not be ensured. Economic performance depends also on people's

---

13 J. Clark Leith, *Foreign Trade Regimes and Economic Development: Ghana* (New York: Columbia University Press, 1974), pp. 164, 45.

attitudes, attributes, and motivations and on social mores and institutions which are often not congenial to material progress.

Effects of Foreign Aid

Official aid to poor countries has often been advocated, especially in its early days, as necessary for breaking an alleged vicious circle of poverty and stagnation. The argument was that poverty sets up virtually prohibitive obstacles to its own conquest and that these obstacles can be overcome, if at all, only at the cost of morally intolerable sacrifices. This notion is fanciful, as is demonstrated by the rise from poverty to riches of innumerable individuals, groups, and societies; by the very existence of rich countries, all of which began as poor countries; and also by the extensive and often rapid progress in much of Asia, Africa, and Latin America long before foreign aid and without widespread hardship.

External donations cannot possibly be indispensable for emergence from poverty. In a sense this is evident from the phenomenon of development as such, because although the world is a closed system and has not received resources from outside, there has been great development one way or the other. If the conditions of material advance other than capital are present, then capital will be generated locally or supplied from abroad on commercial terms. Low income and capital *are* poverty: they are not its underlying causes.

Not only are intergovernmental wealth transfers manifestly not indispensable for development, but they do not even necessarily benefit development or the interests of the population in the recipient countries. As they have operated since World War II, they have probably obstructed rather than benefitted development and general living standards. Under the NIEO, adverse effects are even more likely.

Official wealth transfers represent an inflow of resources in the recipient countries. But the policies of the governments and the wider repercussions of the inflow can easily outweigh any benefit from subsidized resources. As we have seen, many, perhaps most, aid-recipient Third World governments have pursued economic policies ranging from the wasteful to the inhuman. It is conjectural what policies they could or would have adopted without outside support. What is not in question is that many aid recipients have pursued and still pursue social and economic policies extremely damaging to the well-being of the population and to its material progress. The ability to carry out such policies has been bolstered by aid, which indeed has often been necessary to keep these governments financially afloat and to conceal from their people the worst effects of some of these policies, at least temporarily. Ethiopia, Indonesia, Sri Lanka, Tanzania, Uganda, and Zaire are some of the more obvious examples.

International official wealth transfers promote concentration of power, extension of state control, and general politicization of life in the recipient countries. The resources go to governments and enlarge state power and patronage compared to that available in the private sector.[14] This effect is reinforced by frequent preferential treatment of governments with persistent balance-of-payments difficulties or engaged in so-called development planning and other measures that politicize their societies. Strengthening of coercive power and intensified politicization of life in the Third World may be the most important and pervasive adverse repercussion of official aid.

There are also other adverse effects. Official aid underpins the anomalous policies of Third World governments in restricting the inflow and deployment of private capital and expropriating both foreign and domestic capital, while simultaneously complaining of its shortage. The balance-of-payments deficits encouraged by official aid serve both as effective appeals for external assistance and as convenient justification for specific controls that are politically congenial to governments but that discourage productive enterprises and provoke the flight of capital. Other untoward repercussions of these transfers include the propagation of the idea that material advance depends on external

---

14 Government economic power can be considerable even if public-sector activity is a small proportion of national income. Much of economic activity in ldcs is in subsistence and traditional small-scale agriculture. It is the size of the public sector relative to the exchange economy and not to the total national income which is relevant.

Moreover, the public sector can be small, absolutely and relatively, and yet government can exercise close control over the economy, for example, through state trading monopolies, licensing, and exchange controls.

donations rather than on personal, social, and political factors.

All this does not mean that official wealth transfers cannot benefit development or the population at large. But a favorable outcome cannot be taken for granted, as it usually is in discussions of aid and the NIEO. The contribution of these external transfers is at best marginal, as they mean only that some capital is supplied free or on subsidized terms. But again, lack of capital is not the cause of sustained poverty. Moreover, even apart from the major adverse repercussions on the determinants of development that we have listed, aid resources are normally less productive than commercial capital (the inflow of which is in fact obstructed by official wealth transfers) as their use is not so well adjusted to market conditions, to the supply of complementary factors, and to local conditions generally.

There is thus no general presumption that aid promotes development or helps the population at large. The acute and continuing plight of many aid recipients after decades of aid, the difficulties of many Third World governments in servicing even extremely soft loans (evidenced in the NIEO requirement of debt relief), and the frequent and acute shortage of food and other necessities all suggest that official wealth transfers are ineffective for sustained economic improvement. This accords with expectations, because material progress depends on personal, social, and political factors and not on external doles.

International Income Comparisons

The moral and political imperative to contain, reduce, or close the wide and persistently widening gap in incomes and living standards between the West and the Third World has become a major plank in the advocacy of international wealth transfers. The opening sentence of the prestigious Pearson Report reads: "The widening gap between the developed and the developing countries has become a central issue of our time." In the words of the preamble to the NIEO Declaration: "The gap between the developed and the developing countries continues to widen in a system which was established at a time when most of the developing countries did not even exist as independent States and which perpetuates inequality."

Income differences between the West and the Third World would indeed be both large and increasing if it were true that the material achievement and progress of poor countries were inexorably constrained by poverty itself or by malevolent external forces. But we have seen that this is not so. Moreover, conventional discussion of income differences between the West and the Third World ignores major problems of concept, measurement, and interpretation that affect radically the familiar conclusions.

To begin with, it is inappropriate and misleading to lump together and to average the incomes, living standards, or rates of growth of the Third World, a huge and profoundly diverse aggregate with over one-half of the world's population and with societies ranging from many millions of aborigines to many millions of inhabitants of huge cities. There are even wider differences in incomes and rates of progress within the Third World than within the West. Many Third World countries have in recent decades grown much faster than many Western countries, including the United States and Britain, so that the ratio of per capita incomes between these Western countries and the faster-growing Third World countries has declined. Examples of Third World countries that have grown rapidly are South Korea, Taiwan, Hong Kong, Malaysia, the Ivory Coast, Kenya, Brazil, Colombia, Mexico, and Venezuela. The rapid progress of large parts of the less-developed world and the virtual stagnation of others are simply an aspect of the diversity of the Third World.

In the usual discussions of the wide and widening gap it is common for the Third World to be identified with the poorest countries. But this is obviously mistaken if, as is often the case, the oil states of the Middle East are included in the Third World. There are also numerous regions and groups in other Third World countries that are better off than some groups, regions, and even countries in the West. Further, if the notion of the celebrated gap is to refer to the income difference between rich and poor countries and not to that between the West and the Third World—itself no more than a collectivity of non-Western countries—then the size of the gap is bound to be arbitrary. There is a gradation in national incomes and no clear or self-evident break between the poorest rich country and the richest poor country. The choice of the dividing line, and hence the magnitude of the income difference, is arbitrary.

There are also major, indeed basic, conceptual problems involved in income comparisons between widely different societies. For instance, the national income statistics and comparisons that are staples of the advocacy of the NIEO are unadjusted to allow for differences in age composition. The proportion of children is much larger in the Third World than in the West. The incomes and requirements of children are usually much lower than those of adults. Comparisons that do not take age composition into account confuse differences in income with differences in age, and this obscures the interpretation of the evidence.

Again, in national income calculations major items of expenditure are treated as income when in fact they are necessary to earn income; that is, they are costs rather than income, as, for instance, the cost of traveling to work. These items are usually much more important in the West than in poor countries. The much greater importance of intrafamily services and of subsistence production in the Third World, activities that are apt to be ignored or greatly underestimated, further biases these comparisons. The use of conventional foreign exchange rates in international income comparisons is another major source of underestimation of incomes in the Third World.

These various biases and errors are far greater than is usually acknowledged. They have been investigated in recent years by Professor Dan Usher, an economist who lived and worked for several years in Thailand. In an article published in 1963, Usher argued that while conventional statistics put per capita income of the United Kingdom at fourteen times that of Thailand, living standards in the United Kingdom were more like three times that of Thailand.[15] He developed his arguments in a subsequent book, of which the principal conclusions are sufficiently significant in the present context to be quoted at some length.

Using Thailand as an example this book shows that statistics

---

15 Dan Usher, "The Transport Bias in National Income Comparisons," *Economica*, May 1963, p. 140.

like those may contain errors of several hundred per cent.
...discrepancy is not due primarily to errors in data....the
fault lies with the rules [of national income comparisons]
themselves...[which] generate numbers that fail to carry
the implications expected of them....

Many village communities seem to have attained a standard
of material comfort at least as high as that of slum dwellers
in England or America. But at my desk I computed statistics
of real national income showing people of underdeveloped
countries including Thailand to be desperately if not impos-
sibly poor. The contrast between what I saw and what I
measured was so great that I came to believe that there
must be some large and fundamental bias in the way income
statistics are compiled.[16]

And even Usher's estimates do not fully take into account
differences in age composition.

Major shortcomings in population statistics are also
pertinent, as are occasional manipulations of the statistics
for political purposes. Nigeria, a relatively advanced African country, provides an example. The "politically embat-
tled census of 1963" yielded an officially reported count of
55.6 million. According to most observers, a more reliable
estimate was 37.1 million, the 1952–53 figure compounded
at 2 percent per annum. "The censuses of 1962 (nullified)
and 1963 were carried out under conditions of considerable
political tension, where the pressure to inflate figures for
purposes of parliamentary representation and control of
the federal government was very great."[17]

In spite of the size of errors and biases affecting international income comparisons (which, as we have seen, can
amount to several hundred percent of reported income differences), academic and official publications are full of
estimates of per capita incomes of Third World countries

---

16 Dan Usher, *The Price Mechanism and the Meaning of National Income Statistics*
(Oxford: Clarendon, 1968), intro.

17 P. Kilby, *Industrialization in an Open Economy: Nigeria, 1945–1966* (Cambridge:
Cambridge University Press, 1969), p. 4. The UN estimate of the Nigerian population of mid-1974 is 61.3 million; the Nigerian estimate is 72.8 million. In discussing this general issue, O. Morgenstern quotes an unnamed civil servant:
"We shall produce any statistic that we think will help us to get as much money
out of the United States as we possibly can. Statistics which we do not have, but
which we need to justify our demands, we shall simply fabricate." *On the Accuracy
of Economic Observations* (Princeton, N.J.: Princeton University Press, 1963),
p. 21.

and even of the entire Third World, which purport to measure incomes and income differences to the nearest dollar and income changes to a tenth of a percentage point. Such estimates have often been invoked as a basis for far-reaching policies, including the determination of the volume and allocation of official aid.[18]

The unreality of recorded national income differences and changes is underlined by changes in life expectation. In recent decades, mortality has declined much faster in the Third World than in the West. Over the last 25 years or so, both the absolute and the relative differences in life expectation between the two aggregates have narrowed substantially. Thus this gap, which is relatively unambiguous, has certainly narrowed and not widened. At the same time, the higher survival rate in the Third World has increased the difference in conventionally measured per capita incomes by increasing the proportion of children and aged in the Third World. But the resulting widening of the gap reflects an improvement and not a deterioration: most people like to live longer and see their children do so. Thus in interpreting the much-deplored population explosion it must be remembered that income statistics normally do not allow for changes in age composition and, possibly more important, do not include health, life expectation, and the possession of children among the components of welfare, so that they often register as deterioration a change which is an improvement, and conversely.

But even if the errors, biases, and other inadequacies were absent, and even if the concepts underlying income comparisons were firm, income differences would still not provide a sensible basis for policy. Even when statistics are reliable and unambiguous, they register only one quantifiable aspect of a situation, often to the neglect of other pertinent aspects, including the history of the situation. For instance, incomes can become more equal as a result of such radically different changes as a relative decline in the

---

18 It might be argued that the errors and biases will matter little if their incidence and size remained largely unaltered over time. A recorded widening of per capita income differences could then be said to indicate a real widening (though the recorded gap at any time would be subject to serious error). However, age composition and the importance of subsistence production, for example, change over time.

birth rate of the poor, a relative increase in their mortality, expropriation of the rich or moderately rich, an increase in capital compared to unskilled labor, or technical change. Yet all these changes would give rise to what is called an improved distribution of income. Reliance on income statistics as a basis for wealth transfers disregards the results both of government policy and of the conduct of the population at large, with anomalous or even perverse results. The policies of many Third World governments have reduced incomes in their own countries and thus increased the extent of income differences between their countries and prosperous countries. The expulsion of ethnic minorities has directly reduced per capita incomes in many countries (besides inflicting massive hardship on those directly affected). Should this impoverishment and the consequent widening of the gap entitle the governments to additional aid? And if this then serves to encourage further expulsions, should this be a basis for yet more aid? Reference to the gap or to any other form of income differences is useless as a basis for wealth transfers unless one considers how the differences have arisen and the likely results of the transfers.

International Redistribution

It is often suggested that the NIEO is no more than a natural extension of redistributive taxation from the national to the international level, a suggestion made superficially more plausible by the frequent references to the need to reduce an allegedly wide and widening international income gap.[19] But there are crucial differences between international wealth transfers and domestic redistributive taxation, differences which mean that these transfers are open to many more objections than domestic progressive taxation.

The adjustment of taxation to personal and family conditions is often imperfect even under domestic taxation because of the arbitrariness of the distinction drawn be-

---

19 In the words of Dr. Nyerere, the rich nations "should not expect to continue to deal with problems of comparative poverty within their own nation at the expense of people abroad who are poorer than their poorest." "Economic Challenge," p. 246.

tween income and the cost of earning it. International wealth transfers are intergovernmental and cannot be adjusted at all to personal and family situations. Many taxpayers in donor countries are much poorer than many people in the recipient countries. Moreover, in the Third World the receipt of aid generally benefits the powerful and the more prosperous, while the poorest groups benefit little and are often harmed. Further, the case for redistributive taxation rests on broad uniformity of living conditions and requirements and also on broad similarities of attitudes and motivations. But conditions and requirements differ greatly in different countries of the world. Again, while internal redistribution of income does not depend in any way on national income estimates, international wealth transfers rely heavily on such estimates, which, as we have seen, are subject to very wide margins of error and major limitations of concept.

Finally, in domestic redistributive taxation public opinion can shape some thinking and exercise some control over the process; under international wealth transfers the taxpayers in the donor countries do not know what goes on in recipient countries and have no control over the distribution of the funds there.

International Egalitarianism and Political Conflict

The promotion by political action of world economic equality at an acceptable level of prosperity is an explicit major purpose of the NIEO. According to the second principle of the NIEO Declaration, "there should be the broadest cooperation of all the member States of the international community based on equity, whereby the prevailing disparities in the world may be banished and prosperity secured for all." The implications of this principle deserve notice.

The objective implies an unlimited, open-ended commitment by the West. Yet as we have seen, while large-scale transfers can despoil the West, they cannot ensure the attainment of prosperity in any particular poor country, let alone the whole of the Third World; economic achievement and rate of progress depend on favorable domestic factors and government policies. But the unlimited commitment is only one of the far-reaching implications of the promotion of worldwide equality envisaged in the NIEO Declaration.

The exercise of political power in itself implies inequality of power. This is coercive power, because, unlike wealth, political power enables its possessors to restrict the choices of others. Attempts to remove or even to reduce substantial differences in income and living conditions imply coercion when these differences reflect aptitudes, motivations, institutions, and circumstances. The extent of the required coercion depends on the degree of standardization to be attempted and on the strength of the forces behind those differences. Because differences in the incidence of the determinants of economic performance, both among and within societies, are deep-seated, political action substantially to equalize incomes and living standards over large areas or even worldwide implies extensive forcible remolding of peoples and societies, far-reaching coercion, and wholesale politicization of life. It implies attempts to remake people both as individuals and as societies. Such attempts postulate not only world government but world government with totalitarian powers.

State action to promote economic equality, social and cultural uniformity, or the acceleration of economic development is widely advocated in the West. This induces Third World governments to claim that they are pursuing such objectives when they establish economic controls and politicize social and economic life. The policies actually pursued often have little to do with their avowed objectives. For instance, economic equality, social justice, concern for the poor, and protection against economic colonialism or other forms of alleged exploitation are habitually invoked to justify expropriation of owners and employees of foreign businesses, ethnic minorities, and local entrepreneurs. While economically productive, these groups are usually politically ineffective or vulnerable, because they are often unpopular not only locally but also with influential groups in the West, including opinion makers. The beneficiaries of these expropriations, often only temporary beneficiaries, include members of the government, their military allies, and their civilian supporters —civil servants, urban businessmen, and professional people, all of whom are usually relatively well off.

These allegedly egalitarian measures are not designed systematically to reduce domestic income differences, let alone to benefit the poor. In many, perhaps most, ldcs, systematic reduction of income differences would not even accord with local mores. And even if such a reduction were the intention, the required organization and information generally would not be available. What does accord with the purposes of most of these governments is a readily intelligible objective, namely, the extension of the power and grip of the rulers, by such means as enfeebling or neutralizing actual or potential opponents, placating their own supporters, and eliminating differences that do not favor the rulers. The same is true of coercive and often brutal policies, pursued in the name of nation building, to eliminate social and cultural differences (including linguistic, religious, and ethnic differences).

Discrepancy between ostensible purpose and actual performance and result is observable also in the imposition of state economic controls in many Third World countries. While such controls were allegedly designed to promote both economic equality and material progress, they in fact serve primarily or even solely to concentrate power in the hands of the rulers and strengthen their grip over the population.

These extensive and often comprehensive coercive policies, liberally supported by Western resources or even made possible by them, have vastly enhanced the role of governments—that is, of politicians, civil servants, and their allies —and have correspondingly increased the prizes of political power and the stakes in political conflict. These trends exacerbate political tensions. They have contributed greatly to the frequency, extent, and often literally murderous intensity of political conflict in the Third World in recent decades, including large-scale civil war in Africa and Asia. Groups and populations that have lived together peaceably for decades or even centuries have been set against each other, as in the Far and Middle East and Black Africa. And although politically ineffective groups, notably ethnic minorities, have suffered most conspicuously from these developments, the interests and the fabric of the lives of the mass of the indigenous population have also been profoundly damaged.

The NIEO will enhance the extent and intensity of these policies with corresponding increase in political tensions and hostilities, both within and between societies. At first it will promote tensions between the West and the Third World. But if the process of international wealth transfers were to continue for any length of time, the beneficiaries would be likely to quarrel over the spoils. Moreover, devotion to the assertion so prominent in the advocacy of the NIEO—that the prosperity of those who are rich has been gained through the exploitation of the poor, and the corollary that wealth transfers are restitution for past wrongs—is likely also to exacerbate tensions among Third World countries. The more successful will be envied even more than they are now, and the hostility will be heightened when the success of the more prosperous can be attributed to specific policies, such as commodity schemes, that are a feature of the NIEO.

Anomalous NIEO Proposals

Major anomalies of NIEO proposals are prominent in four components that are staples of UNCTAD conferences and similar occasions: commodity agreements, debt cancellation, transfer of technology, and multinationalization of aid.

Commodity Agreements

The NIEO Declaration emphasizes the need to achieve a "just and equitable relationship" between the prices of the exports of developing countries and the prices of their imports, with the aim "of bringing about sustained improvement in their unsatisfactory terms of trade." The linking of commodity agreements (or schemes) and foreign aid is evident in the requirement that "improved compensatory financing schemes for meeting the development needs of developing countries concerned" be pursued "until satisfactory terms of trade are achieved for all developing countries." The open-endedness of the developed countries' obligation is evident in that there is no specification either of the "development needs" of the Third World or of what terms of trade would be "satisfactory." Moreover, the terms of trade of different ldcs move at different rates and often in different directions.

Commodity agreements are an inappropriate instrument for resource transfer from rich to poor and are likely to operate perversely.

1. Exporters of primary products are not generally poor (let alone inevitably poor). The OPEC countries are only the limiting case showing how inappropriate it is to identify primary producers, even primary producers in ldcs, with poor people. Rich countries are net exporters of major primary products and their close substitutes. Within the less-developed world, countries exporting primary products are usually among the most prosperous. (And within the exporting countries, the main beneficiaries of commodity agreements are relatively prosperous producers, politicians, and administrators.)

2. Effective commodity agreements penalize potential producers who have to be excluded to ensure restriction of supply. The frustrated producers are usually poorer than the beneficiaries. This applies both within individual countries and internationally.

3. Most major commodity agreements have covered or are likely to cover commodities used in products of mass consumption in both rich and poor countries. The higher prices tax users, often regressively.

4. The operation of commodity schemes requires the allocation of valuable export rights and quotas, which sets up political tension both internationally and within individual countries.

5. The incidence of commodity agreements is often arbitrary and largely concealed, thus differing from the incidence of routine foreign aid collected through the budgetary processes in donor countries.

6. The instability of commodity agreements poses further problems. Success in raising the incomes of the favored producers and countries depends critically on the control of output and supply, not only of the commodity in question but also of close substitutes, whether agricultural or manufactured. The raising of price itself stimulates the search for new sources and new substitutes. Except where the commodity occurs in a few places only, no scheme is likely to succeed in raising the price for long without large sums of money becoming tied up in unsold stocks. And increasing dissatisfaction can be expected

from excluded producers and producing countries, especially where the scheme in the meantime can be seen to raise the price materially. The eventual collapse of an agreement drastically disturbs incomes and prices and is likely to exacerbate tensions within and among the countries affected, besides inviting further demands for external aid.

Debt Cancellation

Large-scale debt cancellation as a form of official aid is again perverse. It is unrelated either to the incomes or to the development prospects of the beneficiaries. Indeed, it clearly favors governments (or their predecessors) who have proved their inability or unwillingness to use resources productively.

A large proportion of the debts of Third World governments (and, until recently, practically the entire indebtedness of African and Asian governments) stems from foreign-aid loans made on concessionary terms, the grant element in which has often been over half the nominal value and sometimes over 90 percent. Moreover, these loans were often supplemented by outright grants. The burden of the debts has already been much reduced by inflation and by substantial default, the latter usually masked by such euphemisms as rearrangement, renegotiation, rescheduling, or consolidation. The demands for further write-offs, usually total cancellation, suggest that the partial defaults were insufficient and that the resources have been used unproductively.

There are other anomalies. The beneficiaries are certainly not the poorest countries, as these have few external contacts and would have few external debts. Third World countries that defaulted on soft loans in the 1960s included, among others, Argentina, Brazil, Chile, Ghana, Indonesia, Peru, and Turkey, which are relatively prosperous. Again, most Third World debtor governments pressing for these write-offs restrict the inflow and deployment of private capital. Other paradoxes include the large-scale expropriation of both domestic and foreign investments in many debtor countries and the practice of many debtor governments to grant aid to other governments. Moreover, a policy of debt cancellation promotes improvidence, for it encourages debtor countries to pursue inflationary policies and so to dissipate foreign exchange reserves, because the consequences of these policies help the pleas for the write-off of debts.

Transfer of Technology

Proposals for the transfer of technology to the Third World are vague about method and objectives. They often are no more than expressions of hostility to the West and to multi-national companies accused of withholding technology from the Third World by patents and industrial secrecy. At the same time, the West generally and the multinationals in particular are accused of introducing unsuitable advanced technology into the Third World and of inducing extravagant consumption habits and cultural dependence in Third World populations, who are assumed to have no minds of their own.

All this is insubstantial. Restrictions on external commercial contacts imposed by Third World governments are by far the most important obstacles to the inflow of productive wealth and resources. Moreover, in much the same way as capital is most productively used by those who have either accumulated it or obtained it commercially, so technology is used most effectively by those who have developed or purchased it. Thus, because the Japanese had to pay for technology or technical expertise, they purchased it selectively and applied it in accordance with the mores, institutions, and market conditions of their society. Gratis or subsidized technology transfer is not readily adjusted to complementary factors, market conditions, and institutions. Altogether, disappointment of unwarranted expectations attached to the subsidized transfer of technology will again exacerbate tensions and promote further demands for wealth transfers.

Multinationalization of Aid

The channelling of wealth transfers through the international organizations instead of bilaterally is much canvassed, chiefly on the arguments that this would make its allocation more objective and that it would remove the recipients' sense of resentment and humiliation, thereby alleviating political tensions. However, multinational aid—a substantial move toward supranational government under the auspices of the United Nations and its affiliates—is open to the same objections as bilateral aid, and to others besides.

A direct relationship between the supplier and the user of capital promotes its productivity. Multinational aid severs any connection between suppliers and users of the subsidized capital. It also deprives legislators and, *a fortiori*, the taxpayers (the real donors) in the donor countries of even the semblance of surveillance or control over the spending of the funds. Nor is multinationalization likely to improve the allocation of international wealth transfers. The methods and criteria of multinational transfers have little to do either with productive deployment of capital or with relief of poverty.

The New Order

The announcement of the NIEO practically coincided with the silver jubilee of official aid, which began with President Truman's Point Four Program in 1949. In those days, the advocates of aid claimed that its aim would be achieved by relatively modest spending over a few years. Today, many billions of dollars later, the volume of official aid continues to expand. Political and economic developments both within the Third World and in the West sustain the demand for ever greater transfers of wealth.

Even if international income differences were to narrow appreciably, which is unlikely, this would not abate egalitarian passions. Tocqueville observed that when social differences have narrowed, the remaining ones appear especially objectionable. This is all the more likely when the reduction in differences have been brought about by political pressure, because there is then no reason for stopping at any particular stage. Once the case for a policy like that of the NIEO for the international transfer of wealth is taken for granted, virtually anything that happens can be instanced in support of its continuation or reinforcement. Indeed, once wealth transfers are under way, the criteria for their maintenance and expansion can be plausibly shifted from, say, income and living standards to growth rates, or to the position of the poorest, the quality of life, the condition of the environment, and so on. Thus, Third

World pressures for large-scale wealth transfers from the West are likely to persist and intensify.

If such pressures are successful, the result will be, not an alleviation of the miseries of poverty, but the spread of totalitarian government and a further erosion of the position of the West. These effects will be greatly intensified if international wealth transfers are combined with egalitarian measures within countries of the West and of the Third World. That such egalitarianism is central to the thinking of prominent advocates of the NIEO is evident in Dr. Nyerere's statement that the "eradication of poverty" envisaged and demanded will involve "a ceiling on wealth for individuals and nations, as well as deliberate action to transfer resources from the rich to the poor within and across national boundaries."[20]

The pursuit of egalitarianism will require an immense extension of the use of the coercive power of governments over individuals, for nothing else would be capable of effecting the substantial homogenization, nationally as well as internationally, of highly diverse nations, societies, groups, and individuals. Any large-scale movement in this direction will transform society. It will create indeed a new international economic order, but it will be an order which gives people neither freedom nor prosperity.

---

20 "Economic Challenge," p. 247.

Harry G. Johnson

World Inflation, the Developing Countries, and "An Integrated Programme for Commodities"

World Inflation

The Concept

It has been known for hundreds of years that inflation is inevitably associated with excessive expansion of the money supply—inflation is always and everywhere a monetary phenomenon. Unfortunately for the public understanding of the subject, for at least as many centuries (over 20) as we have experienced inflation, some people in authority have believed that in their particular case the laws of economics have been repealed, or at least suspended in their favor. And there have always been those among the educated public who trust mistakenly to their own common sense

Reprinted, with some changes, by permission of the author and the Banca Nazionale del Lavoro, from the *Banca Nazionale del Lavoro Quarterly Review*, December 1976.

about the world and think inflation is caused by someone, somewhere, antisocially raising prices or wages; consequently, they see the solution in the fallacious belief that if only that someone were stopped from selfishly and greedily raising prices or wages, inflation would go away. Thus, understanding of the recent and current world inflation has been clouded and confused by the assertion that inflation is due to the irresponsibility of trade unions, the profit-seeking greed of monopolists, the rising prices of food demanded by selfish farmers, or the monopolistic raising of the price of oil by the Organization of Petroleum Exporting Countries (OPEC). None of these arguments is correct, because they all refer to changes in *relative* prices—the price of one good in terms of others, a problem of "real" or "barter" economics—whereas inflation is a matter of the prices of *all* goods rising in terms of *money*—a problem of monetary economics. But they all have great psychological attraction—to the politicians and their officials, who thereby gain an excuse for collecting their paychecks without doing the job they are being paid to do; and to the man in the street, who is conditioned to the belief that his government knows best what is good for him and that if something goes wrong it is the fault of some other civilian who is not loyally doing his social duty.

Inflation is a matter of excessive creation of money. How then can there be such a thing as a world inflation, when different countries have their own money and its supply is controlled by independent national central banks? This question, too, is a source of basic misunderstanding. Just because a country is a country and its central bank claims to be independent, does not mean that it really is independent and that it has control over its own rate of inflation, or that its inflation can be explained by domestic developments special to that country and not shared with other countries. On the contrary, if, as was the case up until 1973, each country maintains fixed rates of exchange between its currency and other countries' currencies, the result is exactly the same as if there were one world currency: there is one world inflation, attributable ultimately to too fast a rate of growth of the world money supply as a whole. Each member country in the world monetary system has to have roughly the world rate of inflation, whatever it misleads itself into thinking it can achieve by its own policy independently of the other countries in the system.

Up to February 1973, with a brief few months of "dirty floating" of exchange rates in the latter half of 1971, the countries of the world maintained a fixed exchange rate system and in consequence enjoyed (which is not the right word) a world inflation. The proximate cause of the world inflation was excessive monetary expansion in the United States—highly contagious because of the central position of

TABLE 1
WORLD INFLATION

Year	ANNUAL RATES OF CHANGE		
	World Money Stock	World Nominal Income	World Price Level
1950	0.1	4.0	-1.2
1951	6.6	14.3	7.6
1952	6.3	7.4	3.2
1953	4.4	5.8	0.7
1954	3.7	2.5	1.0
1955	4.1	8.7	0.4
1956	3.2	6.9	2.1
1957	1.1	6.0	2.8
1958	2.0	2.2	4.0
1959	3.9	6.6	-0.8
1960	3.0	6.8	3.1
1961	4.0	6.0	1.7
1962	6.1	7.8	2.3
1963	7.0	7.0	2.4
1964	6.8	8.4	2.2
1965	6.4	8.2	2.7
1966	5.7	7.9	3.3
1967	6.5	6.4	2.8
1968	8.3	8.2	3.8
1969	6.7	9.1	4.8
1970	7.6	8.5	5.4
1971	13.6	10.2	4.9
1972	15.3	14.1	4.3
1973	13.4	18.4	7.1
1974	10.4	9.0	11.8

SOURCE: Hans Genberg and Alexander K. Swoboda, "Causes and Origins of the Current Worldwide Inflation," mimeographed (Geneva: Graduate Institute of International Studies, November 1975).

the United States in the world economy. This expansion was associated initially with the failure to finance its escalation of the war in Vietnam by the requisite increase in taxation and then with subsequent failures of U.S. monetary policy. The consequence was not only inflation in the U.S. and the world economy but inflationary financing of the war, partly at the expense of the citizens of other countries who often did not—and even whose governments did not—publicly approve of the war itself. But the financing of the war in Vietnam was not by any means the whole story. There is abundant evidence that other advanced countries also became generally more willing to resort to inflationary monetary policies. This was partly, perhaps, because money was plentiful in the world economy and balance-of-payments deficits were consequently less risky, but it was also due to the increased emphasis on equity in the distribution of income and the rapidly mounting concern about "the environment." The latter are fundamentally the eventual legacy to the contemporary world of the resistance of American youth to being drafted and deprived temporarily or permanently of their share in the "affluent society."

Be that as it may, the world economy in the late 1960s embarked on a phase of world inflation (see tables 1 and 2). The result of the international monetary strains thus generated was the collapse of the international monetary system itself, the so-called Bretton Woods system of fixed exchange rates, alterable in cases of "fundamental disequilibrium," set up after the Second World War in order to prevent the reemergence of the 1930s' problem of world deflation.

National vs. World Inflation

Can one still talk of a "world inflation" when there is no longer a world monetary system and a world money? Strictly and logically speaking, one cannot; in a world of floating exchange rates, countries regain their national monetary independence, and any inflation they have is entirely their own doing and their own choice. Since they again have control over the supply of their national money, they are free to pursue any inflationary or deflationary policy they choose—"inflationary" and "deflationary" being defined by

TABLE 2
AVERAGE ANNUAL RATES OF INFLATION, 1955–70 AND 1970–75

1955–1970		1970–1975	
SELECTED INDUSTRIAL COUNTRIES			
Germany	(2.4)	Germany	(6.2)
Canada	(2.5)	United States	(6.8)
United States	(2.5)	Canada	(7.3)
Belgium	(2.6)	Switzerland	(7.7)
Switzerland	(2.6)	Sweden	(7.9)
Australia	(2.7)	Norway	(8.4)
Italy	(3.2)	Belgium	(8.4)
United Kingdom	(3.6)	Netherlands	(8.6)
Netherlands	(3.7)	France	(8.8)
Norway	(3.9)	Australia	(10.3)
Sweden	(3.9)	Italy	(11.3)
Japan	(4.5)	Japan	(11.3)
France	(4.6)	United Kingdom	(13.0)
Average	(3.3)	Average	(8.9)
Range	(2.2)	Range	(6.8)
SELECTED LESS-DEVELOPED COUNTRIES			
Guatemala	(0.5)	Tunisia	(5.2)
El Salvador	(0.6)	Egypt	(5.9)
Panama	(0.8)	Iraq	(6.3)
Malaysia	(0.9)	Panama	(7.2)
Singapore	(0.9)	Malaysia	(7.3)
Iraq	(1.9)	Sri Lanka	(7.4)
Greece	(2.0)	El Salvador	(7.8)
Thailand	(2.1)	Morocco	(8.3)
Sri Lanka	(2.1)	Guatemala	(8.4)
Tunisia	(2.7)	Thailand	(8.8)
Morocco	(2.7)	Iran	(9.5)
Syria	(2.7)	Singapore	(10.5)
Ecuador	(2.8)	Syria	(11.2)
Egypt	(2.9)	Paraguay	(11.6)
Mexico	(3.0)	India	(11.7)
Pakistan	(3.0)	Mexico	(12.1)
Iran	(3.4)	Spain	(12.1)
Nigeria	(4.1)	Taiwan	(12.2)
Philippines	(4.7)	Greece	(12.3)
Ghana	(5.4)	Peru	(12.8)
India	(5.8)	Ecuador	(13.5)
Taiwan	(5.8)	Nigeria	(14.2)
Spain	(6.8)	Philippines	(15.1)
		Pakistan	(16.8)
Average	(2.9)	Average	(10.3)
Range	(6.3)	Range	(11.6)

SOURCE: International Monetary Fund, *International Financial Statistics*, 1972 Suppl., and April 1976.

comparison with the average of the other countries or those countries with which they do most of their international business. (One should be careful to note, however, that countries maintaining a fixed rate on the U.S. dollar, as Mexico does, or on a major European currency have chosen whatever inflation obtains in the country to whose currency they have pegged their own.)

In strict logic, then, the concept of world inflation lost its meaning with the collapse of the international monetary system in February and March 1973. But strict logic is not always the best way to understand economic phenomena: one has to bear in mind also the time dimension of adjustment to changing economic circumstances; the strength and persistence of traditional habits of thought, especially among those old enough to occupy positions of power; and the political convenience of myths about the nature of the world, and especially about the sources of problems that are uncomfortable for politicians and policymakers.

To be specific, the world inflation was well under way before the collapse of the international monetary system in early 1973; and inflation (and for that matter serious depression), once well under way, is both difficult and time-consuming to stop. It was, in fact, not until 1975 or 1976 that sharp differences began to emerge, in the statistics (see table 3), between those countries that had been seriously determined to stop inflation and those that had not—or had become so only later. Earlier, it made some sense to continue to refer to world inflation—in the precise sense that all countries were faced with a common problem of coping with the domestic impact of an inflationary process that had originated as a worldwide and previously unavoidable phenomenon.

Apart from that fairly logical distinction between a common cause and a common set of consequences, the collapse of the international monetary system into a floating rate system was quickly followed by two events that need not have had, but that governments generally allowed to have, inflationary consequences. One was the "oil crisis" and the resulting fourfold increase in the price of oil. The other was the sharp upward surge of the prices of foodstuffs—a reaction to a "real" shortage associated with the fact that the upward phases of the business cycle in the major countries

TABLE 3

VARIATIONS IN NATIONAL INFLATION RATES

Year	Percentage Points*
1960	9.2
1961	9.0
1962	17.7
1963	19.4
1964	14.2
1965	12.1
1966	10.5
1967	6.4
1968	11.2
1969	14.5
1970	13.8
1971	14.1
1972	14.5
1973	12.4
1974	37.0
1975	34.1**

SOURCES: Federal Reserve Bank of St. Louis, *Rates of Change in Economic Data for Ten Industrial Countries* (Belgium, Canada, France, Germany, Italy, Japan, Netherlands, Switzerland, United Kingdom, United States), (May, 1976); David I. Fand, "World Reserves and World Inflation," *Banca Nazionale del Lavoro Quarterly Review*, no. 115 (Dec. 1975), pp. 347–69.

*Sum of absolute deviations from world rate of inflation.

**Preliminary estimate.

were unusually and exceptionally closely synchronized, while world output of foodstuffs was abnormally low. Usually some countries are in the downswing, bottom, or early upswing phases of their business cycles while others are at the crests of their booms. As mentioned, both of these developments involved changes in *relative* prices and need not necessarily have been allowed to give an upward boost to all money prices in general, let alone a continuing inflationary impetus. But allowing them to add to the inflationary impetus was the easiest way out for policymakers, especially in view of the political sensitivity of their constituents to rises in the price of food, on the one hand, and the price of energy for heating and transport, on the other.

In these circumstances, it was obviously politically very convenient for policymakers to endorse the view that inflation was a world problem that they were powerless to control, to take credit for doing their best in the face of insuperable difficulties, and to confine their actions mostly to gestures and to denunciations of unpopular groups who could be accused of taking unfair advantage in protecting themselves against the common inflationary misfortune. In this connection, it was particularly useful that the oil crisis could be blamed (not really accurately) on the Arab countries, which most people had not included as full members of the "Third World" and which for various reasons of history and religion tended to be regarded in the Western world with contempt and dislike mixed with uneasiness and distrust. It was also politically useful that for most countries, and even in the United States with regard to some important commodities, foodstuff prices tended to be governed by or identified with import prices, so that domestic inflation could be easily identified with rising prices of imported food and hence with a "world inflation" caused by forces outside the country's control. This identification is, of course, fallacious, because it neglects the role of the country's foreign exchange rate in fixing the domestic money equivalent of the foreign prices of imported goods—rising foreign prices can be quite consistent with falling domestic prices if the exchange rate is appreciating sufficiently rapidly. But it was easier to blame "world inflation" than to call attention to the domestic monetary and other policies that ensured a base-rate of domestic inflation and allowed rising import prices to aggravate that base-rate.

These remarks illustrate the third point mentioned earlier, concerning the political convenience of the myth of world inflation in that it excused policymakers from taking the unpopular anti-inflationary measures allowed them after February 1973 with the freedom of exchange rates to float. But greater weight should, in my view, be given to the second factor mentioned, the strength of customary modes of thought among those senior enough to occupy positions of power in the making of economic policy. Though the international monetary system of fixed exchange rates collapsed into a floating rate regime in early 1973, policymakers in the new system—both at the national government level and at the level of the International Monetary Fund—seem to have had, and to continue to have, virtually insuperable difficulty in freeing their minds from the idea that the floating rate system is only a temporary arrangement pending a return to a fixed rate system. Worse, they cannot free their minds from the idea that the system the world now has still is, and works in the same way as, a fixed rate system. Thus, for example, a country's policymakers may think in fixed-rate terms, expect rising external prices to cause internal inflation, and conduct their domestic monetary policy to accommodate the domestic inflation they expect, for fear of causing domestic unemployment if they try to stop the domestic impact of world inflation by domestic deflationary policy. The result of this thinking will be that the country will have domestic inflation, and its exchange rate will remain fairly stable. In other words, the results will be more or less the same *as if* the country had a fixed exchange rate and had to conform to the world inflation. And it will therefore appear, quite wrongly, that a floating rate system works just like a fixed rate system and is governed by the same logic.

It is worth noting, too, that the same semblance of identity between a fixed and a floating rate system can be achieved by several other types of failure to understand and take advantage of the freedom for discretionary domestic monetary and anti-inflationary policy offered by the system of floating exchange rates. For example, exporting and import-competing industries, whose leaders quite understandably think in terms of partial economic equilibrium, naturally tend to regard any appreciation of the currency as imposing a competitive international disadvantage on them; and they will press the government, probably successfully, to hold down the exchange rate, which will automatically require the support of an expansionary (and inflationary) monetary policy. As another example, if a certain differential between domestic and world interest rates is regarded by the monetary authority as normal and desirable, to be maintained by monetary policy, the country will have to follow a monetary policy producing roughly the same rate of inflation as the rest of the world, to prevent the normal "real" relation between national interest rates from being disrupted by differing expected inflation rates and associated expectations of future exchange rate changes.[1] As a

---

1 Technically, we can write

$$i_d = r_d + \pi_d \; ; \; i_u = r_u + \pi_u \; ; \; e_d = \pi_d - \pi_u$$

where i is the money rate of interest, r the real rate, π the expected rate of final and still more obvious example, if policymakers act on a belief that there is some "correct" or "natural" (or some other value-laden or chauvinistic adjective) value for their currency in terms of the U.S. dollar or some other major currency, they will for practical purposes have committed themselves to a fixed rate system even though their exchange rate is nominally free to float. And so long as policymakers think and act in this way, as they have to a large extent been doing, it will remain legitimate to use the concept of a world inflation—even though the economist who does so thereby both helps to perpetuate a myth and fortifies the intellectual ossification that is in any case the incurable occupational disease of the economic policymaker.

World Inflation and the Developing Countries

I turn now to the problems posed for the developing countries by the world inflation. To begin with, though, it would help to clear out of the way certain problems that are incorrectly identified with and regarded as being caused by the world inflation.

In the first place, the rise in oil prices has necessarily had a serious effect on the real incomes of the non-oil-producing developing countries—which is almost all of them outside the Middle East. But the monopolistic increase in oil prices had very little to do with the world inflation. One cannot say that it had nothing to do with the world inflation, because well before the increase was introduced the members of OPEC had become increasingly restive about the fact that oil prices were fixed in terms of U.S. dollars—albeit with an "inflation factor" consisting of an agreed annual price increase designed to compensate for American inflation. (Incidentally, the inflation factor was fixed at 8 percent per annum, which at first seemed far too high but for three years or so before 1976 turned out to be somewhat below the actual.) But continuing inflation in the major countries after 1973 served to *reduce* the real burden of the oil price increase, and in fact, oil prices in money terms have

---

inflation, and e the rate of change of the exchange rate defined as the price of U.S. dollars in terms of domestic money, and the subscripts d and u refer to domestic and United States variables; then $i_d - i_u = r_d - r_u$ requires $\pi_d = \pi_u$, which implies managing monetary policy so that $\pi_d = \pi_u$ and $e_d = 0$, i.e., stability of the exchange rate on the U.S. dollar.

started to come down, as various observers predicted they would ultimately have to in real terms. The main reason for this prediction was that the need for revenue would eventually break cooperation among the members of OPEC and lead to covert or overt price cutting. This elementary economic logic, amply verified by past experience of price-raising cartels, was not generally accepted at the time, though both continuing inflation and the general recession involved in the process of trying to stop it have sharpened the results of the logical reasoning: OPEC member needs for revenue have expanded more rapidly than many commentators thought possible, partly as a result of the wastes involved in crash spending programs and partly as a result of the effect of continuing inflation on the money costs of real programs. At the same time, depression has cut the demand for oil in spite of the mistaken efforts of democratic governments to keep domestic energy prices down while appealing to the public to be economical in their use of energy. In the longer run, oil prices are likely to wind up significantly higher than they were during what may be called the coal-into-oil revolution of the 1950s and 1960s but substantially lower in real terms than they were in the two and a half years following the "oil crisis." In any case, however, the real economic problems associated with oil pricing have to be distinguished from the monetary problems of world inflation.

Second, the problem posed for the developing countries by world inflation has to be clearly separated also from the rapid fall in relative prices of foodstuffs and raw materials since the peak reached a couple of years back. The recent fall of relative prices of primary products has been exceptionally rapid and severe for a number of developing countries, both because the peak of the usual boom was exceptionally high and because the subsequent recession has been exceptionally severe owing to the determination of certain key advanced-country governments—specifically, the United States, Germany, and Japan—to fight and beat inflation thoroughly, in spite of the transient cost in terms of unemployment and low production. Both elements—the high peak associated with world inflation and the low trough associated with determined anti-inflationary policy—have to be borne in mind in assessing the implications of recent experience for the developing countries. The peak was a cyclical peak, and the trough is a cyclical trough. Unfortunately, it has been my observation—based on the behavior of farmers in advanced countries, but easily transferable to understanding the attitudes of spokesmen and theorists for developing countries—that all farmers everywhere are firmly convinced that the highest price they have ever received ought to be the lowest price they should ever get for their products. This attitude, incidentally, is usually accompanied by the idea that since man cannot live without eating, he should pay as much for his food as he can be made to pay without starving to death.

Again, however, these issues have nothing to do with world inflation, except perhaps in providing historical evidence that can be misinterpreted to make a case for compensation for alleged injustice. Nor does the condition of world inflation add any strength to arguments for efforts to raise the real prices of primary products by cartelization, more attractively packaged as "an integrated commodity policy" or a "new international economic order." These arguments are the subject of the next section; for the present purpose, it is sufficient to note that such arguments concern the real relative prices of commodities *and* that there is no reason to suppose that the money prices of such commodities persistently lag behind a general inflationary price movement. (This is in possible contrast to the prices of manufactures, which are not determined in organized commodity markets.)

What special problems, then, if any, are posed for developing countries by the fact of world inflation? One type of problem has already been touched on: the effect of unexpected inflation, or an unexpected acceleration in the normal rate of inflation, in reducing the real value of exports contracted for long in advance in terms of fixed money prices. This problem, it might be recalled, arose during the short-lived 1950-52 Korean War–boom in primary-product prices; but at that time—such is the influence of fashion on popular and governmental economic thinking—the official complaint, at least in southern Asia (the beneficiary of boom prices for rubber and tin), was that high commodity export prices were bad because they raised the cost of living for urban workers and diverted the farmers away from the government's objective of achieving self-sufficiency in foodstuffs. The successor governments of the independent developing countries have since then, of course, become much more sophisticated, in the sense of appreciating that there is no reason why high prices for commodity exports should be passed along to the stupid farmers. Instead, they are creamed off for spending on and by the educated government bureaucracy in the name of promoting economic development, social justice, or what have you.

The problem of the loss of real export proceeds because of unexpected inflation is, however, necessarily a transient one. Once inflation gets to be expected, either money contracts will come to be roughly indexed to provide the real prices bargained for, or producers (and even their governments acting for them) will cease entering into long-term contracts and will take their chances on the market when the product is ready for delivery. The longer-run problem, as students of the economics of inflation in the advanced countries have come to realize, is the disturbing effect of unexpected variations—accelerations and decelerations—in the rate of inflation itself. The rate is also associated with changes in public opinion and governmental policy with respect to the relative importance of avoiding inflation or of achieving whatever objectives inflation helps in the short run to promote. These changes can result in variations in both the rate of inflation and the level of economic activity. Note that I have put this point in a rather complex way, because research into the theory and empirical measurement of the so-called Phillips curve trade-off between inflation and unemployment has verified that there is no such trade-off in the long run, while more recent research on the basis of the "rational expectations" approach has emphasized that it is only unexpected changes in governmental policy that have leverage over the behavior of the real economy. The point can be put in another, somewhat different, way, related to Latin American experience with endemic severe chronic inflation—experience, incidentally, that is little known or analyzed by the leading economists of the advanced countries. It is that, once inflation of this endemic but "stop-go" type gets a firm hold on an economy, it becomes more important to the economic individual to reach informed guesses on probable changes in the rate of inflation and in the government policies that determine it than to evaluate the kind of market, demand, and cost information that is by traditional economic analysis assumed to be the strength of a competitive, relatively free economic system (a description used here to include the contemporary Western-style "mixed" private and state enterprise system). And this in turn gives rise to both a great deal of inefficient decision making, unconducive to economic development and modernization, and to apparently blatant injustice in the distribution of income and wealth.

It is true enough that a number of developing countries, especially but not exclusively in Latin America, have long persisted in creating this problem for themselves. They have further compounded its development-inhibiting effects by domestic price-intervention policies aimed at shielding the real incomes of significant social groups from the effects of inflation. In addition, they have practiced international economic intervention policies aimed at preserving a fixed exchange rate in spite of domestic inflation at a rate much faster than the slow upward trend of world prices. But the less-developed countries as a group have, until the emergence of world inflation, had the important, though underappreciated, advantage of trading with an advanced-country world characterized by fairly steady, sustained economic growth at fairly stable (more accurately, slowly rising) prices. This favorable climate for economic development is what has been destroyed, at least temporarily, by world inflation. And it is, in all probability, far more important for the development of the developing countries than either the various impediments to their development posed by protectionist trade policies in the developed countries or the various "countervailing monopoly" and collective monopoly policies now being demanded by the United Nations Conference on Trade and Development (UNCTAD) pressure group, under the rubric of "a new international economic order."

Reforming the International Economic Order

The Emphasis on Commodities

One of the major consequences of the world inflation and related developments has been the increased international political stridency of the demand of the Group of 77 in the United Nations and UNCTAD for "a new international economic order" (earlier described as "a new world trade order") designed to right the alleged past wrongs inflicted on developing countries by the prevailing GATT (General Agreement on Tariffs and Trade) system of liberal international trade. The "oil crisis" of 1973 and the subsequent quintupling of the dollar price of oil lent massive (but in large part illusory) support to the idea that great income transfers from the wealthy countries could be extracted by cartelizing primary-product marketing, even though oil is a uniquely strategic commodity and in its case cartelization has been facilitated by the divided interests of the multinational petroleum companies. The boom and subsequent collapse of primary-foodstuff prices provided new support for the belief that competitive world markets unjustly prevent primary producers from obtaining "fair" prices for their products. Finally, "indexing" as a means of reducing the uncovenanted arbitrary income redistributions inherent in the process of unexpected inflation has been a major issue among monetary experts in the developed countries, providing an opportunity to confuse commodity-market-instability problems with inflation problems. They have used the blanket term "indexing" to include the quite different objective of fixing the real relative prices of primary commodities in terms of manufactures.

Commodity agreements as a solution to the various problems of primary-product exporters are not a new idea.[2] In one form or another, they have over a half century of experience behind them, all of it a history of failure—of the various commodity agreements that have been attempted, only the latest tin agreement survives, and only in a truncated fashion, and tin has the peculiar advantage of involving fairly large-scale enterprises. Yet there is still abundant faith in commodity agreements as a panacea,

2 The popularity of international commodity agreements as a solution to problems of primary producers goes back to the interwar period, when it was an obvious extension of the 1920s' British policy idea of "rationalizing" industry and, slightly later, an obvious idea for benefitting primary producers in the Commonwealth and the Empire. It derived some support from its long-time advocacy by Mr. St. Clair Grondona, was endorsed at one point by Keynes, and became a standard prescription of many Oxford graduates and dons, presumably through the continuing advocacy of R. F. Harrod.

and, as is usually the case, the faith rests either on ignorance of past history or on the obstinate belief that what went wrong last time is attributable either to lack of will or cleverness or to unwillingness to commit sufficient financial resources to the enterprise—but never to inherent difficulties that could be understood in terms of elementary economic analysis.

Nor is "an integrated commodity policy" a new concept. In fact, the UNCTAD Secretariat has been attempting for over a dozen years to endow the concept with concrete meaning, but the task has proved impossible, because the objectives sought are inconsistent at even the most elementary level of economic analysis. They include stabilizing prices in the short run, raising prices in every run, achieving prices that would be "fair" and "just" to producers while not being unfair to consumers ("equitable to consumers and remunerative to producers," in the current catch-phrase), maximizing profits from exports, maximizing foreign exchange earnings from exports, and achieving "parity" (though it is usually not called that) of real income for primary-product and manufacturing-goods producers.

The "integration" part of the "integrated commodity policy" is only too obviously a political integration, UNCTAD-style—that is, the description as an "integrated" and therefore a presumably considered and attention-deserving policy, of a ragbag of individual policies that might, like any politician's election platform, command an electoral majority by promising something for everyone. In short, the word "integration" applies, not to the policy, but to the demand for something for nothing for everybody who thinks he deserves it. The latest demand for an integrated commodity policy, to be discussed below, has exactly the same features of being "integrated" only in the sense of demanding the creation of a monopoly. A sufficient number of would-be monopolists can make the exploitation of consumers by producers politically appealing to a majority of producers. The policy attempts also to enlist the support of the consumers, as willing accomplices in their own exploitation, by deliberate misapplication of concepts of fairness and justice derived from unconnected areas of economic discussion. (The most noteworthy example is the attempt to misapply the concept of "indexing," discussed above.)

Before proceeding to detailed consideration of the proposed commodity policy, it is relevant to note the extent to which that policy, and the demand for a so-called new international economic order, of which it is a part, is based on ancient history. Its true inspiration is politico-economic analysis, particularly the Prebisch world-vision, of the economic phenomena of the Great Depression of the 1930s. In this conception, the trend in the terms of trade between commodities and manufactures inevitably turns against commodities. Since this is attributed to the industrialized countries' presumed monopoly power to force down commodity prices in terms of manufactures, the counteracting policies required are, on the one hand, forced industrialization and, on the other, countervailing monopolization. Even UNCTAD's own so-called experts have been unable to document this theory statistically, except by the intellectually shady process of taking each successive peak of commodity prices, reached under world boom conditions, as the floor from which to make subsequent measurements. Its strength can only be accounted for by a deep emotional and political need to find an external scapegoat for the condition of economic backwardness, a need that must be reckoned with in a rational consideration of proposed, ostensibly economic, policies. One aspect of the Prebisch world-view is specially worth mentioning, since its significance has only come to be appreciated recently and imperfectly. The historical experience of deep world depression from which the Prebisch vision originates was a phenomenon of the Keynesian short run, during which, for practical purposes, population as well as technology can be safely assumed to be constant. Any longer-run proposition or policy proposal concentrating on the terms of trade as a strategic variable cannot hope to comprehend the economic forces at work without paying great attention to the role of population, and particularly to the classical Malthusian presumption that, unless checked, population tends to breed to the level of subsistence. Population helps determine the international division of the gains from trade— including the possibility of altering this distribution by the organization of producer (or producer-country) monopoly power.

An "Integrated" Commodity Policy

The Integrated Programme for Commodities,[3] proposed in 1975, has four general objectives:

(i) to encourage more orderly conditions in general in commodity trade, both with regard to prices and the volume of trade, in the interest of both producers and consumers; (ii) to ensure adequate growth in the real commodity export returns of individual developing countries; (iii) to reduce fluctuations in export earnings; and (iv) to improve access to markets of developed countries for developing country exports of primary and processed products.

These are restated in relation to commodity arrangements as follows:

(a) Reduction of excessive fluctuations in commodity prices and supplies, taking account of the special importance of this objective in the cases of essential foodstuffs and natural products facing competition from stable-priced substitutes;

(b) Establishment and maintenance of commodity prices at levels which, in real terms, are equitable to consumers and remunerative to producers...;

(c) Assurance of access to supplies of primary commodities for importing countries, with particular attention to essential foodstuffs and raw materials;

(d) Assurance of access to markets, especially those of developed countries, for commodity exporting countries;

(e) Expansion of the processing of primary commodities in developing countries;

---

3 Quotations and paraphrases in this section are taken from: "An Integrated Programme for Commodities: Specific Proposals for Decision and Action by Governments," Report by the Secretary General of UNCTAD (TD/B/C.1/193), October 28, 1975. Supporting documents are TD/B/C.1/194–97. It is sometimes argued, with apparent seriousness, that the wording and argument of documents of this kind should be disregarded as politically constrained pronouncements and that instead the economist should either concentrate his attention on the internal staff documents that are presumed to provide the scientific basis for the propaganda publications (but which unfortunately are generally not available for public scrutiny) or assume that such documentation exists and supports the propaganda publications. This argument is both disingenuous and inadmissible, quite apart from the published evidence that the UNCTAD directorate has deliberately suppressed expert scientific studies whose findings disagree with its published propaganda. The secretariat of an international institution must be held responsible for the scientific quality of the documents it puts into circulation, and it is certainly no part of a professional economist's responsibility to connive at that secretariat's efforts to pass off propaganda as scientific work.

(f) Improvement of the competitiveness of natural products vis-à-vis synthetics;

(g) Improvement of the quantity and reliability of food aid to developing countries in need.

However, "to ensure that no developing country experiences an adverse net effect from commodity pricing policies pursued within the integrated programme, differential measures in favour of developing importing countries... should be an accepted feature of international commodity arrangements established within the programme." These provisions would include "special measures for 'least developed' and 'most seriously affected' developing countries which are exporting or importing members" of arrangements within the integrated program. Specifically mentioned are exemption from sharing the financial costs and risks of stocks and preferred treatment in the allocation of export quotas.

Priority is to be given to 17 commodities of importance to developing countries in international trade, covering three-quarters of their exports from their agricultural and mineral sectors (*excluding petroleum*), with particular attention to 10 "core commodities": cocoa, coffee, tea, sugar, hard fibers, jute and manufactures, cotton, rubber, copper, tin. (The other seven are bananas, wheat, rice, meat, wool, iron ore, and bauxite.)

The specific proposals of the secretary general of UNCTAD for international action are as follows:

(a) The establishment of a common fund for the financing of international stocks;

(b) The setting up of a series of international commodity stocks;

(c) The negotiation of other measures necessary for the attainment of the objectives of the programme within the framework of international commodity agreements;

(d) Improved compensatory financing for the maintenance of stability in export earnings.

The common fund and the international stocking policies are regarded as the core of the program. The "other measures" essentially remove any "integrative" element of the program such as might be provided by a standard format for the individual stocking arrangements, leaving the common fund—described as "essential if impetus is to be given to the building up of international stocks of major storable commodities"—as the only integrative feature. The provision for "improved compensatory financing" for stabilizing export earnings is an indirect recognition of the fact that stabilizing—and even, on average, raising—the prices of commodities is an indirect and inefficient way of stabilizing and possibly increasing the flow of disposable income to the developing countries. Taken as a whole, the action program can without blatant unfairness be described as a demand for a massive investment of funds by the developed countries to underwrite experiments with and promotion of individual commodity-by-commodity agreements. The UNCTAD Secretariat and its developing-nation clientele are committed to these experiments in spite of an uneasy half-recognition that international commodity agreements —aside from the difficulty of devising and operating them— are an exceedingly doubtful instrument for promoting economic development.

The common fund, intended to encourage the development of stocking schemes by assuring finance, is crucial to the whole policy. The total sum mentioned is $3 billion—$1 billion of capital and $2 billion of loans. Although the point is made that the common fund would need less finance than the aggregate of the individual stocking schemes, how significant this pooling effect would be is doubtful, for two main reasons. One is that the fund is envisaged, not as a common pool of finance, but as a source for financing the individual commodity schemes; hence, there is no assurance that surplus financial assets in one scheme will be available to finance stocks of commodities in other schemes. The other reason is that the economies achievable by pooling finance are greater or less according as the financial needs of the pooling members vary inversely or directly with one another; and, as studies by Richard Cooper among others have shown (and as is evident from the business-cycle-related behavior of commodity prices in general), there is probably not that much scope for such economies among commodity agreements. (Pooling of foreign exchange reserves might offer more gains.) Mention should also be made of two mysterious allusions to presumptive advantages—the increased "bargaining strength" of the common fund and "redressing the balance between the developed and the developing countries."

Turning to stocking arrangements, the relevant paragraph reads as follows:

> International stocking measures are proposed for export commodities subject to natural variation in supply (e.g. tropical beverages, sugar, cotton, jute and hard fibers). They are also advocated for commodities with a history of disruption in output or demand, and where international stock management would help to prevent temporary restriction of production, wastage and uneconomic investment (copper, tin and rubber). Furthermore, security of basic food grain supplies at reasonable prices, entailing the creation of international stocks of wheat and rice, is in the interest of developing countries as importers, among other measures for assistance with food trade problems of importing countries.

The problem of storage of food grains against famine or scarcity conditions will not be dealt with here, since it is in principle a different problem from commodity price stabilization in general. In a manner that one has to learn to tolerate as measuring the economic illiteracy of the UNCTAD economic secretariat, the first two sentences of the above paragraph lump together two different economic problems —instability of supply and instability of demand—that require quite different solutions. It is unnecessary to repeat elementary economic analysis demonstrating that, apart from certain exceptional cases of constellation of demand and supply elasticities, stocking aimed at stabilizing prices will reduce the instability of producer incomes when the instability of prices is due to random or unforeseen cyclical demand shifts but will increase that instability of incomes when the instability of prices originates on the supply side. The later section of the document on "compensatory financing" in fact recognizes that "more stable world prices may not always [sic] stabilize earnings for an individual country if its export supply is adversely affected by poor crop conditions."

The section on "other measures for individual commodities" stresses supply management (including export quotas and uniform export taxes) and concludes that "By means of stocking, supply management or trade commitments, or by combinations of these measures, it should be possible, for some commodities at least, to achieve the objective of maintaining prices at adequate levels in real terms." Nevertheless, "in some cases it might not be possible to prevent a deterioration in the trend of prices in real terms, especially if world inflation continues to be relatively rapid." There is no explanation of why commodity prices, whose volatility it is the objective of the program to counteract, should be stickier than other prices in adjusting to inflation. This is curious, especially given the emphasis often placed in Prebisch-style arguments on the rigid, administered nature of the prices of manufactured goods. The main point, however, is that the argument of this section changes the intended purpose of commodity agreements from price stabilization for the commodities covered by the agreements, to the maintenance or raising of their real prices in terms of manufactured goods (or other goods in general). In other words, it becomes the maintenance of what in the history of American agricultural policy was described as "parity" between farm and industrial prices. As a later reference indicates, moreover, this objective is confused, either in ignorance or deliberately, with the notion of "indexing" of prices.

The section on "compensatory financing" refers generally to the "inadequacy" (undefined, except by implication) of existing provisions and asks for more emphasis on a commodity orientation and on real export earnings and for more liberal terms, including a grant element for the poorest countries.

Critical Discussion

Contemplation of the Integrated Programme for Commodities suggests any number of questions, of which only three general ones are raised here. The first is whether the developing-countries group, in its own interests, is well advised to press for a "new international economic order" based on the effort to exploit monopoly power in particular commodities on a "fair shares" basis. This is to be achieved, somehow, by agreement among exporting and importing nations with varying interests in particular commodities. The second, closely related, question is why it is that political figures (including the staff of UNCTAD) are so insistent on formulating questions of "exploitation" or, more neutrally, of "justice" in terms of schemes for rigging prices and adjusting supplies and production, in spite of the virtually axiomatic elementary economic principle that prices neither define the true problem nor provide an effective way to its solution. With respect to both questions, one might well venture the judgment that the ideas of Raúl Prebisch, especially as institutionalized and vulgarized through UNCTAD, have become an increasingly powerful obstacle to cooperation in the promotion of development. Specifically, sympathy with aspirations for development now has to be demonstrated by the acceptance of economic nonsense and the endorsement of proposals that not only maximize the prospective costs and minimize the prospective return for the developed countries but are certain to create dissension among them (witness the need to develop a new category of especially disadvantaged countries to reflect the differential impact among developing countries of the oil price increase).

The third question is why so little attention has been paid to the means by which an integrated program for commodities might be implemented. Instead, great effort is expended on arguing for new institutional arrangements and discussing the problems they are intended to deal with and the objectives they are intended to serve. As an apparently simple but in fact almost insoluble question, what should the manager of a commodity stock actually do, in his day-to-day operations, in order to smooth out price fluctuations? As shown by a protracted discussion of practical operating rules in the *Economic Journal* in the early 1950s, there is no easy solution, *even if* one vastly oversimplifies the problem by assuming that producers act in ignorance of the fact that the stockpile manager is operating to affect prices. One can, of course, assume that producer incomes do not matter, that the real purpose is to stabilize and increase the taxes that governments of developing countries can extract from their primary-commodity producers. Although that assumption is only too congenial to some varieties of economic-development specialists, it both prejudges the issue of what "development" means and how it is best achieved and makes nonsense of the moral rhetoric about the obligation of the rich to contribute resources to the poor.[4] To approach the point from a different angle, it is rather ironic that, at the same time as central banks and commercial banks have been abandoning, respectively, their conviction that they know how to intervene to stabilize exchange rates and their belief that they can outguess the private exchange speculators, the developing countries have been demanding changes that assume that international organizations can easily manage the very similar markets in commodities.

In view of these considerations, it seems that it would be most undesirable to accept the proposition that what is required is the organization of commodity trade in a series of stocking agreements reinforced by measures to restrict output and raise prices or to fix real prices of commodities in terms of manufactures or import goods in general. It would be equally undesirable, on the part of both the developed countries and the economists advising them, to implement that acceptance in the concrete form of subscribing a large sum of investment capital to finance commodity schemes. It would also disregard what comes close to being a professional consensus among those who have looked carefully into the problems that are supposed to be remedied by commodity policy. That consensus can be summarized briefly in two general principles. First, insofar as stability is concerned, compensatory financing related to unexpected shortfalls of foreign exchange earnings (and possibly, in some cases, excesses of import expenditure) is the most effective approach. Second, insofar as resource transfers from richer to poorer nations are concerned, aid related to needs and capacities to pay is far superior to transfers related to exports and imports of particular commodities. Awareness of either principle is scarcely reflected in the assertion that existing compensatory financing arrangements are "inadequate."

If we need, "constructively," to make some concession to the proposition that commodity arrangements could, under favorable circumstances and with intelligent manage-

---

4 There is nothing morally commanding about a presumed obligation of taxpayers and consumers in countries whose average citizen is well off to surrender resources to the governments and ruling elites of countries whose average citizen is poor—especially if the latter's poverty is maintained and increased by his government's policies.

ment, ease the problems of the governments, perhaps even the publics, of developing countries, one approach might be to contribute resources generously to further research on the management principles and operating rules required to achieve what such agreements are intended to achieve. What does a price-stabilization stocking arrangement have to do, in terms of deciding when and how much to buy or sell, to be successful in achieving its objective? How should it conduct its operations to minimize the destabilizing effects of its running out of cash or out of commodity?[5] Another important question, raised by the prospective simultaneous existence of agreements covering a majority or all of the commodities most important in developing-country trade, is the requirement of consistency among the actions of the different stocking schemes, for example, those projected for coffee, tea, and cocoa (or even more seriously, among the 17 major commodities, those for hard fiber, jute, and wool). This kind of question becomes far more significant if the objective of the commodity agreements is to raise and not to stabilize prices. In that event, questions would also arise about the development effects of export quotas, taxes, and related arrangements for restricting exports or production. The UNCTAD literature tends to ignore the effects of such adjuncts to price-raising schemes: the creation of uncertainty for production-planning and investment decisions by producers, not to speak of the reduction of income-earning opportunities for at least some groups of producers.

Another approach, though one not likely to command much interest in the confrontational setting of the United Nations and with the limited economic understanding of

---

5 Some experts believe that the problem with commodities is that there is not enough speculation, in the sense that speculation takes too short-run a perspective and hence tends to produce destabilizing "bandwagon" effects on prices. An alternative way of putting this point is that markets function reasonably well in fair weather but go wild when disasters strike. If this proposition is accepted, it raises very serious doubt about the probable effectiveness of commodity-stock arrangements; such arrangements necessarily assume that a stock of finite size, related to normal trade volumes, is sufficient to provide the desired degree of stability, whereas the contention is that it is deviations *outside* the normal range of variation that cause the serious trouble—and would in turn require a capacity for market intervention far transcending that of a normally constituted buffer stock.

the UNCTAD staff, would be to concentrate on some fundamental questions. Why do commodity prices fluctuate as much as they do? How far and in what respects have such fluctuations had the undeniable adverse development effects that UNCTAD lore—and earlier popular beliefs about the development problem—invariably and sweepingly attribute to them? What, if anything, can be done to mitigate the fluctuations by tackling the basic causes rather than the symptoms (in the form of price fluctuations themselves)? One might suggest that both the instability and the low level (by comparison with aspirations or expectations) of the commodity-export earnings of developing countries are associated with limits on access to alternative income-producing opportunities. In the exporting developing countries, this is a consequence partly of the low level of economic development itself, as reflected in relative current scarcity of industrial skills (including the skills required by modern agriculture) and partly of a rapid rate of population growth, which both inhibits the development of skills and creates an elastic supply of low-income-earning labor. This, in turn, would suggest a constructive, although indirect, response to less-developed-country demands: substantial support for population control policies and for programs of mass elementary education with an emphasis on vocational training.

Prospects

What chances are there, if any, of a return to what seems in retrospect more and more of a "golden age" in world economic development, the period of stable growth of the late 1950s and early 1960s? And what, if anything, could developing nations do to support and facilitate a restoration of such conditions?

On the first question, I am sorry to have to say that I am rather pessimistic. There are two reasons for this. The first has already been touched on in relation to Latin American experience. It is the danger of the world economy settling into a quasi equilibrium of stop-go inflation, in which political democracy is maintained by letting first the stable-money advocates and then the growth, full-employment, and social justice school take turns in setting the levers of economic policy. The key question here concerns the political situation and likely political developments in the United States in the 1976 election. The Ford administration of 1974–76 managed to stick fairly firmly and consistently to the policy of not allowing recovery from the recession to override the need to break inflationary expectations and the inflation process. But this was partly due to administration preoccupation with other issues, which left the way relatively free for independent restrictive monetary policy. Demands for faster expansion or, more insidiously, for further cushions against the effects of unemployment that would threaten to destroy its anti-inflationary lesson-value, have been mounting; and the successor administration, which at the time of writing is widely expected to be a Carter administration, may well attempt to accelerate recovery by inflationary monetary expansion.

The other reasons for doubt concern the current lines of evolution of the international monetary system and are too complex to go into fully here. Briefly, the International Monetary Fund was specifically designed to forestall reemergence of the international liquidity shortage that underlay the Depression. It has ever since been on the side of expansion of international liquidity as a cure for the world's ills, even though the problem has become the converse of the 1930s' problem—namely, excessive expansion of international liquidity, supporting world inflation. And this proinflationary stance has been reinforced by the natural tendency of the IMF, like other international and quasi-governmental national institutions, to try to strengthen its political support and acceptability by catering to the special interests of politically powerful groups of constituents. Specifically, it has been cultivating support in two areas by potentially extremely inflationary devices. First, it has been steadily enlarging its role as a lender of international liquidity on concessionary terms to developing countries with balance-of-payments difficulties. Second, it has collaborated in the development of a compromise between the European desire to restore gold to a significant role as a form of international liquidity and the American desire to demonetize gold and reduce it to a commodity like any other, a compromise that, stripped of its technical detail and mystery, amounts to adding official gold reserves back into the total of usable international liquidity at something like four times their original monetary value.

What, if anything, can the less-developed countries do to facilitate a return to conditions of stable world economic growth? Again, my answer has to be pessimistic. There is little these countries can do other than encourage or oppose policies adopted or recommended in the advanced countries, on grounds of an overall world interest that should be given consideration along with national self-interest. Unfortunately, however, the attitudes of the developing countries have an indirect influence, inasmuch as national self-seeking on their part sets a tone or climate for national self-seeking by the individual developed countries. In this respect, one can, if one wants to be brutally realistic, discern a tragic sequence. The self-seeking of the developing countries—or, more accurately, of those of their politicians and intellectuals who have concentrated their attention on seeking painless development and affluence, by speechifying with high moral indignation in demand of special transfers and treatment on the basis of alleged past economic wrongs—this self-seeking has gradually closed off one after another of the avenues of genuine help from the advanced countries. Thus, the demand for aid without strings has increasingly turned into the reality of less and less aid of any kind; the demand for unilateral trade preferences for the manufactures of the developing countries in the markets of the advanced countries has turned into the reality of carefully restricted access to markets and the development of a neo-neocolonialism in the form of affiliate membership in the European Economic Community. The demands for control over technological transfer and over the activities of multinational corporations in developing countries is likely to mean the gradual retreat of the multinational corporation and its technology from operations in the developing countries (with the probable exception of the Southeast Asian countries of Chinese cultural origin, which are tough enough and confident enough to take their chances in free international competition). On the specific problem of world inflation, the danger is that the developing-country group will be so fascinated with their rediscovery of the age-old fallacy that the creation of money is a way of getting something for nothing—something real for something paper—that they will provide indirect support for international and advanced-country domestic monetary policies that will guarantee the continuation of world inflation on a stop-go basis.

In conclusion, I offer a speculative thought for readers to contemplate. Since the industrial revolution, the world economy has enjoyed two periods of fairly steady and sustained economic growth—a long one following the end of the Napoleonic wars and a much shorter one following the end of the Second World War and the Korean War. In each case, the expansion period was ended—and succeeded by a period of inflation, depression, economic nationalism, *ad hoc* policymaking and general economic confusion—as a result of a war that very soon after its start was fairly clearly seen by thinking people as having been a ghastly mistake. The thought I offer is the very simple one that if economists want to achieve a better and deeper understanding of the economics of peace and growth, they need to devote more time and effort than they have yet done to the economics—and the politics and sociology—of war and its economic disturbances.

Karl Brunner

The New International Economic Order:

A Chapter in a Protracted Confrontation

For a century, Marxian literature has predicted the collapse of capitalism and outlined the process that would ultimately destroy a social system organized by markets and based on "private property in the means of production." But most Marxian propositions that permitted some assessment have been falsified by events, which were, of course, suitably reinterpreted *ex post facto* in order to save the language required for the "revolutionary purpose." Adjustments in Marxian theory and rhetoric have included a recognition of the role of the intelligentsia and the instrumental use of mass education facilities. The attention of the "socialist struggle for human liberation and the termination of pre-history" gradually moved beyond the "industrial proletariat" to address and incorporate other social institutions or groups.

The crucial function of intellectuals in the erosion of capitalism was fully understood by Joseph Schumpeter. The doctrine of the "march through the intellectual institutions" emerged in Germany almost two decades after Schumpeter's prophetic analysis. His account of the role played by "pro-

Reprinted, with some changes, by permission of the author and *Orbis,* from volume No. 20 of *Orbis, A Journal of World Affairs,* published by the Foreign Policy Research Institute.

fessional articulators" in the evolution of capitalism toward destruction still offers remarkable insights and many stimulating suggestions for contemporary readers. The intelligentsia's role also underlies a more recent phenomenon that cannot be subsumed under the standard Marxian scheme. The socialist assault on capitalism, apart from the entrenched and well-observed aggressive hostility of the Communist bloc, has been spearheaded in recent years by the Third World. We owe some recognition of this circumstance to Daniel P. Moynihan's searching examination in a widely and properly acclaimed article.[1]

The exposure of intellectual elites in the Third World to the influence of Western intellectual traditions extended the "Schumpeterian process" to non-Communist regions outside the established industrial nations. The socialist rhetoric cultivated by representatives of many "new countries" can hardly be missed. Socialist conceptions, moreover, are unmistakably revealed by the trend in economic policy and the prevalent forms of economic organization. This evolution may have affected the position of the United States in some respects. For many years the world's intelligentsia has nurtured an anti-American attitude and expressed political sympathies adverse to long-run U.S. interests. As the leading capitalist country, the United States is a major affront, or possibly an obstruction, to socialist aspirations. Still, without the vast institutional apparatus offered by the United Nations organization, the evolution sketched above would probably have minor significance for the United States. The socialist infiltration and exploitation of the UN apparatus give leverage to the anticapitalism onslaught. The United States thus faces a serious and protracted conflict bearing on fundamental societal issues.

The evolution of the United Nations organization offers a good example of the "institutional weapon." Institutions are created according to some well-meaning intentions, but, once created, they determine incentives guiding their use and development in very different and unanticipated directions. Over the past fifteen years the UN has increasingly suggested or approved ideas involving coercive transfers of

---

1 "The United States in Opposition," *Commentary*, March 1975; reprinted in this vol.

wealth from the "developed" to the "developing" countries. This bias increasingly confronts the United States with a fundamental conflict concerning the future of American society. The institutional facilities of the United Nations are systematically used to launch persistent and wide-ranging assaults on the "injustice and oppressiveness" of U.S. capitalism, which contrasts so sharply, it is implied, with the glowing "justice and liberation" achieved in "socialist countries."

One wonders whether the media and our representatives understand the seriousness of the challenge. The traditional bureaucracies and diplomats in the State Department seem either unwilling or unable to cope with the situation. Any forceful attention to the challenge violates the traditional pattern of diplomatic procedures, and this may explain the blandly uncertain stance cultivated on many occasions by U.S. representatives.[2] Such uncertainty may also be conditioned to some extent by institutional incentives that determine an overlapping range of interests for national and international bureaucracies and operate to weaken the attention devoted by some national bureaucracies to *national* interests. It also explains the reaction of bureaucracies and old-line European diplomats to former Ambassador Moynihan's statements. Moynihan apparently understood the nature of the challenge and the prospects of the confrontation. Substantially more than bland acceptance of socialist condemnatory rhetoric is involved in this failure of U.S. administrations and representatives. The rhetoric accompanies persistent attempts to expand the institutional apparatus of international organizations. Moreover, such expansion would gradually impose, at least in explicit intention, increasing constraints on our domestic arrangements. The "march through the international institutions" thus becomes one of the means eventually to overcome U.S. capitalism and to transform American society to the levels

---

2 The report published by the correspondent of the *Neue Zürcher Zeitung* in August 1975 on the occasion of the UN Conference on Crime Prevention held in Geneva is most revealing in this respect. It summarizes the onslaught on Western countries and the United States in particular and notes the silence among Western representatives, stating specifically that they refused to respond to the barrage in order "to avoid polemics." This attitude reveals a serious failure to comprehend the new international reality or a serious misjudgment concerning the strategy with which to meet these onslaughts.

of "justice, equality, and liberty" allegedly achieved or achievable under the socialist theories guiding many representatives of the Third World. Even if the rhetoric were just an instrument to encourage the U.S. intelligentsia's supply of guilt feelings and thus to foster transfers of wealth, such transfers require institutional arrangements modifying the longer-run nature of our society.

International Socialism

The general pattern governing UN institutions may be exemplified by two resolutions adopted by the General Assembly on May 1. The Assembly adopted the "Declaration on the Establishment of a New International Economic Order" designed "to eliminate the widening gap between developed and developing countries." The declaration recognizes that "remaining vestiges of...colonial domination... and neocolonialism in all its forms" are among the "greatest obstacles to the full emancipation and progress of the developing countries." It also asserts that an "even and balanced development" is impossible to achieve "under the existing international economic order" and emphasizes that the inherited economic order "is in direct conflict with current developments in political relations." It is then proposed that developing countries participate actively, fully, and equally "in the formulation and application of all decisions that concern the international community." And so we read that "international cooperation for development is the shared goal and common duty of all countries." The "broadest cooperation of all States,...whereby the prevailing disparities in the world may be banished," should be forthcoming, and the "full permanent sovereignty of every State over its natural resources and all economic activities" should be respected.

Secondly the General Assembly launched itself on a supplementary resolution introduced as a "Programme of Action on the Establishment of a New International Economic Order." Colonialism and neocolonialism are again properly exorcised and condemned. The actions proposed are subdivided into categories covering trade and raw materials, transportation, the international monetary system, regulation of multinational corporations, and an array of means strengthening the UN system in the field of international economic cooperation. The provisions under the first item are intended to assure larger real revenues from exports and more aid and financial contributions in one form or another. Transportation costs are to be lowered (somehow), at least for the developing countries. In the range of international monetary problems, developing countries are to be "fully involved as equal partners" in all decision making. Return to a system of fixed exchange rates is mentioned with some emphasis. This proposal requires supplementary attention to the provision of international liquidity, with a link to financial grants for developing countries. The "link" is thus naturally tied to the restoration of fixed exchange rates. The last section of the action program lists an extensive schedule for utilizing or expanding UN institutions and in this manner raising the leverage to be exercised by Third World countries.

In case some innocent reader of the UN resolutions misses the meaning of the exercise—with its beautiful phrases about justice, peace, equality, liberty, and humanity, enunciated by representatives of a large assortment of minor and major tyrants—we can fortunately refer to the useful interpretation supplied by a self-styled moralist. On March 17, 1975, Gunnar Myrdal delivered his Nobel Memorial Lecture, "The Equality Issue in World Development." Myrdal's world view opens with the old "colonial empires" neglecting or possibly exploiting their less-developed regions, which "stagnated in poverty." The spreading independence of the postwar period encouraged an awareness of the inequality between developed and other countries. A moral issue emerged, and it should dominate our attention. Myrdal acknowledges that some aid was given over the years, but he finds such aid thoroughly inadequate and usually given for the wrong motives (except, of course, by Sweden). Both morality and rationality, in his view, demand the establishment of a new world order, which should be designed to remove inequality and introduce an egalitarian justice.

The moral requirement follows from the egalitarian principle, and the rationale from Myrdal's judgment that substantial reductions in Western societies' consumption levels are "in the best interests individually and collectively" of all members of these societies. Implementation of such moral and rational demands requires national planning to achieve lower levels of consumption, thus releasing resources for transfer to the developing countries. He notes that the West, in particular the United States, would have to be prepared "to initiate and cooperate in planned intergovernmental action in a way pointing towards 'a new world order' asked for by the underdeveloped countries, which in turn would necessitate the rational restriction of our lavish utilization of resources." The new world order thus introduces a system of "integrated national planning" for the sole purpose of effecting a massive transfer of wealth from the industrialized nations to the majority of members of the United Nations. Myrdal understands quite clearly that this "new order" cannot be realized without vast institutional changes covered by the expression "national intergovernmental planning." He observes in passing that an economic organization relying on markets seems not to be conducive to "rational actions" bearing on consumption demands.

The issue confronting the United States is thus clearly defined. We are addressed by a majority of members of the United Nations and "intellectual or moral leaders" to accept in essence and initiate a transition into a socialist world and a socialist society. It may be appropriate at this point to clarify the use of the term "socialist" in this discussion. Two closely associated characteristics of social organization crucially determine important aspects of human life: the extent to which allocation and use of resources are guided by market prices, and the range or content of private property rights. There is no society without markets and some price-guided activities and, similarly, no society without private property rights (or entitlements) to resources or use of resources.[3] It is important in this respect to understand the nature and consequences of an "entitlement structure"; consequences vary substantially with the range, explicit-

---

3 Observers of the German Democratic Republic note that janitors at the Leipzig Trade Fair charge about $80 for "private use right" to a toilet for the fair's duration. Speedier access to medical doctors requires side-payments; so does more rapid attention by automobile mechanics. Along with the official and formally decreed system, an informal market system has emerged based on de facto entitlements of the janitor, the medical doctor, mechanics, and others. They all control *some* dimension of resource use, which determines opportunities for transactions.

ness, predictability, stability, and tradeability of the entitlements.

Socialist programs essentially lower the various dimensions of private entitlements and also lower the range open to market determinations. This description implicitly rejects the Lange-Lerner conception of a market-oriented socialist society. Their notion is certainly possible, but it should be recognized that it possesses little empirical relevance. The erosion of private entitlements to resources and their use is usually accompanied, as a matter of empirical fact, by the replacement of markets and market-determined prices with a political-administrative allocation mechanism. This attrition of private entitlements, according to socialist literature and rhetoric, is a necessary condition for the transition from "prehistory to human history"—a necessary condition to assure human dignity and a "meaningful level of the quality of life."

This view has infiltrated the discussion at UN conferences on a wide range of issues, be it population, food, pollution, or crime. It is also clearly reflected in the documents emerging from UNCTAD, UNIDO, or the General Assembly bearing on the proposed New International Economic Order. The challenge confronting the United States should be fully recognized and accepted. We should also unhesitatingly accept the criteria advanced for judging a social organization, viz., criteria stated in terms of "human dignity and the quality of life." It is true that these terms are vague and somewhat ambivalent and thus require further circumscription for adequate analysis, but this is hardly the purpose of the current discussion. It is sufficient here to emphasize most decisively that the case for capitalism should not shirk these standards. On the contrary, usefully formulated in a nonevasive mode, they should be fully embraced as the relevant standards of our judgment.

In this respect, there is indeed a moral issue in the choice between social organizations, and it subsumes a cognitive obligation to analyze with reliable means the *comparative* operation of different institutional structures. This analysis extends to the human patterns fostered by different arrangements, the attitudes reinforced, and the values permitted. It is in these very terms that the case for capitalism should and can be made. But so far we see little evidence that U.S.

representatives at international organizations and conferences understand the nature of the challenge or find it useful to fit the confrontation into their accustomed political
game. Their neglect is, in my judgment, not entirely harm-
less for our long-run interests.

Explaining Social Relations

A dominant and basic theme of much of the rhetoric offered
by the Third World is the Marxist-Leninist idea of exploitation. By the Leninist extension of Marx's original notion to
international relations, the difference in wealth between
Western industrial nations and the Third World is explained
in terms of a colonial history, or more generally, in terms of
subtle and pervasive forms of political coercion. Western
exploitation impoverished the Third World and enriched
the Western nations. The story is impressionistically plausible and has influenced public attitudes substantially
beyond faithful members of the Leninist branch of the
Marxist church. One frequently encounters the assertion
that the colonies and politically dependent territories stagnated in poverty, with progress occurring only after independence. Myrdal's Nobel lecture elaborates on this theme,
and the rhetoric of the above-mentioned UN resolutions
clearly reflects this view.

"Decolonization" is introduced as a necessary and primary condition of economic progress. Such progress seems
impossible to achieve under a colonial regime. But it also
appears that abolition of colonialism is not sufficient. The
socialist doctrine claims that exploitation continues in new
forms, covered by the term "neocolonialism." Neocolonialism emerges whenever private transactions occur between
"developed" and "developing" nations. It occurs in particular whenever private corporations do business in developing
nations. In a sense, the label is attached to every transaction
proceeding with the expectation of a *quid pro quo*. Abolition
of neocolonialism thus involves by definition the desired
transfer of wealth to the Third World—a flow of real resources
without a *quid* for the *quo*.

It is clear that these notions offer opportunities to justify
an extraction of wealth. They also offer to established elites

and bureaucracies in the Third World opportunities for enrichment.[4] These opportunities are partly conditioned by the somewhat bemused responses encountered among members of our intelligentsia. The basic theme likewise justifies the developing countries' claim to "reparations" as compensation for the "obvious damages" wrought by colonialism and neocolonialism. The flexible definition of "neo-colonialism in all its forms" and the claim for reparations embodied in the UN resolutions back up an open-ended invitation and provide incentives to use expanding UN facilities for an unending stream of action programs that will raise political pressures on Western governments. The persistent demands also maintain the attention of Western media and professional articulators.

The prospects of a protracted confrontation suggest that the socialist rhetoric with its apparently substantive claims should not be blithely disregarded in the manner cultivated by U.S. representatives at UN happenings. It seems important that the claims and the associated rhetoric be forcefully and explicitly contested. One wonders occasionally whether Western representatives are sufficiently aware of the dubious case underlying the standard rhetoric. Some general indications of the weakness of the socialist claims would seem appropriate in this context.

We should note first that, according to socialist doctrine, "exploitation" occurs whenever resources (means of production) are owned privately. All transactions occurring under capitalist arrangements are thus necessarily exploitative. The extent of exploitation can be measured by the portion of national income absorbed by ownership of resources. It is important to recognize that this language has a motivating purpose, directing moral-political actions. It implies that abolition of "private property in means of production" liberates the working mass and generally raises economic welfare and human dignity. But while the Marxian story is plausible, as are many other stories, it fails precisely in its most vaunted virtues. Marxian writers emphasize the superior insights into crucial social relations summarized

---

4 The reader may wish to refer to Omotunde Johnson's instructive investigation, "The Economics of Corrupt Government," *Kyklos* 28 (1975), fasc. 1.

by the *Produktionsverhältsusse*—the relation between men determined by their relation to productive resources. But the Marxian account misses completely the important entitlement structure shaping the political, social, and economic process and therefore fails to offer any systematic account of political-economic events or processes under socialism.

It is not a matter of chance that socialist writings and the rhetoric about the socialist state barely penetrate beyond some essentially metaphorical or metaphysical elaboration mixed with a touch of the Nirvana approach. Neither is it a matter of chance that Marxian, and more generally socialist, literature cultivates a "Karamasov fallacy." One notes instances of injustice, frustration, or unhappiness advanced as evidence against capitalism. One also notes that in a socialist country specific groups of the population enjoy more decent housing than before the "socialist liberation." This is suggestively used to prove that the whole pattern is generally improved. Although such comments and observations are a useful ploy in a political struggle, they provide little information bearing on a systematic assessment of alternative institutional arrangements and economic organizations. Such assessment is not possible within a Marxian or socialist framework. The doctrine offers no intellectual handle on and no analytic perception about the working of socialist institutions, no understanding of the incentives emerging under these institutions and the resulting nature of the social process. It therefore usually fails to offer any relevant interpretation of the problems typically arising under socialist organizations. The permanent agricultural crisis in the USSR offers a good example of the general situation.

Attempts by Marxian philosophers to struggle seriously and honestly with the institutional workings and modes of behavior determined under socialist regimes reveal in explicit detail the flaws of Marxian sociology. The sociological model of man used in this literature obscures reality and prevents intellectual access to men's responses to the incentives provided by different institutional arrangements. It is unable to explain the system of side-payments and "unofficial or private" transactions arising under socialist institutions, the patterns of corruption dictated by these arrangements, the power structure or the nature of political competition, and similar problems.[5]

Comparative Merits of Capitalism

A semireligious attitude or commitment, which frequently replaces the necessary analysis and evidence, is scarcely conducive to a useful and rational assessment of alternative social systems. But such an assessment over a broad range determines the essential case for capitalism. It is not a case based on guaranteed and uniform justice, happiness, liberty, and the like; rather, it emphasizes that a system based on wide-ranging private property rights diffuses arbitrary power more effectively than any alternative social organization. While "justice, liberty, and equality" are not guaranteed, such a system offers more opportunities, and more persistent opportunities, for justice. And it offers them at a lower cost—that is, at a lower level of forfeited or sacrificed human values. It also opens up more alternatives, again at a lower cost, than the institutional arrangements typically imposed by a socialist regime. In particular, it holds out a broader range of alternatives for work and in lifestyles, which erodes patterns of servility and subjugation.

The "open institutions" of capitalism do not assure equality, but they loosen established and inherited inequalities to a larger extent than the "closed institutions" of socialist societies, which are justified with an egalitarian rhetoric. Moreover, the private cost of dissent—expressed in terms of opportunities sacrificed by engaging in political, intellectual, moral, or artistic dissent—is certainly positive in *any* social system ever realized or still to be realized. This circumstance frequently encourages a peculiar blindness, revealed by absolutist assertions that freedom or liberty is equally missing in most social systems. But the occurrence,

---

5 An examination of this sociological model may be found in a paper prepared by William Meckling for the Second International Interlaken Seminar on Analysis and Ideology (June 1975): "Values and the Choice of the Model of Man in the Social Sciences," *Schweizerische Zeitschrift für Volkswirtschaft und Statistik*, 1976. A full session of the Third International Interlaken Seminar on Analysis and Ideology (June 1976) explored the issue still further with papers presented by coauthors Gerard Gäfgen and Hans Georg Monissen and by Willi Meyer. Among the serious writings by Marxian philosophers are some published by the group at the University of Belgrade—with specific reference to Stojanovich.

even under the best of circumstances, of positive private costs of social dissent should not blind us to the large differences in these costs. Their magnitude is systematically associated with the prevailing pattern of the entitlement structure, and they tend to vary with the range, content, and reliability of private property rights. A persistent erosion of such rights eventually raises the cost of dissent and nonconformist behavior in politics, morals, literature, and the arts.

Lastly, the greater opportunities and wider range of alternatives available at lower cost to the average man under a system of private property rights assures better protection of human dignity than can be expected under an essentially political-administrative apparatus. The manifest preference of established bureaucracies and intellectual elites in the Third World for socialist arrangements should be quite understandable, for the attrition of private property rights and the replacement of markets with political-administrative institutions raises the power of both bureaucracy and elite. An extensive reliance on markets erodes such powers and lowers opportunities for wealth transfers and enrichment via political activities. Some members of the elite and the bureaucracies recognize the potential for large rewards—at the cost of the average citizen—under socialist arrangements.

A suitable and highly articulated rhetoric obfuscates the transfer of internal wealth to established elites and bureaucracies. It is also an important instrument in the intellectual offensive directed at international wealth transfer. Under the circumstances, it is vital to understand precisely the human achievement of the social organization covered by the "capitalism" label. We will undoubtedly find pockets of oppression and injustice in capitalist economies. The world's intelligentsia has persistently emphasized the evils perpetrated in Chile, in Greece under the military junta, in Rhodesia, South Africa, and Spain, and possibly also in Brazil. One can indeed observe oppression in these countries, and the cost of dissent is probably higher than elsewhere in Western Europe or the United States. But in its hysterical rhetoric, the world's intelligentsia has apparently abandoned a sense of proportion in judging the human situation. The cost of nonconformist behavior in these countries is substantially below the level prevailing in countries accepting the Marxian faith or in numerous socialist countries claiming membership in the Third World.

This observation justifies no complacency about our own institutions or acceptance of the social patterns in the above countries, but it needs some emphasis. It reminds us that a wider range of private property rights is not sufficient to remove substantial political constraints on individual activities. Yet these countries also offer useful elaborations on our theme. For one thing, within them, an important area of daily life associated with individuals' work and economic activities remains free from detailed coercion and harassment. Political discussions within small or private groups are to a substantial extent feasible at little risk and very small cost. There is intermittently even a measure of public discussion of nontrivial social or political issues. Moreover —and this is a crucial point—the persistence of a diffuse range of private and reliable entitlements lowers the survival probability of the confining political system. The pervasive property rights prevent an "institutionalization" of the political system and thus raise the chance of transition to a political-social organization with greater freedom, that is, entailing a smaller cost for nonconformist behavior.

We notice some serious discussions and a hopeful expectation about Spain's emergence from the ossified forms of a Falangist dictatorship. Similar developments in Chile and Brazil are not entirely improbable. Does anyone seriously contend that Yugoslavia will "open its institutions" after Tito's death or that the Soviet Union will let "a thousand flowers bloom" after Brezhnev's death? The answer is obvious, and the difference in opportunities and prospects is anchored in the prevailing entitlement patterns. We are eventually led to realize that a *Gulag Archipelago* typically emerges under a socialist regime, and with it develops the systematic use of arbitrary terror to browbeat citizens into well-patterned conformity.[6]

---

6 A short comment should be added apropos of Rhodesia-Zimbabwe and South Africa. That apartheid involves a wealth transfer to the white population was clearly recognized by the South African labor unions in the 1920s. At the time, the market operated toward gradual integration, and this occurred most particularly on the "marriage-market." But recognition of the internal wealth transfer implicit in apartheid should not blind us to the fact that the economic welfare of the blacks in South Africa, on the average, probably exceeds the levels reached (or descended to) in any other African country.

It seems important to stress that patterns of subjugation and servility fostered by vast political-administrative machineries lower access to alternatives over a wide range of life. The emergence of such machineries is implicit in Myrdal's program. His authoritarian position is clearly revealed by his peculiar conception of "rationality"—meaning that his judgment and the judgment of his friends should prevail. The average consumer "needs to be told what's good for him." Myrdal effectively exemplifies the group of professional articulators who fail to appreciate that most people have a definite idea concerning the quality of *their* life. Many prefer life-shortening consumption habits to the chance of experiencing senile uselessness. Many prefer skiing, mountain climbing, car racing, or flying to a safe, stodgily "rational" existence. Myrdal brought into focus a central issue of our time by pointing up the arrogant claim of "intellectual and moral leaders" to control the fate of our societies. Proposals to institute a comprehensive administrative control apparatus are a natural consequence of this claim and of the supporting view that most people are ignorant and incapable of addressing their own interests.

Colonialism and Neocolonialism

In this context, the colonialist theme so ardently cultivated by the Third World deserves our particular attention. It determines the moral fervor and offers a justification of the claim for a New International Economic Order, but the rhetoric of "colonial" or "neocolonial" exploitation by Western industrial nations is a legend substantially falsified by historical events. According to the standard exploitation thesis, poverty and economic stagnation should increase in relation to the density of transactions with capitalist economies. Yet we systematically observe the opposite. Over the past hundred years, regions with the least commerce, the

---

One should also note the intriguing statement made in Mozambique by one of the black leaders of Rhodesia-Zimbabwe. Making clear that a rigid socialist regime will be instituted in Zimbabwe, he warned particularly that it would have no room for assorted competing black politicians whose socialist ideology is suspect. A comparison of future patterns in Mozambique, Zimbabwe, and Angola with the life patterns feasible in "oppressive white Rhodesia" or apartheid South Africa will certainly be interesting.

smallest exposure to capitalism, and only marginal transactions with Western nations have remained the poorest and most truly stagnating areas (e.g., Ethiopia, Afghanistan). Almost without exception the colonies experienced substantial economic progress under colonial status and benefitted from a net flow of real resources from industrial economies. The dramatic expansion of population, the improvement of life expectancy, the appearance of public transportation and modern cities, resulted from economic relations with the West. Western investments raised real income beyond the levels that would otherwise have been achieved. This description holds regardless of the regular repatriation of certain profits earned on these investments. Similarly, the use of exhaustible resources contributes to rising real income, at least over time. And with suitable reinvestments of savings accruing from raised levels of real income, real income could be raised permanently.[7]

We conclude that there is little merit in the well-publicized idea that Western countries effected a transfer of wealth from the colonies to their own economies, a transfer impoverishing the colonies and enriching the mother countries. The remarkable economic progress of capitalist economies over the last 150 years seems to support the exploitation thesis, but only if one fails to recognize the parallel development in the colonies. When real income per capita in Western economies rose persistently, this economic progress, in spite of Marxian predictions to the contrary, also benefitted the colonies. In any case, all the relevant indicators show an increase in economic welfare for these regions. In contrast to some popular beliefs, trade *is* mutually beneficial. Moreover, decolonization often produced economic stagnation and even economic decline. The sub-Saharan region, Sri Lanka, Burma, Uganda, Bangladesh, and Pakistan are outstanding examples of this. Other countries may fare a little better, but even those like Algeria or India show little progress in comparison with previous phases of their economic evolution, whereas a colony like Hong Kong has continued to thrive.

---

7 This issue is discussed effectively by Peter Bauer, who for many years has studied the problems confronting developing economies. See his "Western Guilt and Third World Poverty," *Commentary*, January 1976; reprinted in this volume.

These divergent patterns exemplify the irrelevance for economic progress of colonial status and decolonization. Such progress is crucially conditioned, instead, by the policies and institutions developed. The comparative stagnation following decolonization in numerous cases resulted from a pronounced shift to "socialist programs and institutions" or from a rapid increase of political instability and uncertainties about the "social rules of the game."

A notion evidently cherished in UN resolutions refers to a member country's right to "sovereignty over its resources." One might respond with a shrug of the shoulders and easily assent to an obvious meaning. But the phrase involves a rather specific meaning subtly associated with the exploitation thesis. "Sovereignty over resources" is realized by "nationalization" and suitable ownership by "government." Moreover, "determination of one's own economic fate" is exercised by a system of political-administrative controls over the size and allocation of (nonhuman and human) resources. The rhetoric cultivated by the UN resolutions thus supports a concentration of de facto entitlements to the use of resources in the hands of a ruling oligarchy and its articulators and bureaucracies. "Sovereignty" and "determination" involve the establishment of a socialist economy with eroded private property rights and a political-administrative machinery replacing markets over a wide range of activities, subjecting the vast majority of inhabitants to the political machinations of a ruling oligarchy using these means to foster its political position and enrich its patronage and clientele.

Still, the notions appeal to wide circles wherein it is apparently difficult to grasp that a developing economy could hardly advance its welfare better than by letting foreigners buy its natural resources and thus involve their active interests in economic development. Whether this inflow of foreign capital necessarily leads to political influence and domination depends very much on the prevalent institutions. Foreign business firms will invest in political influence and manipulations only to the extent that such investments are expected to bear returns. The "relative density" of government in society is the crucial factor. In the face of a comparatively small government sector and modest regulatory powers, investment in political manipulations brings little return and remains on a small or even vanishing scale. The political problem posed by foreign business firms operating in a developing country results essentially from the established and pervasive influence of bureaucracies and government officials. It increases with a socialist trend in policy and institutions, becoming an "endemic disease" of such institutions as the operators of the government's administrative machinery find it advantageous to exploit opportunities determined by their position. Yet such (illicit) transactions probably raise general economic welfare above the levels achievable in the context of a rigid "sovereignty over resources" and a militant "determination of economic fate."

The exploitation theme also shapes the issue raised about terms of trade. It is occasionally asserted that Western industrialized nations manipulate the terms of trade to their advantage and impoverish the raw-material-producing Third World. But the terms of trade of primary producers were, according to Sir Arthur Lewis, much more favorable in the 1950s than for the previous eighty years, and they improved even further in the late 1960s. The overall picture covers a diversity of experiences for different parts of the developing regions. Moreover, deliberate manipulation of the terms of trade by industrial nations for their benefit implies rising export tariffs on manufactured goods in conjunction with rising import tariffs on raw and primary materials. Yet we find no such pattern. There remains the obnoxious fact that the United States, Australia, and Canada are major suppliers of some primary commodities on the world market. Under the circumstances, "manipulation of the terms of trade" should be dismissed as a politically useful fabrication.[8]

An Alternative

The conflict regarding the foundations of social and economic organization cannot be exorcised with pious platitudes. We may prefer tranquillity, serenity, undisturbed quiet with all contentious engagements far removed, but the issues bear on our lives and the prospects for our society.

---

8 Bauer's discussion of this issue (ibid.) is again noteworthy.

What should be the position of the United States on these issues? Certainly it would be desirable for Washington to reexamine the trend emerging in recent years in various UN organizations. We should seriously question the wisdom of blandly following this trend with only muted reservations. But what might be a feasible alternative to a thoughtless accommodation? An alternative action program expressing the long-run interests of the United States, in my judgment, involves five major strands.

The U.S. economy forms a vital center of the world economy, and the consequences of American domestic policies are felt throughout the world. Financial instability in the United States contributed substantially to the emergence of world inflation in the late 1960s and early 1970s. Financial policies pursued in the United States also determined the final breakdown of the system erected at Bretton Woods, and they eventually produced—reinforced by the massive transfers of wealth engineered by OPEC—the "stagflation" observed in Western economies. Such economic vagaries and uncertainties impose severe adjustment costs on many countries. Restoration and maintenance of financial stability is thus the first obligation U.S. policymakers should accept. This means that Washington must evolve a set of policies and institutions assuring stable monetary growth at a noninflationary level and a controlled budget with at most a modest deficit. Restoring a reliable pattern of financial stability would require a major political effort and a considerable break with recent and current trends.

The second and third strands of a positive program would be directed toward a substantial opening of our economy. All trade barriers should be removed or drastically lowered. Import quotas of any kind and obstacles to imports should be systematically abolished—this action including the reduction and removal of tariffs. The elimination of trade barriers would offer other countries opportunities to sell their products and acquire the means to finance an increasing range of imports while substantially helping to expand their real income levels. The same policies would also contribute to a more efficient use of resources in the U.S. economy and would in the longer run benefit U.S. residents. Moreover, the systematic removal of trade barriers should be supplemented by a removal of all barriers to private investments in foreign countries or obstructions to private loans made available to foreign businesses and residents. The flow of capital would depend to a large extent on conditions in foreign countries and particularly on the predictability and stability of the rules of the game applied to foreign business and foreign investors. The policies and institutions of the Third World would thus form a major determinant of the capital flow and of the contributions made by industrial economies to the rate of development.

As for the fourth item on the program, it is imperative that the United States formulate a coherent conception of the conditions relevant to economic growth and rising welfare. Uncertain growth and "stagnating poverty" are not the result of a colonial history or the consequence of "neocolonialism in any of its forms." Over the postwar period, most developing countries settled on a course of policies and a pattern of institutions systematically obstructing or retarding their economic development. In a growing number of countries, economic reality has been sacrificed to ideology. Representatives of the U.S. government should learn to argue a coherent case for alternative programs and policies that would release the shackles imposed on developing economies. These programs and suggestions should be formulated with the full acknowledgment that members of the Third World have the right to proceed according to their own lights. But their insistence on policies and institutions obstructing their development and lowering their welfare sets on the Western nations no moral obligation to bail them out with a massive transfusion of resources. The manifest failure of government-offered economic aid has revealed its wastefulness and inefficiency.[9] All aid should be replaced by voluntary transactions executed on open capital and credit markets.[10]

---

9 See Peter Bauer's "Politicization of Knowledge: Development Economics," prepared for the First International Interlaken Seminar on Analysis and Ideology (June 1974) and subsequently published in *Schweizerische Zeitschrift für Volkswirtschaft und Statistik*, 1975.

10 The pervasive concern about a permanent food crisis should stimulate U.S. representatives to present alternatives to the established agricultural and land-tenure policies of the Third World. Tanzania recently accepted the Soviet model and collectivized agriculture. The resulting effect on her agricultural output is predictable. Subtler ramifications bearing on agricultural output and population emerge from other land-tenure systems. Arthur DeVany demonstrated, for in-

Attention to policies emphasized in the previous paragraph introduces the last item in a positive agenda. U.S. representatives (and, it would be hoped, even some intellectuals) should forcefully contest socialist claims in the world market for ideas. The case for capitalism as a set of flexible institutions best designed to assure a continuous striving for human dignity and human achievement requires some impassioned articulation. We should not hesitate to offer a vision of our humane potential, though this may involve some radical changes of established procedures and well-entrenched habits, as revealed by the first press conference of Ambassador Moynihan's successor. According to European press reports, Ambassador William Scranton emphasized that there are no fundamental issues of principle that would lead to a confrontation between the United States and major portions of the world. This view may simply represent the standard verbalism of a "diplomatic bureaucracy," but the fact remains: we *are* confronted with a serious challenge and a severe test of our understanding of fundamental issues of social organization. Why U.S. representatives persistently fail to recognize or to admit the existence of an underlying confrontation is therefore a puzzlement. Of course, our own domestic trend has veered sharply in the direction implicitly advocated by the New International Economic Order, and perhaps this leads many politicians and professional articulators to respond sympathetically to the socialist rhetoric supplied by UN organizations and the Third World. But the longer-run cost measured in human values will be high on this road. We can still learn; we can offer to the world a vision of human opportunities and human dignity.

---

stance, in an interesting study using Mexican data (prepared for the April 1976 Carnegie-Rochester Conference on Public Policy) that the ubiquitous usufruct system creates incentives lowering output and raising the average family size. See "Land Reform and Agricultural Efficiency in Mexico: A General Equilibrium Analysis" *International Organization, National Policies and Economic Development* (Amsterdam: North-Holland Publishing Company, 1977).

Contributors

Peter T. Bauer is Professor of Economics, London School of Economics (University of London) and Fellow of the British Academy. He is also a Fellow of Gonville and Caius College, Cambridge. He has published several books and many articles on economic subjects. His latest book is *Dissent on Development* published by Weidenfeld and Nicolson, London 1972, 1976 and Harvard University Press, Cambridge, Massachusetts 1972, 1976.

Karl Brunner is Professor of Economics and Director, Center for Research in Government Policy and Business, Graduate School of Management, University of Rochester and Permanent Guest Professor, University of Bern, Switzerland. In recognition of his contributions to monetary theory, he was awarded the "Doctoraat Honoris Causa" degree from the Catholic University of Louvain in 1976. In addition to his work in monetary theory, he has written several articles on public policy topics, and is the co-organizer of the Carnegie-Rochester Public Policy Conferences and co-chairman of the Shadow Open Market Committee and the Shadow European Economic Policy Committee. He is the founder and editor of the *Journal of Monetary Economics*.

Harry G. Johnson was the Earl Grey Distinguished Professor of Economics at the University of Chicago at the time of his death in 1977 and had previously held a joint professorship in economics at the London School of Economics and Political Science. Harry Johnson held visiting appointments at numerous universities throughout the world and traveled extensively to lecture and offer advice. He published several hundred articles and several books in international trade theory and policy, monetary economics, price theory and development economics.

Rachel McCulloch is associate professor of economics at Harvard University. Her research has produced several articles on international trade theory and policy and the economics and politics of the new international economic order.

Daniel Patrick Moynihan was elected to the U.S. Senate in 1976. Prior to that he was ambassador to India and the United Nations and Professor of Political Science, Harvard University.

In addition to his professional publications he has written extensively in periodicals for diverse audiences. His books include *Maximum Feasible Misunderstanding, The Politics of a Guaranteed Income, Coping,* and (with Nathan Glazer) *Beyond the Melting Pot.*

Basil S. Yamey is Professor of Economics, London School of Economics (University of London) and a Fellow of the British Academy. He has published several books and many papers on economic subjects. His latest book is *The Economics of Futures Trading* (with B. A. Goss) published by Macmillan, London 1976 and Halstead, New York 1976.